D1601229

All music is what awakes from you
when you are reminded by the instruments.

"SONG FOR OCCUPATIONS"
WALT WHITMAN

HAWAIIAN SON

The Life and Music of Eddie Kamae

James D. Houston

with Eddie Kamae

ʻAI PŌHAKU PRESS

DISTRIBUTED BY
The Hawaiian Legacy Foundation
Ho'okupu Project
P. O. Box 8230
Honolulu, Hawai'i 96830-0230
www.hawaiianlegacy.com

PUBLISHED BY
'Ai Pōhaku Press
contact via
www.nativebookshawaii.com

Illustrations are from the collection of Eddie and Myrna Kamae
unless otherwise noted on pages 257–258.

LCCN 2004104395
ISBN 1-883528-28-3

Designed and produced by
Barbara Pope Book Design, Honolulu, Hawai'i
Printed and bound in China

Contents

Part Three

opposite

Near Volcano, on the Big Island, this venerable koa *tree is Eddie Kamae's trusted* kupuna *(wise elder).*

This book is dedicated to the memory of
Mary Kawena Pukui
1895–1986

Me ke aloha pau ʻole

These concrete steps are all that remain of Mock Chew's house, which once stood across the road from Sam Li'a's birthplace in Waipi'o Valley.

Foreword

Rain beat down on the corrugated overhang. The beach was empty, and beyond the beach the famous bay was empty, no canoes, no swimmers, no surfers. The water was stippled with a million raindrops, and we sat around a breakfast table trying to talk, though we couldn't hear much in this sudden Hawaiian downpour.

I was there to meet Eddie Kamae, whose music I had known for years. I had listened to his records. When Eddie sings, his voice is full, penetrating, lyrical: you hear echoes of the chant and feel the pulse of old genealogies. Offstage he is the most softspoken of men. He speaks in a manner the Hawaiians call *nahenahe*—soft and gentle—and that day he was not inclined to raise his voice just because it was raining so hard half of what he said was lost in the relentless clatter. He was in his late fifties then, with silver hair, smooth brown face, shrewd and kindly eyes that saw right into you.

This was the summer of 1984. Eddie had read one of my stories—or so I'd been told—and thought I might be the one to help him with a film he hoped to make. Film work was not my specialty. But I welcomed the chance to meet him. I would have paid money to shake his hand. He is the Willie Nelson, the Woody Guthrie of Hawaiian music: composer, band leader, legendary instrumentalist. As a young man he developed a jazz picking style that forever changed the status of the *'ukulele.* He became its reigning virtuoso. In the early days of the Hawaiian cultural renaissance, back in the 1960s, his band "The Sons of Hawaii" had played a leading role.

We had an elegantly laid railside table at the Halekūlani:

Eddie and his wife Myrna, myself and my wife Jeanne, and our mutual friend, Jeannette Paulson, founding director of the Hawaii International Film Festival, who had chosen this spot for us to get acquainted. Off to the left Diamond Head was a shadowy blur behind the sheets of rain that pummeled the water and the hotel lawns. As we exchanged pleasantries, sipping our orange juice and Kona coffee, waiting for our orders, I had to slide my chair up closer to Eddie and then lean in to hear his words.

"I want to thank you for your story," he said.

"I thank you for reading it."

"It made me cry."

I didn't know what to say.

"It's my story, too," he said, touching his chest. "Your father. My father."

The way he said this, the open honesty in his face, along with a reverence that came into his voice, brought me to the edge of sudden and inexplicable tears. I was moved. I was flattered. I was astounded. I had imagined—I realize now, as I think back upon that day—implicitly I had assumed that we'd led entirely different lives.

The story he'd read was about growing up in San Francisco, the son of a father from an east Texas farm town. As a kid I was ashamed of his downhome ways, his music in particular. A painting contractor by trade, he had a passion for the steel guitar and always had a country/western band going on the side. In my ears then, this was Okie music. And I was not an Okie. I was from the City by the Golden Gate. It was only after he passed away and I found myself playing upright bass in a bluegrass band that I finally came to understand his musical passions, thus where he had come from, and where I had come from, too.

I titled this story, "How Playing Country Music Taught Me to Love My Dad." A Honolulu literary journal had recently reprinted it, and our friend Jeannette had passed it along to Eddie, who now turned toward me again.

"You know, when I was growing up here in Honolulu, my father always loved Hawaiian music. He wanted me to play it.

Nothing would have made him happier. But I was like you. I thought I was smarter than him. It sounded too simple. I liked jazz and swing and the Latin numbers." His right hand strummed against his shirt. His left hand fingered invisible chords.

"For a long time that's all I played, until certain things happened, and I saw that my father was right all along . . ."

He stopped talking and gazed out into the rain, with a little reflective smile that seemed to say he was going to continue.

When he didn't, I said, "So is this what your film will be about? Your father?"

"Maybe."

Again I waited. But now the papayas had arrived, the eggs, the Portuguese sausage, the croissants, the rare jam made of *pohā* berries. After the salt and pepper had been passed around, and the ketchup and the hot sauce, Eddie said, "I had a second father. An old Hawaiian man. A musician. A composer. A sweet man. A country man. He lived a kind of life that was tied to the old time. I want to make a documentary that would honor his life and his music and what it means."

"Where did he come from? Where is he now?"

Eddie spent a couple of minutes on his eggs and sausage, then said, "He passed away a few years ago. He was almost a hundred. He was born in Waipi'o over on the Big Island, back in 1881. And that interests me a lot because my father was born there too. I don't know if you have seen Waipi'o. It's a special place. I want to make a film that could catch the feeling of this place."

"Wait a minute," I said, pulling my chair up so close we were shoulder to shoulder. "Am I hearing this right? You say he lived almost a hundred years?"

"Yes. He was my teacher, you see. But he was more than that. Somehow the island spoke through him . . ."

In Hawai'i, when something makes your scalp tingle and arm hairs prickle, they call it "chickenskin." As Eddie began to tell the story of the old man's life, I felt lifted off my chair by uncanny forces.

A year earlier I had spent a semester as visiting writer at the University of Hawai'i and had begun to understand the ongoing struggle between two views of Hawai'i's spectacular terrain: as a source of economic power, and as a source of sacred and spiritual power; as a package of commodities to be bought and sold in the international marketplace, and as an ancestral habitat to be honored and revered. I had been looking for a way to write about it, maybe fiction, maybe nonfiction. Just before leaving home for this summertime return to the islands, I had made a long note to myself about a novel with a central character whose life would span a hundred years of Hawaiian history. His story would start on the Big Island, which is the most mysterious island and in its way the most compelling, since the active volcanoes are there. It is also the newest and the wildest island. I had imagined a man born in the 1880s, caught in the turmoil of a century of profound cultural change, but with a spiritual anchor and deep grounding in the island of his birth.

Eddie's mentor was a man named Sam Li'a. While his story was not word for word my imagined scenario, it was so close to the outline for my as-yet-unborn novel that I experienced half an hour of unrelieved chickenskin. Though I had not met Eddie until that morning, I felt an overpowering sense of kinship, as if we had known each other in another life.

He had never made a film. It was the old man's story that called to him and his own deep need to make a record of it, to share it. By the end of breakfast the squall had passed. Diamond Head stood against the southern sky. I told him yes, it would be a privilege to take a look at the footage gathered so far and listen to his tapes of Sam Li'a singing his songs, and maybe we could talk a little about how to shape the material, where to begin, and so forth. As I said this, I already knew that some kind of path was opening up and that I would follow it as far as it went. Whether my imagined novel had been a form of premonition or mere coincidence, it seemed too strong a signal to ignore.

I didn't really need a second signal. But I got one anyway. We had all left our cars with valet parking. While we stood in the breezeway outside the lobby, waiting for the cars to come around, an attendant pulled up in a blue Datsun. I almost stepped toward it, thinking it was mine, though of course it could not be mine, since I was a driving a rental and my blue Datsun was back home under the carport in Santa Cruz. I caught myself in time and watched with amazement as Eddie opened the passenger door so that Myrna could slide in. His car was the exact duplicate of the one I drove in California, right down to the tweed upholstery: a baby-blue 1978 Datsun 510 with dark blue interior, the four-door sedan.

I told this to Eddie, and his eyes opened wide. "Wow! How long you had it?"

"I bought it new."

"Me too."

Then he smiled a dazzling smile of pleasure. "You sure this is not your car?"

He leaned down to the open window. "Hey, Myrna, look in the glove box. Check the registration."

We all laughed, and he and I shook hands with that strangely tribal recognition of anyone who shares your color and model and make.

And that was not the end of it, not by any means. That night back in our hotel room, my wife and I were asleep when out of nowhere the radio began to blare forth a Hawaiian song. We both sprang up in the darkness.

"What's that?" she cried.

"It's the radio."

"Why did you turn on the radio? It's two in the morning."

"I thought you turned it on."

"It sounds like Eddie."

"It is."

When we're in Honolulu, I always keep the radios tuned to the all-Hawaiian-music station. This happened to be a clock radio. Maybe the wake-up timer had mistakenly been set for 2 A.M. Maybe it was a freak moment in the history of electronics. Whatever the explanation, Eddie's band was playing "Mauna Kea," one of their perennial hits, about the Big Island's snow-capped peak, and Eddie's voice was filling our hotel room.

Jeanne lay back down and said, "Well, that settles it."

"Settles what?"

"Anybody who can turn our radio on in the middle of the night from the other side of town is somebody you have to pay attention to."

And so we began to meet, starting the next afternoon. In the shaded front room of his Waikīkī apartment, we listened to tapes of Sam Li'a chanting in the ancient Hawaiian way, the quavering voice of a man in his nineties, yet hauntingly strong, as if rising right out of the valley of his birth to cross the centuries—a voice from the 1880s reaching our ears in 1980s Waikīkī.

Waipi'o looms large in Hawaiian lore and legend, one of a series of deep valleys that notch the Big Island's northern shore. To reach it you drive out from Hilo along the rain-drenched Hāmākua coast. You drive to the end of the pavement, where a dirt road takes you down to sea level, a road so steep that rental vehicles are forbidden to attempt it unless they have four-wheel drive.

In Eddie's front room we looked at footage of drop-off cliffs that frame the valley floor, the taro ponds, the jungle curves of Waipi'o stream. We saw Hi'ilawe, a famous double waterfall that inspired one of Hawai'i's most often played love songs.

For me, all this was a nostalgic flashback, since Jeanne and I had spent part of our honeymoon there some thirty years earlier. We were married in Honolulu, then hitchhiked around Moloka'i, Maui, Lāna'i, and the Big Island. Waipi'o seemed a magical place to us, gorgeously tropical, yet fearful, too, as if laden with the spirits of ancient lives. Farmhouses were scattered here and there, but they were all empty, abandoned. Few had lived in that valley since the great tidal wave of 1946, which rushed a mile inland and covered the trees.

Eddie was delighted to hear that I had already been affected by Sam Li'a's valley. When I told him I had a whole box of color slides from Waipi'o, his face lit up.

"You say from 1957?"

"Lot of taro then, but no people," I said. "Old farmhouses, rock walls, the empty beach . . ."

"Pictures from that time are hard to find. Can you make me some prints?"

I told him it would be an honor. Once we were back home, I dug out my old slide collection, printed up a dozen shots, and sent them off. Eddie's letter came right away, full of thanks, commenting on one photo in particular:

> *I especially like the photo with the concrete steps that lead to Mock Chew's house, with Hi'ilawe Falls in the background. That's a perfect shot. Right across the road is where Sam Li'a was born and raised. Both houses are not there any more. The steps that lead up to Mock Chew's house are the only remaining landmarks from these houses, and I plan to film these steps, mentioning that this is all that remains and that the home of Sam Li'a was only a few yards across the road.*

With this letter came another rush of chickenskin. I had photographed Mock Chew's house for the view of the falls, and also because underneath its broken-down porch I had found an old *poi* pounder—a valued artifact among anthropologists and once a basic implement in all Hawaiian households, carved from porous lava rock and used to pound taro root. When we returned from that long-ago roam around the islands, I brought it with me. For all those years it had been a feature of my bookshelf in Santa Cruz. Now I had met Eddie Kamae, inviting me to work with him on a documentary film about an old man born in Waipi'o valley in 1881. Twenty-seven years ago I had taken a photograph of an abandoned house in a deserted valley at the end of the coast road on the north shore of the Big Island, while standing on or near the very spot where Eddie's mentor was born and grew up. And I had carried away with me, from right across the road, a stone implement and kept it close to my writing desk—my Waipi'o valley souvenir.

Once again my scalp tingled and my neck prickled and my arm hairs stood out, as I asked myself what kind of Hawaiian karma was going on here.

Nineteen more years have passed, and still I ask myself that question, though I now know that in Eddie's world, seemingly uncanny connections are not at all unusual. Here in California, where I spend most of my time, you have to be careful telling stories such as that one. Certain people stand silent and glance away in embarrassment, or wag their heads as if to say you have made one too many trips to the tropics. But where Eddie lives, sychronicities abound and premonitions are a feature of daily life. He inhabits a Polynesian world where the past and the present coexist, where the dead often speak to the living, where bones have voices and rocks have life, where the line between humans and the rest of nature quickly falls away, as birds become messengers, and rain squalls too, and unexpected winds, and a shark may well be your guardian ancestor.

(Just to set the record straight: soon after meeting Eddie I took that *poi* pounder back to the valley. They say all the rocks from the Big Island belong to that island and ought to stay there. I'd had mine long enough. I didn't want to push my luck. If I was going to work on a project about Waipi'o, I needed to clear the air. It's a mysterious and powerful place. I flew over there, drove out to the bluff, hiked down the *pali* road with my *poi* pounder wrapped in ti leaves, asked the valley and the island to forgive me for removing this piece of stone from where it belonged, and put it back where I'd found it. When I mentioned this to Eddie, he said, "Maybe that rock was ready to go back home and figured out a way to get you to take it there.")

As of this writing we have worked together on seven documentaries about various features of Hawaiian music and cultural tradition. When he asked me recently if I'd be interested in collaborating on a book, it was like that first day at breakfast: it was something I had already started thinking about and had even made some notes about.

This curve of islands in the middle of the Pacific was once the most isolated place on earth. Its unique and inescapable geography has made Hawai'i a trans-oceanic crossroads, a center for trade, travel, and military strategy. For Hawaiians, as for so many native peoples around the world, it has meant a complex struggle for cultural definition and survival, going on now two centuries and more. Eddie Kamae is among those who, by pursuing his own singular path, has found a way to reclaim his heritage and in so doing inspire others. He came of age at a time when Hawaiians had been made to feel like second-class citizens in their own homeland, when the use of their native language had been prohibited in schools and in public offices. Today, with honors heaped around him, he is recognized as a "living treasure of Hawai'i." This book tells the story of his life and career. It's a Polynesian odyssey, measured by the numerous teachers he has met along the way, dancers and singers, storytellers, healers, elders, and *kūpuna* who have guided him in his long quest to find the source of a rich musical tradition and thus to find himself.

James D. Houston
Honolulu/Santa Cruz
December 2003

Part One

Aia no i ka mea e mele ana.
Let the singer select the song.

Hawaiian Proverb

Waikahalulu is the pool in Nu'uanu Stream
where Eddie fished as a boy and learned to swim.

Edward Leilani Kamae
at age fifteen

1

Origins

ne of Eddie's earliest memories is the sound of his mother's voice. Hawaiian was her first language. She spoke it with a soothing, lilting roll he calls *palupalu,* a word sometimes used to describe the roll of the sea, or the sound of small waves lapping a sandy shore. To his young ears it was a kind of singing.

"On her way to the market," Eddie says, "she would call out to everyone she passed, all her neighborhood friends, even the policeman directing traffic. 'Hoo-eee,' she would call."

Born Alice Ululani 'Ōpūnui, she grew up on Maui, where even today the voices of locals are softer and more leisurely than you tend to hear in Honolulu. Her family's land was on the leeward side of the West Maui Mountains. She met her husband there while he was enrolled at Lahainaluna, famous as the first boarding school in Hawai'i, established by missionaries in 1831, back in the days when Lahaina was still a mid-Pacific whaling stop and the capital of a newly united Hawaiian kingdom.

Samuel Hoapili Kamae came from Kapulena, a country town near Waipi'o, on the Big Island's north shore, but after finishing high school in 1912, he never went back home. He didn't want to fish or farm or pull taro or work on a sugar plantation. At Lahainaluna, where the first Hawaiian-language newspaper had been published in 1834, they still had a press, and he had learned printing. With this trade and his young bride, he decided to try his luck in the big city.

Sam Kamae was one-fourth Cherokee. His father, Samuel Sr., had been born in Sacramento in 1856, the son of a Cherokee woman and an adventurous Hawaiian who had sailed to

Eddie's father, Samuel Hoapili Kamae (1890–1956), in Honolulu, circa 1920.

California, as had so many others from these islands in the days before and after the Gold Rush. Eddie's father was six feet tall, with pronounced cheekbones that gave him an Indian look. He had a great fondness for wrestling matches, especially when an Indian wrestler came to town. Sam always had two season tickets so he could bring along one of his sons, and it was a rare treat for young Eddie to accompany his father to the Civic Auditorium to see "Chief Thunderbird" or "White Cloud." Sam Kamae was a quiet man who didn't talk much, but these matches would ignite him. "I watched him stamp his foot and slap his hands against his knees when the Indian jumped into the ring and started dancing his war dance. As a boy, it was a very special moment for me, to see my father happy."

Edward Leilani Kamae grew up in what he calls "a camp" of some thirty houses, located a bit west of downtown and a few blocks inland from Honolulu harbor. Their district was named Kauluwela, which literally means "the hot stick used for spreading oven stones." These were one-story frame houses, with walkways on two sides. It was a little working-class compound, mostly Chinese, a few Koreans, one Japanese family, and one Hawaiian family, the Kamaes. All the mothers kept an eye on all the children. As Eddie recalls, "No child was off the hook. You would get it if you were naughty, a swat on your butt, or your ears would be pinched. All of us grew up with respect for the elders, no matter who they were or where they came from."

The older kids also rode herd on the younger ones. By the time Eddie came along, in 1927, there were already three brothers and three sisters in the family. Three more brothers would follow him. He remembers learning how to swim when the older boys threw him into the water at Waikahalulu, a popular swimming hole and waterfall on Nu'uanu stream. "We would cry, but they were in control. You cry, but when you hit the water you automatically swim like a dog. Next day you are in the pool again, swimming with your friends and not afraid any more."

He remembers catching *'o'opu* and *'ōpae* in that pool (goby and freshwater shrimp) to sell to elderly Chinese in the neighbor-

hood—"my first business venture." He remembers selling the *Honolulu Star-Bulletin* at the corner of Hotel and Maunakea Streets, and diving for coins thrown from the deck on Boat Day, when the big passenger ships would pull into the harbor.

And he remembers the day his mother noticed a young Chinese fellow who slept every night in a nearby park. He looked to be about fifteen years old. She sent Eddie to bring him to the house, and she told him, "You don't sleep there any-more. You sleep here." They took him in and fed him, and the family of twelve became a family of thirteen. "From that day on he was my brother. It was the old Hawaiian way of doing things," Eddie says. "You *mālama* those around you, you care. Years later my mother told me something I still think about.

All these little things we do for each other, we feed them more than food. We are feeding the soul."

In the summertime, there were trips to visit the family place on Maui. They would take deck passage on an inter-island cargo barge, Eddie's mother and three or four of the kids. In those days, the mid-1930s, it would be an overnight trip from Honolulu to the pier at Lahaina.

His grandmother lived in a large frame house shaded by mangoes, with a view east toward the mountains and the high central peak, six-thousand-foot Pu'u Kukui. For Eddie it was a trip to the country to see his *tūtū*, Kauhai Likua. At age seven, eight, or nine, he would not yet know that as a young woman in the late nineteenth century she had danced in the court of King Kalākaua. He would not yet know that when she disappeared into a shack behind her house, she spoke to Laka, deity of the *hula*. Though he witnessed the frequent rainbows above the misty valley that climbs toward Pu'u Kukui, he would not yet know the powerful role these mountains play in Hawaiian mythology, as the birthplace for the *mo'o,* the sacred lizard goddess Kihawahine, who sprang forth from here to cross the ocean and link Maui with Polynesian islands thousands of miles south and east. For the youngster growing up in Honolulu, it was too early for such things to register. But like his mother's voice, it would all be there waiting for him; it would all come back, when the time was right.

opposite left
At Kaumakapili Church, Honolulu, in 1953, Eddie's brother Joe is flanked by his daughters, Kathy (left) and Jo. Behind them are Eddie's mother, Alice Ululani 'Ōpūnui, and father Sam.

opposite right
Eddie's grandmother, Kauhai Likua (1868–1938).

At Farrington High School, in Kalihi, on the city's west side, Eddie got by, but the classwork never held his attention for long. His passions were elsewhere: making money and making music. His long love affair with the *'ukulele* began at age fifteen. One evening his oldest brother, Sam, a driver with Honolulu Rapid Transit, discovered an instrument left behind on the back seat of his bus. It was the end of his last run. The lost and found office was closed. Instead of turning it in, he brought the uke home and gave it to his brother. From that day onward, Eddie was hooked. He just liked the sound of it, the size of it, the feel of the strings, the hum of the wood.

Another brother, Joe, was Eddie's first teacher, passing on the basic chords and strums. Joe was already singing and playing guitar at parties and at local variety shows. Before long Eddie was good enough to chord along behind him, much to his father's delight. Listening to Hawaiian music was the elder Sam's favorite pastime. He encouraged Eddie to follow in Joe's footsteps. But the tunes Eddie was learning seemed too simple, too easy. Many of the traditional Hawaiian songs, based on *hula* chants, used two chords, sometimes three. The *hapa-haole* tunes, written in the 1920s and 1930s—like "Sweet Leilani" and "Lovely Hula Hands"—seemed vapid and unchallenging. On the radio he liked to listen to classical music and to swing—Benny Goodman, Glenn Miller. Eddie strummed along behind Joe, listening, learning, but he also started dipping into guitar and piano books, picking up what he could about chord structure and music theory, looking for something else, something more.

Meanwhile, from other brothers he had learned another kind of lesson, one they in turn may have learned from their father. Though Eddie wouldn't find this out until many years later, Sam Kamae had a small enterprise going on the side, handling bets from around the neighborhood in a popular Chinese game of chance called Chi-fa. Instead of betting on a lucky number, players would rely heavily on dreams, riddles, and hunches to guess each day's lucky word. It was a citywide game, wherein a winner could collect a dollar-fifty for each nickel invested. As a local bookie, Sam would take ten percent off the top of whatever he collected.

"So maybe it ran in the family," Eddie says now. "In those days I didn't know what my father was doing. But I saw how my older brothers used to gamble. Whenever they lost, I would feel sad. One time my brother lost a lot of money all at once, and I really felt bad for him. He didn't feel so bad, but I felt bad. I figured I had to learn more about gambling so this wouldn't happen to me too. I got the hang of it pretty fast, and I started running my own dice game. All the time I was learning how to play the *'ukulele,* I had a dice game too, going all the way back to junior high."

At Farrington his game room was the boys' lavatory. He would bribe the janitor to show up early, before morning classes began, and open the doors, so the teenage gamblers could gather among the sinks and stalls to place their bets. As banker and dice-master, Eddie kept himself in decent clothes and ample pocket money—until the beginning of his senior year, when the dice took an unexpected roll.

It was 1945. On August 4 Eddie turned eighteen. Ten days later the Japanese surrendered, and World War II was over. But young men were still eligible for the draft. Now Eddie needed a student deferment to stay enrolled, and the principal at Farrington wouldn't approve it. "He said, 'I'm going to let you go into the army,'" Eddie recalls. "'It'll make a man out of you.' But the main thing is, I think, he was relieved. If he could get rid of me, he could get rid of the dice games and clean up the school."

Assigned to the Quartermaster Corps, Eddie was sent to New Caledonia, a long narrow island in the Coral Sea, as far south of the equator as Hawai'i is north of it. New Caledonia had been a staging area for some of the major battles of the war, and provided the setting for many of James Michener's stories in his wartime memoir, *Tales of the South Pacific.* Eddie spent his months there crating up supplies and equipment for shipping back to the States. Anything being left behind, or marked for disposal, he and his crew would give to the Melanesian locals. "The army didn't believe in giving anything away," he says. "But we would see the natives, and if we had something we were supposed to get rid of that they could use—pots, pans, utensils, tables, clothes, anything—we gave it all to them. In my unit we were all from Hawai'i, local boys. Why throw 'em away, we said, give 'em to the island folks. And every day they waited for us."

Two years later he was back in Honolulu, honorably discharged. With support from the G.I. Bill he re-enrolled at Farrington High, where he finally completed his senior year, only to learn that he was one credit short of graduation. He could make it up, he was told, in a summer session course. But halfway through the first meeting he got up and walked out, never to return. The lecture was boring him; it was stifling to sit in the summer heat; and Eddie was almost twenty-one. If he hadn't graduated by this time, he reasoned, maybe he didn't need to graduate. A diploma did not interest him nearly so much as the call of his music.

In the South Pacific he'd had plenty of time to practice. He had developed his own repertoire of instrumental solos, among them Hoagy Carmichael's "Stardust," and the uptempo Latin favorite, "Tico Tico." He started attending weekend music sessions at a place called Charlie's Cab Stand, on South King Street, near 'Iolani Palace. It was a large open shed, where a platform would be set up at one end. On Saturday afternoons musicians and singers gathered from all parts of the island and jammed into the evening. Most of them, like the cab drivers, had other jobs and performed for the joy of it, taking turns, all impromptu, urged by a crowd of listeners like Eddie's father, who brought him there soon after he came home from the army.

The first time Eddie took the stage and played one of his specialty numbers, he got an ovation. Money suddenly appeared at his feet, quarters and dollar bills, thrown by the festive crowd. He was back the next weekend, and the weekend after that. One Saturday at Charlie's Cab he met up with another *'ukulele* aficionado, a fellow about his own age named Shoi Ikemi, who shared his belief that the instrument was yet to be explored to its full potential. They began to rehearse together, working out duets of a complexity no one thought possible on what had heretofore been mainly a rhythm instrument. One would take the lead, backed by the other, as they offered a captivating mix of Latin tunes and pop standards. When they tried out their act at Charlie's Cab Stand, they were a sensation.

Called The Ukulele Rascals, Eddie and Shoi were soon in demand at parties and fundraisers, such as the annual Policemen's Benefit at McKinley High School auditorium. It was Eddie's first large public performance, a local revue, with various Hawaiian singers, dancers, and musicians, and The Ukulele Rascals stole the show. They played five songs and came back for four encores. The next thing they knew, they had an offer to play weekends at Lau Yee Chai, a restaurant and lounge on Kūhiō Avenue in Waikīkī. Hired to warm up the room for a featured trio, the Rascals quickly built their own following.

In 1948, Eddie teamed up with Shoi Ikemi to form The Ukulele Rascals.

Listeners couldn't get enough of them. Eddie and Shoi played there for six months.

What was going on? Two young guys with *'ukulele,* who didn't even sing: how could they pull crowds in, week after week? In part it was their ingenious arrangements and new level of technical skill. In part it was the *'ukulele*'s unique role in the Hawaiian islands.

Originally from Portugal, it arrived by ship, carried in the hands of sailors who preferred this four-stringed miniature guitar for long voyages where space on board was limited. They called it the *braguinha,* named for the northern town of Braga. Students of Hawaiian musical history have pinned down the year the *braguinha* arrived (1878), and they can name the fellow who brought the first one ashore: João de Freitas. The Portuguese sailors played with pride and vigor. Hawaiians took to it immediately. They called it *pila li'i li'i* (little fiddle), and then came up with the name that stuck, *'uku lele* (jumping flea).

It became the favorite instrument of King David Kalākaua, a talented musician and composer. He learned to design and build his own. In 1886, when he celebrated his fiftieth birthday at a large "Jubilee" on the lawns in front of 'Iolani Palace, *'ukulele* were used for the first time to accompany *hula* at a public occasion. Within a few years it had joined the guitar and fiddle to become a central feature of what was soon to be called "Hawaiian music." Before long the instrument itself would become an emblem of Hawai'i, and the playing of it has been more honored and attended to here than anywhere else, including its country of origin.

Outside Hawai'i the *'ukulele* has had an image problem that dates back to the days of Cliff "Ukulele Ike" Edwards. While he was the first to spread its popularity across the United States, in the 1920s and 1930s, he was often depicted wearing a caved-in hat or grinning from the cover of a collection such as *Ukulele Ike's Comic Song Book.* In later years the parody singer Tiny Tim, during his time in the international spotlight, would strum lamely on his *'ukulele* to accompany high-pitched hits such as "Tiptoe through the Tulips." In his hands it was a toy, a prop for a novelty act.

Not so in Hawai'i, where school kids take *'ukulele* classes, viewed as a necessary part of an introduction to their island heritage. Devotees practice all year long to perform at *'ukulele* festivals or to compete in local and statewide contests. It is surely the only place in the world where a master of this instrument can become a culture hero.

One of the earliest was Jesse Kalima, who proved that the *'ukulele* could not only drive the rhythm but also shine as a solo instrument. In 1935, when he was fifteen, he won the Territorial Amateur Hour Contest with his now classic version of "The Stars and Stripes Forever." This rousing Sousa march is not by any means a Hawaiian song. But when it was played by a Hawaiian, on the islanders' favorite instrument, it was cause for general celebration. During the years when Eddie Kamae began to practice and listen, Kalima's early solo hits were in the musical air: "Dark Eyes," "Jealousy," "Under the Double Eagle."

When The Ukulele Rascals started pulling them in at Lau Yee Chai, something more had been added. They had moved the *'ukulele* to the forestage, to headline a musical act. And Eddie had developed an original, innovative picking style that enhanced single-string or double-string melody with simultaneous chording. He had been listening to Charlie Christian and Django Reinhardt. He had been listening to Xavier Cugat and the South American bands, finding strums for the complex Latin tempos.

Eddie had also started working with a new professor at the University of Hawai'i. Barbara Smith had recently joined the faculty and would soon found the Ethnomusicology Study Program. A friend had been impressed with one of her classes, so Eddie—who'd never before set foot on the campus—knocked on her office door one day and introduced himself. They soon struck a deal, trading *'ukulele* lessons for private tutoring in chord structure and music theory. He learned to read scores and sharpened his approach to certain classical pieces that caught his ear. To a repertoire that included Hoagy Carmichael and Cole Porter, "Lady of Spain" and "Granada," he added a sound no one had heard attempted on *'ukulele*—"Malagueña," from the *Andalusian Suite* by Ernesto Lecuona, portions of Ravel's *Bolero,* an adaptation of Rachmaninoff's *Second Piano Concerto.* In the world of Hawaiian performance, twenty-one-year-old Eddie Kamae was going where musicians had not gone before.

In 1949 he and Shoi got word of auditions for a variety show that would tour the United States. Bandleader Ray Kinney would star, in those days an enormously popular singer and showman with fans from coast to coast. The auditions were held outside Honolulu at the home of one of Kinney's backers. Dozens of acts tried out. The Ukulele Rascals dazzled everyone, as usual, and made the final cut, joining a troupe of singers, *hula* dancers, and Kinney's traveling band.

For the youthful virtuosi it was an honor and a great break, since the end of the tour would bring them to the Lexington Hotel in New York City. In the 1930s Kinney had spent four years at the Lexington's Hawaiian Room, then the nation's prime showcase for Hawaiian performers. Eddie's mother and father joined the many friends and family members who came down to the wharf to drape them with *lei* and tearfully wave as they boarded a steamship for the West Coast.

Starting in San Francisco, they worked theaters like the old Tivoli on Market Street. First a feature film would play, then the revue would do its show, twice, sometimes three times a day. Looking back now, Eddie calls it "the last days of vaudeville." The band would accompany Kinney's melodious tenor. In *lei* and swirling skirts the dancers would take the stage, and then the Rascals.

They traveled by bus down the coast to Los Angeles, Hollywood, and San Diego, then headed north to Oregon, up to Seattle, and across the border to play Vancouver. Often the theaters were packed. Kinney was a big draw. Born in Hilo, he was among the best known performers of his day, Hawaiian or otherwise. During World War II he had toured 157 military bases. By the late 1940s he had cut over five hundred records with Decca.

Eddie looks back on those days with amazement. "I just couldn't believe it. For the first few weeks, everywhere we went, it was sold out. When our turn came, Shoi and me, we just got up there and played our songs, all the Latin numbers and specialty tunes we loved. Kinney's arrangers had the band behind us some of the time, horns and rhythm, so we sounded better than ever."

While the shows were exciting, life on the road soon lost its shine—the endless bus rides from city to city, the low-budget hotels around the corner from the theater. From Vancouver they traveled south into Idaho and Utah. As the crowds began to thin out, the show's precarious financial status began to reveal itself. They were actually living off each day's receipts. A low turnout at the box office could mean low rations for the cast. Eddie recalls the morning a hotel had to hold his bags because no one had paid for his room. One day he didn't have enough to buy his own breakfast. When the producer refused to advance him some pocket money, Eddie went across the street, pawned his *'ukulele,* and told the producer, "If you plan to put on a show tonight, you'd better go over and get me out of hock." And he did. But Eddie knew this couldn't last much longer.

The weather finally made up his mind. After a loop through North Dakota, they headed back into the Rockies. These were big, famous mountains, bigger than any others he'd seen, but they weren't his mountains, and to his Hawaiian eyes they looked cold, cold, cold. Fall was turning to winter. Snow whitened the higher peaks. They were getting ready to do a show in Longmont, Colorado, north of Denver, when the fingernails on Eddie's right hand snapped off from the cold. Without them he couldn't pick. "To play that night," he says, "I had to go buy some false fingernails and glue them on. After the show I said to myself, 'That's it.'"

In his mind's eye he was seeing another set of mountains, the emerald peaks of O'ahu on the day they had steamed out of Honolulu harbor, the steep, mist-laden Ko'olau range rising up to dwarf the buildings downtown. He wired his father for airfare. He showed Ray Kinney his fingers and told him his life on the road had come to an early end. It was also the end of The Ukulele Rascals. Shoi stayed with the revue a while longer, until they reached Chicago, where he fell in love. As for Eddie, he'd seen enough of the mainland to last him quite a while—from Mexico to Canada, from the coastline to the Great Plains. New York City was too far away, and getting to the fabled Lexington Hotel seemed a lot more trouble than it was worth.

A DANCER AND A HEALER

My grandmother, Kauhai Likua, was a woman of the older time. Born in the 1860s, I think. She was recognized early as a beautiful dancer. That's how they picked the ones who would dance at the king's court in Honolulu, for events at 'Iolani Palace and all that. When you were very young, they saw the grace in your body, and you started training with one of the hula *masters. Later she came back to Maui and passed on what she knew to Emma Sharpe, of the Farden family, who also grew up in Lahaina, and became one of the great dancers and* kumu hula *of my mother's generation.*

Originally her family's land was farther back toward the mountains, and higher up, at a place called Ka-ua-'ula, which means "red rain," maybe for the way the red volcanic soil can color the water. Lots of streams back there, where the water comes down from the West Maui Mountains. The plantation people wanted more access to the water. So my grandmother traded them for the land we used to visit in the summer, where we still have family living and where she is buried, in closer to Lahaina. The highway runs past there now, but when I was a kid there was no highway yet—to the east, just open fields, then the sugarcane, then the mountains.

She was famous as a healer, you know. When I was growing up in Honolulu, we never went to a doctor or anywhere near a hospital. If somebody got sick, we could call my grandmother, and she would come over from Maui. She knew all about herbs and medicinal plants. She could take one look and know what was wrong and what to do.

Her husband, my grandfather, he was a fisherman over there on Maui. There is the story of how he comes in from fishing one day with bad cramps in his stomach and in his back. Even though he never mentions it to my grandmother, she knows what is wrong and she knows why. She says to him, "You done something to the sharks today." And he just grunts because he knows she was right. Sometimes if he was out fishing for 'ōpelu *and it looked like the sharks were going to harm his catch, he would drop dynamite into the water. He didn't want to hurt them, just scare them back. But* *maybe this time something happened, and that's why he got the cramps and the backache. For all the folks over that way, the shark is their '*aumakua, *their family guardian.*

And there was another story I heard, this one from my auntie, my mother's sister, about the time a state senator from the other side of the mountain comes to Lahaina to ask my grandmother for help. This is back in horse and buggy time. Today Maui is filled with cars from one end to the other. Those days not so many cars yet, and this senator he comes in a horse and buggy, begging Kauhai Likua to help. So she and her daughter ride their horse all night, around the mountain, to a house where this woman, a relative of the senator's, is having fits. When two strangers walk in, she jumps up onto the table, shouting and waving her arms. She is wild. My grandmother applies a protective oil to herself and to her daughter, so whatever sickness possesses this woman won't pass to them. Then they wrestle her down off the table, and my grandmother tells her daughter to hold the woman's legs against the floor, while she holds her arms. For a long time she prays in Hawaiian—that was what she spoke, you know, she never did speak English her whole life. She prays in Hawaiian until this woman's body relaxes and she rolls over and falls asleep. After that the woman is okay. The senator is weeping, he is so grateful. He pulls a roll of bills out of his pocket and hands some money to my grandmother. But she won't take it. Give it to the community, she says, and she gets on her horse with her daughter and they ride back to Lahaina.

Eddie with the Martin "Standard" 'ukulele
he played in the 1950s.

Awakening

The mainland tour had soured Eddie on the music business. If that's what it took to be a working performer—all-day bus rides, one-night stands—he'd find some other way to make a living. During his army time in New Caledonia, and in the first year after discharge, he'd always kept a dice game going on the side. To bring in some money, he turned to gambling, around Honolulu, and also on nearby Moloka'i, where Filipino fieldworkers staged cockfights every weekend. Amid the noise and fervor of the fighting pits, Eddie and a Chinese partner set up a dice table and also took bets on the roosters. As their cover, to provide a legal reason for these regular weekend visits, they invested in a local chicken ranch.

The money was good, and they might have kept it going for quite some time. But petty gambling eventually slipped toward petty crime, and they got caught in a marketing scheme, trying to pass off vials of cornstarch and flour as household medicine. Convicted of conspiracy to defraud, Eddie was sent to O'ahu Community Correction Center, a low-security facility in Honolulu's Kalihi district, where he spent the next three years.

In jail he went back to the *'ukulele.* "I didn't know how I was going to last three years in there," he says. "My uke was my companion and my way to find some peace of mind. Music got me through."

The worst moment was the day his mother and father came to visit. "They only came once, and I never forgot it. I didn't know what they were going to say, their son getting arrested and jailed like that. My father was a quiet man. He never said much, but what he said, you knew he meant it. For a long time he looked at me. Finally he said, 'Well son, you just make the most of this.' That's all. Then he turned and they walked away.

"It was the only time they came while I was in there. What stayed with me was the look in his eyes. They just held me and looked through me and told me things he would never say with words. Something about the way he looked straightened me out right then and there. It was not what he said, but what I saw in my father's face. I guess I was around twenty-seven or twenty-eight. I knew I could never again do anything that would disgrace his name or disgrace my family.

"Just before I got out of there he passed away. So I never got to tell him what was on my mind. But when I went to see my mother, she handed me an envelope. There was money inside. You see, he figured I would need a car to get around. All he told her was, 'This is for the boy.'"

The years in jail were long, soul-searching years. But once he was out, he had a second lease on life, a new certainty that playing music was all he'd ever wanted to do. He went straight to Waikīkī and auditioned for a show opening at the Biltmore Hotel. Though he'd been out of circulation, Eddie was still regarded as the most influential *'ukulele* stylist of his time. He was hired on the spot as a nightly soloist.

It was a good gig. The Biltmore stood on Kalākaua Avenue, tall and pink, right across from Kūhiō Beach. From the uppermost floor, called the Top of the Isle, you could watch the sky turn to flame out beyond the famous lines of breaking surf. Fans would come early and stay for the show. The dancers were shapely and well rehearsed. The band was smooth. Haunani Kahalewai, the emcee and lead singer, was a popular Decca recording artist, featured for years on the transpacific radio show "Hawaii Calls," and known throughout her long career as "Hawaii's First Lady of Song."

Most nights, after the show, Eddie would head down the avenue to catch the last set at another club, the Queen's Surf, overlooking the beach in front of Kapi'olani Park. He liked to hang out with the other musicians who gathered for late-night drinks. The gifted young pianist Mahi Beamer led a trio in the

 lounge. Upstairs, in the Barefoot Bar, The Eddie Spencer Band included bassist Joe Marshall and singer Gabby Pahinui, known for his charismatic voice and madcap behavior. Gabby had been performing in the clubs and lounges of Waikīkī for twenty years, usually playing steel guitar. But among musicians he was known as the most talented practitioner of a style called "slack key," which in the late 1950s was still heard mostly at backyard parties and family gatherings. Gabby was also known for nonstop weekend jam sessions at his house in Waimānalo, over on the windward side.

"One night at the Queen's Surf," Eddie recalls, "we were sitting there having a drink, and a friend of mine says, 'Why don't you come with us over to Gabby's place?' And I said, 'What for, what's going on?' 'Come on,' he said, 'you'll see.' When we got there it was around four in the morning, and I couldn't believe how many people were there, musicians, neighbors, everybody coming, bringing food, beer, cooking. Anybody wanted to play something, they could play. They're welcome. Gabby was married, of course, with all his kids around, too, so it was always a full house, even when there was no party. But that's how Gabby was. Everybody welcome. And he was right in the center of it. He gets up there laughing and grabs his guitar and calls out to some other guys to come up, play, and it goes on like that for three days.

"If you had a job, you go do 'em, come back, go into Waikīkī, play the Biltmore, then come back to Gabby's, and the same party is still going on. Two days. Three days. Then Sunday, everybody leaves—until the next weekend, and it starts again. It was the first time I heard Hawaiian music in that jam session way, with so many of the old songs, and singing in Hawaiian—everybody just get up, sing, play, dance, whatever. I liked what I heard, you know, but at the time I still wasn't interested in it for myself, except for this one song. At the parties in Waimānalo, when they ask me to get up, I would play this one song I worked out, written by Queen Lili'uokalani. I liked that one. I guess it was the first Hawaiian song I really wanted to play."

Eddie was on the verge of something, though he wasn't quite sure what. He was looking for a new direction, or some larger

At the Biltmore Hotel, in the late 1950s, Eddie was regarded as the most influential 'ukulele *stylist of his time.*

framework for his music. Afternoons he gave lessons at a Waikīkī studio, while getting ready to cut his first album, *Heart of the Ukulele,* which would showcase his favorite pop and Latin tunes. From time to time he and his most talented former student, Herb Ohta, would get together for a beer and talk about ways to expand the *'ukulele*'s audience, as well as its instrumental range. Maybe they would do a book together, or a series of recordings, or set up some kind of foundation. Or maybe all three. They were talking about jazz, folk, the repertoire of American standards, the classics, perhaps a symphonic performance—anything and everything but Hawaiian music itself which, for Eddie, still held only limited interest.

With the exception of this old tune, "Ku'u Pua I Paoakalani."

One night at the Biltmore, before a show, Haunani Kahalewai had shown him the sheet music and told him it was a song he'd enjoy. Later on he picked it out, took a liking to the sweet and heartful melody line, and found himself playing it over and over again. "It intrigued me," he says. "I didn't know why. I wanted to know where such a song could come from."

You might call it the first crack in a doorway that was soon to open wide. Since Eddie was not yet a singer, he didn't pay much attention to the song's lyrics, though they carried a strange resonance for what was about to happen in his own life.

Lili'uokalani, Hawai'i's last queen, was a prolific composer. "Ku'u Pua i Paoakalani" (My Flower at Paoakalani) was written while she was under house arrest, after the 1893 overthrow of the Hawaiian monarchy. Paoakalani—which means "the royal perfume"—was the flower-surrounded home and garden she kept in Waikīkī. During her imprisonment, restricted to an upper room on the second floor of 'Iolani Palace, she is finding solace remembering the scent of those flowers.

In Hawai'i's long tradition of oral poetry, there is always a story within the story, or underneath the story. This one was a *mele inoa,* a name song, probably for the son of the queen's close friend Eveline Wilson, who had chosen voluntary imprisonment, to share the captivity. According to rules laid down by the American and European businessmen who engineered the overthrow, the queen was not allowed to see newspapers or to receive any reports of activities in her former realm. But Mrs. Wilson's son John devised a way to circumvent this edict. Gathering flowers from the gardens at Paoakalani, he would send them into the palace wrapped in pages from the daily Hawaiian-language papers.

In the spring of 1959 you might say that Eddie Kamae was still under the spell of American and European influences. From boyhood the songs he had chosen all came from overseas. For the first time, the news of musical matters much closer to home was beginning to reach him, to touch him.

He lived in Maunawili then, a semi-rural, tree-filled neighborhood on the windward side. On days when he gave lessons in Waikīkī he would drive around the island's eastern corner, past Makapu'u Point and Koko Head. It would have been faster to take the cross-island Pali Highway, which had opened just the previous year, with mountain tunnels to link the windward to the leeward side. But Eddie was used to the coast road, and he liked the shoreline view, on one hand the sparkling sea, on the other the dramatic face of the Ko'olau range, steep spires and verdant gulleys rising so close you could almost reach out and touch them.

The coast road ran through Waimānalo and past the house and yard of friends he sometimes visited, two sisters, Mabel McKeague and Nani Ho. On one such afternoon he decided to stop and say hello. Nani heard his car pull into the driveway and met him on the porch, her face creased with concern.

"Eddie, guess who's here?"

"Who?"

"Gabby."

"No kidding."

"He's sick."

"Oh yeah? How long?"

She shrugged. "I don't know. A week. Maybe more. His wife was going crazy with all those kids running in and out and Gabby laid up. So we keeping an eye on him."

Eddie was shocked by what he saw. In the backyard Gabby Pahinui sat on a chair, taking the sun. He was thirty-eight then, but looked sixty, gaunt and unshaven. He'd lost a lot of weight. His shirt hung from thinning shoulders. Eddie hadn't seen him or been to the jam sessions for several weeks, not since the nonstop drinking and sleepless nights had finally taken their toll. At first glance he thought the endless party had caught up with Gabby, too. But it was more than that. This was worse than dissipation. Some constriction in his throat made it impossible to eat. He could barely swallow. He was living on thin soup, sipping liquids through a straw.

Gabby's face was haggard with fatigue. But as Eddie sat down next to him and they began to talk, a brightness came into his eyes.

"Son," he said, "you bring your *'ukulele*?"

"Sure. I got a couple with me."

Gabby's broad, charming smile lit up the yard. "Go get 'em. Play some music with me."

As he walked to his car, Eddie wasn't quite sure what would

OLOMA
GOLF
Gabby

come of this. They'd never played together, just the two of them, and their tastes seemed very far apart. But the idea seemed to lift Gabby's spirits, so he was happy to chord along for a while.

As it turned out, Eddie didn't make it into Waikīkī that day. They played through the afternoon and into the evening. He stayed overnight, and they played through the next day, then the next. It was one of those magic times musicians live for, when the chemistry is right and unforeseen connections begin to ignite the air. Gabby—accomplished on every stringed instrument—was impressed by Eddie's versatility and technical expertise. And Eddie began to hear something he had previously not been able to hear, to feel something that until this meeting he had not been able to feel, or perhaps had not been ready to feel. It was in Gabby's strum, his sense of rhythm, with its echo of old *hula* drumming. It was also in his voice.

After a couple of days the music had somehow loosened Gabby's throat. He could take light food, and he began to sing his favorite songs. Gabby knew thousands of songs, including many American pop standards and all the *hapa-haole* tunes and tropical ballads so often requested at the hotels: "Beyond the Reef," "My Little Grass Shack," "Red Sails in the Sunset." But the songs he loved were written by Hawaiians and reached back to an older time—"He'eia," "Haleakalā," "Ka Ua Loku," "Maika'i Kaua'i." He sang them with that poignant breaking and bending of notes that is like the peak moment in flamenco singing or in blues, as it slides between exuberance and lament, the untranslatable, skin-prickling delivery that would soon make Gabby the most famous Hawaiian singer of modern times.

"I heard the soul speaking," Eddie says, "and in almost an instant I understood what my father had tried to tell me about Hawaiian music. I wish now he was there so I could say, 'Dad, you were right all along.' But he had already passed away, so he never got to hear me play the music he always wanted me to play. He would have grinned real wide to hear me say it was not about all those things I used to think were so important, music theory and sophisticated chords. There in Waimanālo, just the two of us, Gabby is pouring out his heart, and the

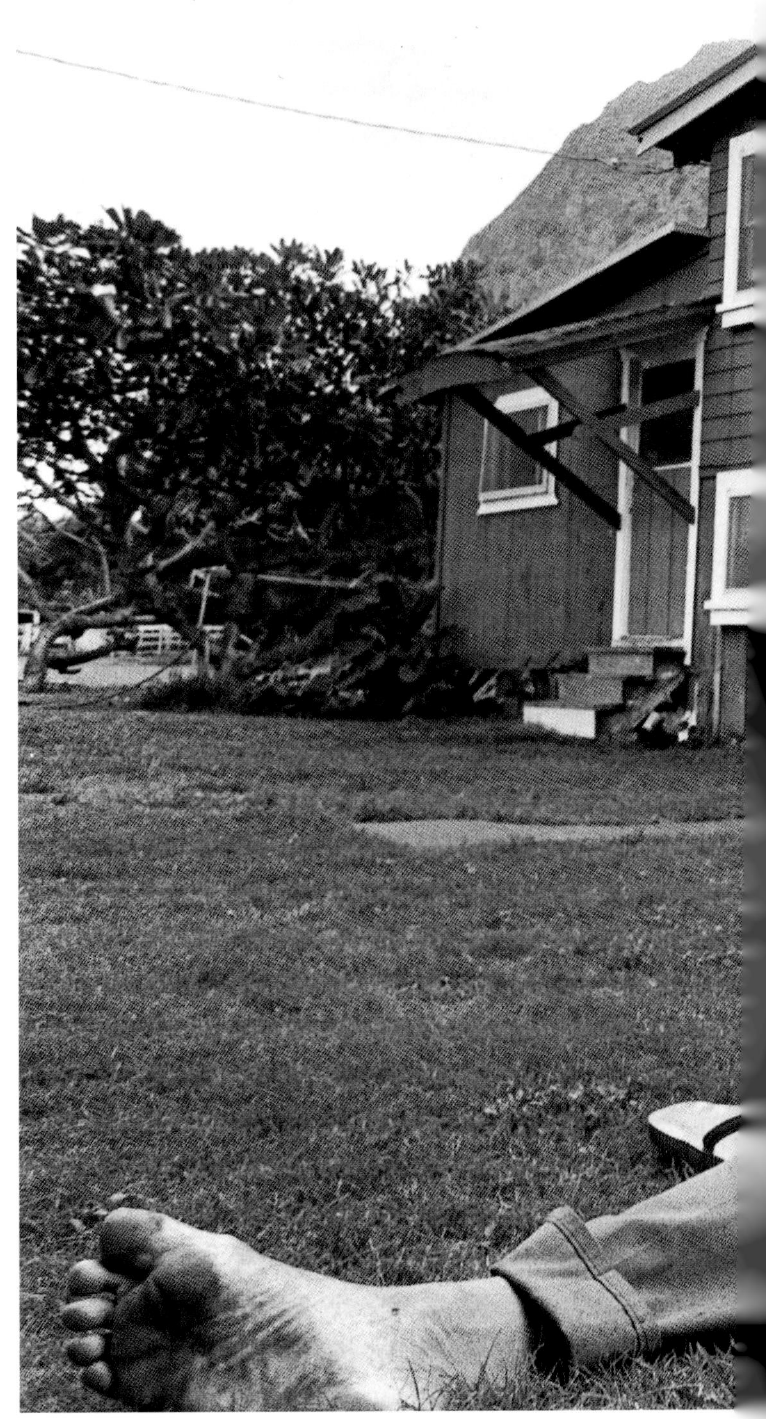

Gabby Pahinui (1921–1980) at home in Waimānalo, circa 1975. When he sang, Eddie says, "I heard the soul speaking."

Morris

In Gabby's Waimānalo kitchen, The Sons of Hawaii jammed, rehearsed, and talked story.

whole history of Hawai'i is in his voice. For me it was like a religious conversion."

For both men these days of music were opening the way to new possibilities. As Gabby's mood improved, he began to chew again and eat regular meals. A week later he was strong enough to walk down the road to the house of someone Nani and Mabel wanted him to meet, an elder in this mostly Hawaiian community, a *tūtū* man who might be able to diagnose his condition.

Eddie went with him. The old man was seated on his porch in a straight-back chair, white-haired and dignified, watching them approach. As Gabby reached the topmost stair, the old man stopped him with his eyes. His voice was frail and graveled, yet full of authority.

"You," he said. "You make a lot of promises you don't keep. That is why you have this *pilikia,* this trouble. People get angry. They wish bad things on other people. Sit down."

Gabby stepped across the porch and sat down next to the

tūtū man, who took his hand and held it as he said a long prayer in Hawaiian. Then with unblinking eyes, looking straight at Gabby, he said, "From now on, don't promise to do something you might not do. If you have to say something, say 'Maybe.' That way you don't have to do anything you don't want to. And other people can't get angry with you breaking your promise and then wish the worst on you."

Gabby was contrite, nodding his head as if to say, 'Yes, I know exactly what you mean.' He was like a young boy in church, talking to the minister.

"Mahalo," Gabby said, standing up. Tears were in his eyes, tears of regret and gratitude. "Thank you, *tūtū*."

The old man released his hand. "Now you can go."

In the days that followed, as they continued playing—working out arrangements, exploring more songs—Gabby continued to improve. Within another week he had moved back home, to his house on Bell Street, three blocks away. He had his appetite again. He was putting on weight. Eddie thought it was what the old man had said. But as time would tell, the words of the *tūtū* man contained a lesson Gabby would never quite learn.

What brought him back was the music itself. It was feeding them both, nourishing them both. "We'd wake up at five in the morning," Eddie recalls, "go out in the yard or to the beach and just play all day. We'd have a few beers, sit back and play till it got dark. We'd have dinner and play for the rest of the night. It was really a happy time."

They both knew something rare was going on. Each man's instrumental skill released something in the other, opening new areas of expression. For Eddie it was partly what he heard in Gabby's voice, partly what he heard coming from his guitar, the slack-key styling Gabby had mastered as no one else had.

The phrase *kī hō'alu* means to slacken or loosen strings as a way to change the tuning. It usually involves lowering the bass and arranging treble strings so that most chords can be played with two or three open strings plucked by a roving thumb. This open chording can make a bigger sound, with an uninterrupted harmonic aura that hums around the melody line as the murmur of surf hums in the air around the islands.

Where the slack-key sound came from is as much a part of Eddie's story as the *palupalu* sound of his mother's voice. The first guitars reached Hawai'i in the 1830s, with the Mexican cowboys brought from Alta California to help Kamehameha III control a runaway cattle population.[1] While Hawaiians learned to rope and ride—and in the process created their unique *paniolo* cowboy tradition—they also learned to pick and strum for songs and dances. They took to the guitar as they would later take to the *'ukulele,* not only playing well, but somehow making it their own. In all likelihood those old vaqueros knew more than one way to tune their strings. The guitar had reached Mexico from Spain, where alternate tunings were, and still are, a feature of the guitar's long history. But Hawaiians would take this feature of the instrument further than anyone else on earth, making slack-key guitar a style and a sound that reveals the spirit of a people and a place.

In the 1930s, when Eddie was growing up, slack-key guitar was still heard mainly as an accompaniment for singing. By 1959 Gabby Pahinui was the best known of a small vanguard of musicians exploring its solo possibilities, using slides, pulls, hammer-ons, harmonics. They were also widening the range of variant tunings, which had become central to the slack-key mystique. Over the years dozens had been developed, some associated with certain families or with districts of certain islands. Often a single tuning would include its own repertoire of songs. With each tuning came separate finger positions and left hand work, which the adept performers had to memorize, since none of this was written down.

Gabby had come of age in Honolulu during the 1920s and 1930s. His given name was Charles. Other musicians nicknamed him "Gabardine" (later shortened to Gabby) because of the pleated slacks he used to wear, and maybe because his kinky hair reminded them of worsted fabric. Like Eddie, he had an early taste for jazz and swing—Benny Goodman, Django Rinehart, Louis Armstrong. But the man who taught him how to play was a little-known and unrecorded guitar wizard named Henry Keawe, born in the 1870s, and a master of the slack-key tunings.

Before joining Eddie Spencer at the Queen's Surf, Gabby had spent eighteen years with the Andy Cummings band, sometimes on rhythm guitar, sometimes on steel. By the late 1950s he was a walking library of Hawaiian melodies and lyrics. He had recently made local history with two recordings that gave new life to what many still regarded as a downhome rural sound: a 33-rpm single of the old love song "Hi'ilawe," released in 1955; and three years later, teaming up with Barney Isaacs, the first-ever album devoted entirely to this style, *Hawaiian Slack Key*. These discs were spinning in backrooms and garages from Kaua'i to Hilo, already shaping the next two generations of Hawai'i's guitar stylists. But during those days in Waimānalo Gabby didn't know this yet. He only knew he was listening for something—a note? a long forgotten song?—and since he'd started playing music every day with Eddie, he felt a lot better than he had before Eddie walked into Mabel's yard.

Toward the end of this month of musical exploration, a visitor appeared. It was bassist Joe Marshall, who had missed seeing Gabby around Waikīkī.

"Hey, pops," he said, walking in the door. "Hey, brother Eddie."

"Marsh," said Gabby, with his welcoming smile. "Come in, come in."

"Where you been?" Joe asked. "How you doing?"

"Doing good. Sit down. Have a beer. Listen to something."

They played a couple of songs, new arrangements they'd just worked out, and Joe was smiling. He had a round face and an impish look, as if always on the verge of laughter. "Gee," he said, "I should've brought my bass."

"Well, go get it," Gabby said. "We'll be here. We got plenty more songs."

"Good idea," said Joe. "I'll be right back."

It was a twenty-mile round trip over the mountain to Honolulu. An hour and a half later Joe was in the room again and tuning up. He had a rich voice and a perfect ear for harmony. Like Eddie, he had grown up in Honolulu, in a big Hawaiian family (ten brothers and sisters), and had been encouraged by his father, who had once played saxophone in the Royal Hawaiian Band. Now thirty, Joe had been playing the Waikīkī clubs for years, before and after army service in Korea. He and Gabby had worked many gigs together and had sung together at the Queen's Surf. So Joe fit right in with what they were doing, backing Gabby on the vocals, anchoring their chords with his easy, steady bass line.

Joe knew right away that this was more than a jam session. He too was ignited by the music, the superb instrumental work, and the chance to pour his heart into Hawaiian-language songs. He stayed the night, and the next night, too, as they all started talking about what they felt emerging here, a "sound" none had heard before yet somehow had been waiting to hear.

But now that Joe's acoustic bass had filled in the bottom of the chords, the need for some other note had opened at the top. Eddie thought they needed a steel guitar. The right steel player, he said, could provide the finishing touch. Joe got excited. He knew a young musician named David Rogers, who had a rare and tasteful style. Eddie and Gabby recognized the name. The Rogers family was famous for its steel players. David's uncle Benny had for many years played and recorded with the Genoa Keawe band.

"You know where he lives?" Gabby said.

"I've been there," said Joe.

"Let's go then! Let's go find this guy!"

They piled into Joe's car and once again he drove over the mountains, this time to Kalihi. As they parked in front of the Rogers family house, another car pulled up to the curb and out stepped a husky fellow with a big, shy grin. In those days David Rogers was still widely remembered as a high school athlete. His football skills, his running and kicking in the local Barefoot League, had earned him the nickname "Feet."

He'd just come back from an afternoon rehearsal. But as soon as he heard what Gabby and Eddie and Joe had in mind, he sensed that here was a chance he, too, had been waiting for. As Joe Marshall would later observe, "Feet was playing a lot, but he wasn't happy with those other groups. He was already searching for the same thing we were searching for, everybody looking for that one thing we can own that is our identity."

Feet knew these three by reputation. At the same time, he had a commitment to another band. What was he to do? Luckily his father was there, George Rogers, a musician known to Eddie and Gabby, an elder statesman of the Hawaiian steel guitar. Maybe George could help his son make up his mind. Eddie asked him if he thought it would be okay for Feet to sit in with them. Then Gabby played a couple of songs from their new repertoire. George approved of what he heard. He appreciated Eddie's show of respect. "Okay," he said at last. "I think my son should go with you folks. Just one thing."

"What's that?" said Eddie.

"Feet don't have his own guitar yet. He's always borrowing mine."

George went out and bought one from a friend, a pancake-style Rickenbacher—a gift to his son, and a kind of advance blessing for the band-to-be.

Back at Gabby's place, Feet joined their ongoing session. He had learned from his father and uncle, yet he did not imitate them. At age twenty-four, he had already perfected his own singular guitar voice. It pulled them together—the bass, *'ukulele,* the pulsing slack-key guitar—completing the sound. As the days went by, as they brought Feet into the repertoire, he also helped to define that sound.

His music is a bit like his manner. "Feet was like my father," Eddie recalls. "He never said much. But when he talked, you paid attention. He saw people for who they were, and he would get right to the point."

There is a busy, flashy way of playing steel that tries to fill each measure with as many notes as possible. Feet's music was the opposite of that. He had no desire to draw attention to himself or be the star. He played with reserve and understatement, with an exquisite purity of tone.

Growing up in a household of musicians, Feet had learned much by example. Coming of age in Hawai'i, he had also picked up a lot by osmosis, since the steel guitar, like the slack-key style, is another Hawaiian invention, this one discovered back in 1885 by an eleven-year-old schoolboy from Lā'ie, over on O'ahu's windward side.

By his own account Joseph Kekūkū (who would later be among the first musicians to introduce steel playing on the U.S. mainland) was walking along some railroad tracks, carrying a guitar, when he picked up a loose bolt and idly slid it across the strings. From that random act, one thing led to another. He began to experiment with a pen knife, with the edge of a straight razor, eventually with a steel bar he made at the Kamehameha Schools machine shop. He needed a bar that fit easily in the left hand as it slid from note to note, while the right hand continued to pluck. The essentials of this instrument, as it has evolved through the decades, found their shape in Kekūkū's early experiments. He laid the guitar on his lap. He raised his strings so the steel could glide without touching frets. He switched from gut to wire strings, in search of a longer, more sustaining note.

Sixty years later young Feet Rogers, like Joseph Kekūkū, was still trying to get more out of the strings. He brought with him a D-major tuning, played only by members of the Rogers family. "How we tune the steel," he once observed, "is kind of like a chant or a family song, you know. It belongs to us, and we have to take care of it, or else it will change like everything else. It's just like my steel, too. It belongs to my father, and I never played one that has the same sound."[2]

For his highest string Feet was using a duplicate of the second string. Slightly thicker, it meant he had to tune it tighter to bring it up to pitch. He found one brand, Black Diamond, that could take this kind of tension. Even then the high string often broke. But the extra tension gave him what he was listening for: a purer ring. In performance Feet would sometimes pull away from a song so that it seemed he'd actually stopped playing. Then, after a few measures of near silence, a single silver note would punctuate the phrasing so hauntingly it filled the room and pierced the heart.

The band didn't have a name yet. When they landed their first gig, in the spring of 1960, they simply said they were "Gabby's group." It was a club called the Sandbox, out on Sand Island Road, across the lagoon from Honolulu International Airport.

Feet knew the manager, Pat Dorian, and knew he was looking for a band, a show, something to replace a Tahitian revue moving on to another club. A transplanted southern Californian who once worked as a stunt man, Dorian had been in the islands for years and loved Hawaiian music. He decided to take a chance, figuring a new band playing traditional songs might have some appeal for his all-local clientele.

It wasn't a fancy place, a big square room with a concrete floor, a bar, a low stage, at the edge of an industrial district and far beyond the tourist loop. No one foresaw the impact this band would have, once they took the stage and word began to spread. They played Thursday, Friday, and Saturday nights. By the second weekend the place was packed, with customers waiting outside to get in. The club's neighborhood regulars were soon surrounded by listeners from all layers of island life—cab drivers and college students, beach boys and politicians, attorneys and fellow musicians, bank officers and corporate executives, side by side with truckers and husky stevedores from the docks who came in straight from work and stayed until closing time. The boys in the band were playing for audiences unlike any they'd seen in their combined years in Waikīkī.

"At the Biltmore or the Queen's Surf," Eddie recalls, "you just never saw this many kinds of people in one place at the same time. They stood for hours in lines that went out the door. I had no idea there was such enthusiasm for pure Hawaiian music, which was all we were playing. Thirty or forty *haole* kids from Punahou School would come in at one time, for instance, sit up in front and sing the Hawaiian words right along with us. If we skipped a verse or mispronounced a word they'd yell out and let us know. Oldtimers, too, started coming in. I mean, *tūtū* ladies from the Queen Emma Society, in their best *mu'umu'u.* I guess it was because we were the only group around in those days playing that kind of music."

Listeners were drawn to the joy in that room, the sheer exuberance of four Hawaiians who found themselves mobbed by fans who shared their passion. And they were drawn to Gabby's showmanship and the naked emotion of his singing.

 Twenty years in Waikīkī, and he had never fronted his own group. Here he could choose what to sing, what to play, and how to play it. With Joe Marshall backing him on vocals, Gabby's voice found new ranges of expressiveness.

Each night they opened with "'Ūlili Ē" (O Sandpiper), an old *hula* song. "They couldn't get enough of it," Eddie remembers. "Sometimes we'd sing it once or twice every set, people banging on the tables until we played it again."

The title names a migratory shorebird, and the name itself imitates the bird's urgent cry as it scurries about, feeding along a wave-washed beach:

'Ūlili ē . . .
'Ūlili ho'i . . .
'Ūlili holoholo kahakai ē . . .

Each verse consists of a four-bar melody that is repeated twice, followed by an eight-bar refrain. At the Sandbox they played it upbeat, with a one-verse intro by Eddie, picking the melody in crisp, full notes. Gabby sang a verse, with Joe and Eddie adding harmony on the refrain. Then Gabby and Eddie picked eight bars together, *'ukulele* and guitar, with Gabby under Eddie's melody line. Gabby sang another verse. Feet took eight bars on the steel. After Gabby sang the third and final verse, the tune ended with an astonishing coda, uke and slack-key guitar in four bars of tight counterpoint, the notes ringing off one another, the kind of synchronized, close-harmony picking that had fueled their four-month jam in Waimānalo.

Just as Gabby had touched Eddie, the band was touching the hearts of all who heard them. Familiar island songs were given new life. Old drumming rhythms had somehow joined the improvisational feel of jazz. Yet this was not a jazz combo. There was no piano, no drum, no horns, nor was there anything like what one would have heard in a hotel lounge downtown: there was no show band in the background. These were all stringed instruments, standard pieces of a small Hawaiian band, played at a superb level of musicianship, while the lead voice of Gabby Pahinui seemed to rise from the earth itself to link these Sandbox nights with the voices of long-gone chanters.

People who were there have claimed they were hearing much more than good music. It was an early signal, they say, an opening note for what would soon be called Hawai'i's cultural renaissance. Such a claim might sound at first farfetched, since we tend to associate the rebirth of a culture with architecture, schools of painting, and literary works. Hawai'i, however, has another kind of history, where music has always been central. In ancient times, the songs, the chants, the dances contained the legends, the genealogies, the stories of origin, migration, love and war and kinship. Hawaiians had no written language. Chanters and dancers were the poets, the historians, the keepers of communal memory. During these early years of reawakening, the voices heard and the songs performed at the Sandbox were among the first to voice feelings yearning to be expressed throughout the island chain.

Eddie and the others didn't see it that way, of course. Not yet. They were high on the sound, but never would have seen themselves as leading any kind of revival. When asked, years later, how he had come by such a vision, as far back as 1959 and 1960, Eddie said, "Hell, if I thought I had to have some kind of vision, I probably would have quit."

At the time it was a chance to do what they loved to do and have a ball doing it. There was always a wild and raucous spirit in the room, with Gabby's antics at the center, as if the all-night parties he once hosted had simply been moved over the mountain to Sand Island Road. He liked to laugh. When the music was going the way he wanted it to go he had a high-pitched laugh of pure delight. He liked to call singers and dancers out of the audience and bring them up onto the stage. He liked to drink, and he liked to borrow drinks. "What did one tonsil say to the other tonsil?" he would ask the crowd once or twice a night. Reaching down to grab some customer's scotch and soda, he would tip the glass back for a long pull, then provide the answer. "Here comes another swallow from Capistrano!"

On one of these nights he had just lifted a glass from a table near the stage when three men in suits walked into the club. One was a Honolulu judge known to many of the customers and known to Gabby, since he'd stood before him just that afternoon while accompanying a wayward son to family court. The judge walked up to the stage and said, "Hello, Gabby." After tilting his head to polish off the customer's beer, Gabby grinned at the judge and leaned into the mike. "Not guilty, your honor."

The customers never tired of this. He was such a charming storyteller and bon vivant, they vied for this attention, even offering drinks so he would sit with them awhile. Gabby spent his intermissions table-hopping, usually for fifteen minutes or so, until manager Pat Dorian rang a gong to signal the start of another set.

Something about that gong gave order to the room, like bells that chime the hour from a village steeple. But after the band had been there a couple of months, Dorian was transferred to Waikīkī, to open another club. The manager who replaced him evidently didn't know about the gong. Or maybe Dorian carried it with him. On the new manager's first night the band took a break that went for half an hour. The boys were waiting for Gabby to get back onstage, but he was holding forth at a corner table, putting away the free drinks. The new manager said to Eddie, "It's been half an hour."

"Don't talk to me," Eddie said, knowing there'd be no music till Gabby was ready to play. "Talk to Gabby. He's the leader."

Forty-five minutes went by. An hour went by. No one had complained. But the chatter level around the club was deafening. The new manager was nervous. He called the club owner, who didn't like to be called at home. The owner said he wasn't paying the band to sit around and drink, so please inform them that this would be their final night.

When Gabby heard they were about to be fired, he leaped onto the stage calling, "Let's play! Let's play!" They finished out the night with a long set and left the crowd cheering for more. But the Sandbox gig was over, ending as suddenly as it had begun, and they were outside in the parking lot, looking across the lagoon at a late flight from the mainland on its final approach, glancing at one another, wondering, Now what?

MISTER SKABADOOZ *Gabby Pahinui was a mystery to a lot of people, but not to me. I worked with him off and on for over ten years, and he was like a lot of performers I have known, who are pulled two ways. Gabby was one of the greatest Hawaiian singers of all time. Some say he was the greatest. He was a musical genius. And he was his own worst enemy. We would get jobs because of Gabby, and we would lose jobs because of Gabby. That was the way he lived his life. It was more than booze. He was an angel with a demon inside of him. He could drive people crazy. Once I was talking with a guy who used to manage a band Gabby was in, and he had this big scar across his stomach from an ulcer operation. He lifted up his shirt and pointed to his scar and said to me, "Gabby Pahinui did that."*

You take the time they staged the first big slack-key concert, downtown at Blaisdell Concert Hall. Some of the younger musicians put it together, and Gabby was the star of the show. Everybody knows how much he did to establish slack-key as the most authentic Hawaiian style of playing. They rehearse everything and put a tight show together. The place is sold out. Some good bands are there to warm up the crowd. Finally Gabby's time comes. While he walks out onstage a band is already playing, and he is supposed to join in. But now he likes the sound of the music so much he puts down his guitar, and he starts to do the hula. *Gabby happens to be one of the best* hula *dancers I have ever seen—you know, that Hawaiian style of male dancing—so the crowd goes wild. But the guys who organized the concert are dying a thousand deaths backstage because the main idea is to honor slack-key, and Gabby decides it's time to dance.*

I remember one day we were in the bar at the Flamingo over on Kapi'olani Boulevard, me and Eddie Spencer, who worked at the rent-a-car place next door, and the head of the Musician's Union, and this real estate guy named Chin Chai. We're in there drinking and having lunch and then playing a few songs. It's an easygoing place. I'm just wearing slippers and a tee shirt, and I have my 'ukulele, *and Eddie Spencer is playing a guitar that belongs to Chin Chai. And after a while Gabby comes in. He just got off from his job with the county, doing road work in those days, so he's in his boots, tee shirt, muddy pants. Nobody was playing music just then, so he says to me, "Son, who owns that guitar?"*

I said, "That guy over by the bar, Chin Chai."

He said, "Ask him can I borrow it."

So I go over and say, "Chin Chai, Gabby wants to borrow your guitar to play for somebody, but he'll bring it back pretty soon."

Chin Chai doesn't even ask where or who. He just says, "Sure, it's okay."

Then Gabby says to me, "Come with me, son, and bring your ʻukulele."

So we jump in my car, and I say, "Where to?"

Well, we drive from Kapiʻolani Boulevard all the way up to Nuʻuanu Mortuary, where all these people are standing around, dressed for a funeral. I say to myself, "Oh no," because I'm just there in my tee shirt, and Gabby in his muddy pants. But it's too late to turn around, so I follow him while he walks up to a guy in a black suit who says, "Gabby, what do you want?"

Gabby names the man who died and says, "I came to play for my friend."

The guy in black goes inside and comes back with a member of the family, another guy in a black suit who looks at our tee shirts and my slippers and Gabby's work boots, and just turns around and walks away. Gabby looks at me with this wild look in his eye that says he's going to do whatever he's going to do.

I say, "Who did you come up here for? That guy in the suit?"

He says, "No."

I say, "Then let's go in. But one thing, Gabby—the minute we walk into the mortuary, you start playing."

He says, "Okay, son, here we go."

People inside are all dressed up, starting to take their seats, and we walk through the doorway, and Gabby starts strumming Chin Chai's guitar, that magic sound, the way only he could do. And nobody gets mad. They don't know what to do but sit there and listen. Then I play my 'ukulele, *and we start singing a sweet Hawaiian song that Gabby knows his friend used to love. We walk down the aisle until we get to the casket. When we finish, we just say* aloha *to Gabby's friend and turn around and walk out again and don't talk to anybody, just go back to the car.*

While we're driving away, I tell him, "Don't ever do this to me again. I don't mind playing if we got decent clothes on, but not with slippers and tee shirt." But Gabby, he just laughs. He's happy, because that's Gabby's way. He doesn't plan ahead. Whatever comes to him on the spur of the moment, that's what he does.

He used to have this word skabadooz, *which meant "anything goes." Sometimes in the middle of a song he turns and says to the rest of us, "Skabadooz," which could mean "I don't remember how we rehearsed this, so just stick with me and we'll get through it one way or another." Here was a guy who made so many people stop and pay attention to Hawaiian music—me included—and you never knew when he was going to change the words in the middle of a song or make up verses or leave out verses. If you don't know Gabby ahead of time, that can really throw you off.*

Joe Marshall would get annoyed with Gabby because Joe went to Kamehameha School and I think he sang in the chorus, and he was a stickler for how the words should go. Joe used to shake his head and call Gabby "Mister Skabadooz," said Gabby had been skabadoozing his whole life and getting away with it. But that was Gabby's way. You never knew what would happen. He wants to drink all night, he drinks. He wants to do the hula *instead of play guitar like everybody paid money to see him do, he dances the* hula *and brings the house down. If a string breaks in the middle of a number, he keeps on playing. Maybe two strings break. Gabby keeps playing. He finds new chords and takes great solos—with two strings gone! He wants to play a song for his friend who passed away, he doesn't tell anybody he's coming. If he's in a tuxedo or muddy boots from his job, he doesn't care. He goes, he sings from his heart, so sweet, with so much* aloha *in his voice he makes you cry.*

3

Guides

Eddie had played a lot of gigs, but none like the one at the Sandbox. Before it was over, doors had opened that would shape the course of his life. Among the fans who showed up night after night was a handsome Hawaiian fellow named Kurt Johnson, a young pilot in the Air National Guard. During breaks, over beers, he and Eddie struck up a friendship. Taken by the sound of the band, Kurt was also touched by Eddie's new-found passion for Hawaiian songs and where they had come from.

Eddie was now the band's researcher, haunting libraries and secondhand stores, looking for song sheets and out-of-print collections, looking for more old melodies, for lyrics, too, and for missing verses. The emotional power of Gabby's voice had awakened a deeply felt connection to the music, and once awakened, Eddie felt compelled to get it right. The music had a history. So did each song. He wanted to know all about these things, though he scarcely knew where to begin.

opposite
Mary Kawena Pukui at Waimānalo, O'ahu, in 1939, making a basket of 'ilima *twigs.*

One night Kurt said, "Eddie, to sing Hawaiian, you must *know* Hawaiian. Otherwise you might not know the right feeling for the words you sing." His mother, he said, was a student of the language, and she had two friends who might be able to help him in this pursuit, if he'd be interested to meet them. Eddie was very interested, especially when he learned that one of these friends was Mary Kawena Pukui, known to be Hawai'i's foremost expert on the cultural tradition.

Kurt made a phone call, and the next evening they were knocking on the door of her modest home near King Street, in midtown Honolulu. Known as Tūtū Kawena, or simply

Kawena, she was then nearly seventy, white-haired and heavy-set, a warm-hearted island woman who wore her learning as lightly as she wore her flowered *mu'umu'u.* She was a master of the *hula* and a storehouse of ancient chants passed down through her family for generations.

Eddie had brought along Feet Rogers. Kawena's daughter Patience was there, too, with her husband. At such a dinner-table gathering, Eddie was ordinarily reticent to speak, yet on this night he found himself doing much of the talking. Kurt had told Kawena about the band, and she wanted to hear more, probing with pointed questions. Eddie described the long jam session in Waimānalo, what he'd heard in Gabby's voice, in the rhythms of his slack-key guitar, and where all this had taken him.

"If someone could explain to me more about the songs I have been researching," he told them, "I could see better where I'm headed. Then maybe I can help Gabby and the boys see it better, too."

It was a call for help. When Kawena didn't respond, he wondered if she was perhaps disappointed in his story. She'd listened carefully to everything he said and to Kurt's animated account of the music and its impact. Maybe she was just too busy to respond. Earlier Kurt had told him how lucky they were to be meeting her this way. "People call Tūtū all the time," he'd said. Only when they were ready to leave, standing in the doorway, did Eddie finally hear her answer. With a wise twinkle of recognition in her brown eyes, she nodded and said quietly, "You can come and see me."

In her softspoken Polynesian way she had extended an open invitation to be available for him as a guide, as a mentor. He thanked her, with his *aloha,* knowing he would soon be back.

Two days later Kurt Johnson arranged a second meeting, this time at his house in Kāne'ohe, on the windward side. He had invited Pīlahi Pākī, another of his mother's friends, widely recognized as a wise elder. She had grown up on Maui, near Lahaina, and had known Eddie's grandmother. Years earlier, while living in Honolulu, she'd heard of an inspired man in south Kona, on the Big Island, who possessed a deep knowledge of the Hawaiian language. Compelled to find him, as if called

Eddie's teacher, Pīlahi Pākī (1910–1985).

to this task, Pīlahi dropped everything she was doing and flew to Kona. The man, named Naluahine, was a fisherman who had lost both legs. He lived alone on a hard-to-reach stretch of shoreline, where he waited for others to come to him. When Pīlahi finally tracked him down, he told her he'd been waiting for her, as one who'd been selected to receive his teachings.

In these two meetings arranged by Kurt, something similar was happening to Eddie. As they sat down to dinner, Pīlahi said, "Where are you in this work Kurt tells me about? And what have you been doing?"

She was a tall woman, with regal stature, and white hair coiffed close around her head. Her commanding eyes held him as he once again told the story of how discovering Hawaiian music had given him a new sense of purpose. This time he'd brought along some new materials, pages of song lyrics which he spread across the table. Pīlahi looked them over and said, "For my Hawai'i, I *laulā* . . ."

She spread one hand wide, in a gesture of generosity. "I give freely. I share what I have. You can ask me questions. Anything you want, from now until tomorrow morning."

Again it was an open offer to be available, but framed in a way that took Eddie by surprise, since he did not yet know quite how to put into words the questions he wanted to ask.

"With oldtimers," he says now, "with the *kūpuna* who followed the Hawaiian style of teaching, they had a certain way of doing things. If you were a youngster or a pupil, you only listen, you watch, you imitate, you keep your mouth shut. In my case, as someone coming in search of advice, it was up to me to ask. Pīlahi said I could ask her anything. But if I don't ask, she doesn't answer. Nobody preaches to you. They just wait. And for me, back then, I didn't know enough yet. So it was my turn now, to go out there and really get serious about the work."

The work. What did this mean? Eddie had become a technical wizard. He could read music and translate notes on the page into chords and melodic lines. His fingers flew around the fretboard. Among those devotees who had tried to emulate his dazzling arrangements on the big production numbers, he had a nickname: "Magua," an Indian word for "fast." But speed, dexterity, technique for its own sake—these were not skills that would get him where he now felt the need to go. His search for missing verses and his urge to get the lyrics right was more than a quest for accuracy, more than the need to satisfy the studious and scholarly side of his nature. The old Hawaiian songs partake of a cultural continuity, and much of it resides in the words themselves. For Eddie, it was a first step toward retrieving what had almost been lost to him.

He remembers that when he was very young, living in the compound in Kauluwela, he slept on a cot in the kitchen. Some mornings he would wake very early and hear his mother and father speaking Hawaiian. While all the children slept, they would sit at the kitchen table, drinking coffee and talking. He would lie there and listen and not move a muscle, having learned that if he spoke or sat up or rustled a sheet, they would instantly shift to English. Though both his parents grew up speaking Hawaiian as a first language, it was no longer something to be passed on to their children. Hawaiian could not be used in school. English was what would get you ahead in the world. To the ears of young Eddie, the voices of his mother and father carried a double message: while he loved the sound and the intimacy of their talking, his parents' native tongue had become secretive and covert, something you had to keep to yourself.

By 1959, when he and Gabby teamed up in Waimānalo, Hawai'i had become the fiftieth state in the Union. In that same year, the first jet flight from the mainland touched down at Honolulu International, reducing West Coast travel time from thirteen hours to five. For people of Hawaiian ancestry these were mixed blessings. Politically and economically, statehood and jet travel would be good for the islands, good for tourism, trade, and investment. But culturally they seemed to be giant steps in a century-long process of disempowerment. Spoken Hawaiian was dying out all through the island chain, along with what remained of traditional practices and arts, such as chant, *hula*, healing, canoeing. Interest in Hawaiian music was at its lowest ebb in decades. Rock-and-roll was taking over. The defining image for the era seemed to be Elvis Presley's hit film, *Blue Hawaii,* released in 1961.

In such a time, in such a climate, the two women who had agreed to mentor Eddie were among the few who had devoted their lives to preserving what they could of a dying language and its lore. While many others kept their eyes on the runway to see what the next flight from the mainland might bring, these two kept their eyes on the deep sources of cultural knowledge, which they believed held the true source of empowerment for their people. They each possessed a kind of authority that is not validated by academic degrees or by any license from a professional body. What they knew, what they carried, had been passed on to them, by voice and by example, from *kūpuna* to *kūpuna,* along with the inner power, the *mana,* that accompanies such transmission.

Descended from high chiefs on Maui, Pīlahi Pākī had spent a number of years traveling through the islands in search of native speakers who could further her study of the language, its poetry, its legacy of oral literature. Kawena's first teacher

Kawena at the Bishop Museum, where she served on the staff for twenty-five years.

was her grandmother, a chanter and healer from the Big Island district of Ka'ū. Her full Hawaiian name was Kawena'ulaokalaniaHi'iakaikapolioPele, which translates to mean, "The rosy glow in the sky made by Hi'iaka who was reared in the bosom of Pele." It linked Kawena by chant and lineage to Pele, Hawai'i's fire goddess and the *'aumakua,* the guardian spirit, of Kawena's family. With such women to guide him, Eddie's "work" could truly begin.

Kawena had recently co-edited the first edition of the landmark *Hawaiian Dictionary.*[1] From her he began to receive his earliest lessons in how meaning can gather around words and images in the old songs. References to birds and flowers, for instance, often signify sweethearts. The words for water and rain *(wai, ua)* might refer to fertility and growth, but sometimes grief; while a cloudburst, a downpour *(ka ua loku),* can be a moment of intensity between two lovers.

"I would take the material to Kawena," Eddie recalls, "and ask her to give me an idea what the story of the song is about. So I can know the best approach to give it, the arrangement. If I know the meaning of the story, I get a better idea for which instrument should do the solo. The story means this and this, she would say, and you can do it sweet. Or joyous. Or nostalgic. Or stately. Or whatever. And then I go talk with Gabby and the boys about my findings."

Some of the results would soon be heard on the band's first album, recorded in Honolulu in 1961. The producer, Don McDiarmid, Jr., was another fan smitten by what he'd heard at the Sandbox. Soon after the gig ended, he approached the band on behalf of his recently formed production company, Hula Records.

As the son of a popular local bandleader and composer, McDiarmid had come to Hawaiian music with his own kind of legacy. (His father, Don McDiarmid, Sr., had started out playing with The Harry Owens Orchestra and, in the 1930s, composed such *hapa-haole* standards as "Hilo Hattie" and "Little Brown Gal.") Having grown up in Honolulu, he knew the varieties of island music. He understood what the band had done, taking these songs he'd heard for years at *lū'au* and family parties and giving them fresh life. To his ears the authenticity of feeling, coupled with the exceptional musicianship, wasn't being heard in the clubs and lounges scattered along the beachfront, and had seldom been recorded.

McDiarmid was among the pioneers of local record production. Not much had changed since the early heyday of Hawaiian music, in the decades before World War II, when production was in the hands of the big mainland companies, RCA Victor, Decca, and Columbia. In the years since the war, half a dozen small companies had sprung up in Honolulu, most of them short-lived and operating by the seat of their pants, setting up their mikes in private homes, church social halls, and high school auditoriums.

When McDiarmid was ready to record the band, there was still no professional studio anywhere in the islands (the first would open in 1967). Cutting an album in Honolulu was a bit like open-cockpit barnstorming in the early days of the airplane: it required a spirit of adventure and on-the-spot ingenuity. He had a two-track Ampex recorder and a friend at KPOI Radio, across the Ala Wai Canal from Waikīkī. He took the band in there at midnight, after regular programming had signed off, and found the space so small that Joe Marshall had to play his bass sitting down, with the instrument across his knees like an enormous guitar.

McDiarmid and his engineer were undeterred by the low-tech conditions. As he and Eddie would later recall, he brought his own musical passion to the mix:

"The blend of the group was what we worked toward on the very first album. We never gave you a sound that you couldn't duplicate when you played live. We could have made you sound like something else that you couldn't duplicate, and that's what happens nowadays, you know. You go to a concert and ask, 'What is that? That's not the guy I got on record!' Well, it's not his fault. The engineers have changed the whole thing. All in all, we tried to keep it as human sounding as we could, and to keep always—the number one thing of everything we did was heart, the heart of Hawaiian music."[2]

With the Sandbox repertoire as a base, they recorded a dozen numbers, all in Hawaiian: a song about the beauties of the northern island of Kaua'i, a song that celebrates Maui, and another about a ship named for Maui's dormant crater, Haleakalā. To compensate for any errors in pronunciation or wording, they printed accurate Hawaiian lyrics on the back of the jacket—a tribute to tradition that no production company had done before.

When it came time to name the album, they had to decide first on a name for the band, still known loosely as "Gabby's group." The story is that Chick Daniels, the legendary Waikīkī beachboy, was heard to exclaim one night, "You guys got the spirit of these islands in your blood! You are all true sons of Hawai'i!"

So that's what they settled on. *Gabby Pahinui and the Sons of Hawaii* was released the following year. After airing the album a couple of times, KPOI Radio got such a listener response, they played it every day for an entire month, the whole album, often several times in a single morning, interspersed with talk about the songs and the musicians. This was something new on local radio, which in those days didn't feature much Hawaiian music. (Five more years would pass before KCCN, the first all-Hawaiian-music station, went on the air.) But the audience was obviously out there, eager to hear what The Sons were doing, and the album would live on, to become a classic. In print now for over forty years, it catches the flavor of those Sandbox days and captures the sound that had announced a new era in Hawaiian music.

Gabby is on the cover, wearing a blue-flowered *aloha* shirt and a huge carnation *lei*. Joe, Feet, and Eddie stand behind him, near the steps of the helmet-shaped bandstand on the grounds of 'Iolani Palace. They are purposely out of focus. Since Eddie was still on contract with the company who'd recently brought out his *Heart of the Ukulele,* his face couldn't appear on the jacket. To keep Eddie company, Feet and Joe stand with him in the fuzzy background.

For this album Eddie had to change his name. With a nod to his windward neighborhood, he chose his alias, "Johnny Maunawili." It didn't trouble him much, since it seemed to be one way to distance himself from the pop standards and adapted classics that had made his early reputation. "I wasn't playing that stuff anymore," he says. "I had lost all desire to play it. Between the time I cut *Heart of the Ukulele* and the time The Sons' first album came out, my musical interests had moved to a totally different place."

TŪTŪ *One day not long after I met Kawena, when I was still living over on the windward side, I heard an old woman singing a song I thought I recognized. But I can't place it. It sounds almost like a song I heard somewhere else, but I'm not sure. The next morning when I wake up, I'm still thinking about it and wishing I asked where it came from. I have to find out something about this song.*

I get into my car and drive over the Pali Highway to Nu'uanu valley to see my friend, 'Iolani Luahine. She was the greatest hula *dancer of our time, trained in the old way. She knew all the chants and* mele, *and in those days she had a position as curator at the Royal Mausoleum, up there behind Punchbowl, where the kings and queens of the nineteenth century are buried. So I drive over to the Mausoleum and knock on the door of the cottage there, not thinking about what time it is, just thinking about that song.*

'Iolani Luahine (1915–1978), Hawai'i's premier dancer, with Tom Hiona in 1961.

'Iolani Luahine, at her Nāpō'o-po'o home in South Kona, circa 1975.

When she opens the door, she is half asleep. Her eyes are kind of red, and she looks at me for a second like I'm crazy to come around at seven in the morning. I think that anybody else she would have shut the door on me. But 'Iolani was like an older sister to me. We knew each other from a long time back. I guess the first time we performed together in the same show was when I was still in high school, backing up my brother Joe. Anyhow, she finally shoves her hair out of her face and manages to say, "Eddie! What are you doing here?"

I say, "'Io, I heard this song yesterday, over in Kailua."

Now she leans forward a bit and opens her eyes wider to get a better look, probably thinking, You woke me up at this hour to talk about a song*? But then she kind of likes the idea. She smiles and says, "What song?"*

While I stand in the doorway, humming it for her, she closes her eyes and listens and says, "Nani Wale E Ka Mahina [The Moon's Lonely Beauty]."

I say, "That's what I thought too. But there's a bridge to this one. Did you notice the bridge? I think it's a different song."

She looks at me and nods and says, "Better go see Tūtū."

Tūtū *is a respectful word for an elder or a wise teacher or sometimes a grandparent. Since we're talking about a song, I know 'Iolani means Tūtū Kawena. I also know she wants to go back to bed. So I thank her and get into my car, thinking, I will go ask Kawena about this song.*

The Mausoleum is really a big lawn, right off Nu'uanu. There's a circular driveway lined with palms, and big memorials spaced around. While I'm passing the memorial that marks the graves of the last royal family—King Kalākaua, Queen Lili'uokalani, and their sister, Likelike—I have the strong feeling I should stop first at the Bishop Museum. It's more than a feeling. It's a signal, a kind of instruction.

I had never been to the museum, even though it was right near where I went to high school. But I make a detour and drive out School Street and park. It is still only eight o'clock. A sign by the front door says they don't open until nine. It looks like nobody is around. But I knock anyway, and pretty soon a white-haired haole *woman comes and opens the door a crack and says, "Yes?"*

It would be easy for her to tell me to come back when they're open. But I don't want to wait. Whatever I'm looking for is somewhere inside. I say, "My teacher, Kawena Pukui, told me any time I go to the Bishop Museum, early or late, to mention her name."

And by golly, it works! Kawena had been on the museum staff for years. Her name is the magic password. A shine comes into this woman's eyes. She opens the door and lets me in. She is the research librarian. When I tell her I'm looking for information about an old Hawaiian song, she takes me right into the library and points me to the Hawaiian music index file.

I don't know the name of the song. I don't know the composer. I'm new to museums. I don't really know where to start. I just pull a drawer open to see what's in there. And the first card I see says "Queen Lili'uokalani." At the time she was the only composer I knew by name, because of the song I learned from Haunani Kahalewai, "Ku'u Pua I Paoakalani." I take that card over to the desk, where the librarian is catching up on some paperwork. She tells me to go to a certain table across the room and wait for her. She gives me a pair of white gloves and a sharpened pencil in case I want to make notes. "No pens in here, please," she says. "No ink."

A while later she comes out with a package about four inches thick and tied with string. I untie the string and open the package and see that it is the queen's manuscripts, over one hundred songs composed by her. And remember, this is forty years ago, long before these were getting rediscovered and published.

Again I don't know where to start. I open to somewhere in the middle, curious about how the pages look. And the first page I open to is the song I came looking for! It's written in Hawaiian, with all the notes scored above the lyrics. By the notation I can tell it is the melody I heard the old woman sing, and the name of the song gives me chicken-skin because it is titled "Tutu."

'Iolani told me to go see Tūtū, meaning Kawena. Now I have been guided to a song written back in the late nineteenth century, about the grandmother of Queen Lili'uokalani.

I go over to the desk and ask if she can make me a copy of this manuscript page. Pretty soon she comes back with the copy and says, "Would you like to see the queen's longhand notes? Her composition pages?"

"I'd love to," I say.

So we go up to another floor where there is a vault for storing the most valuable items. She goes to a shelf and brings out some folders full of loose pages, and says, "Here, this is how she jotted down the first drafts of her songs."

I take them to another desk. I still have my white gloves on, and a flat ruler she gives me for turning the pages, which were very brittle. Again I start in the middle, slide my ruler into the middle of one folder, and I open to the very same song, "Tutu," with the lyrics in the queen's own hand, as she had first written them down, maybe remembering a day when she was watching her kupuna wahine, *her grandmother, her* tūtū, *putter around the house.*

It's a sweet, lilting song about an old woman early in the morning, reading the Bible and praying, and after her prayer, losing her glasses, only to find them propped up on top of her head. It's a whimsical, loving portrait. The oldtime composers, you know, they would compose songs for any kind of occasion, a birth, a death, a war, a voyage, a love affair, a family story—the way poets write poems today. It was their poetry, oral poetry, and the queen was trained in that tradition.

It was a big discovery for me, because that's the day my research work really got its start, going into the Bishop Museum and finding those manuscripts—thanks to Kawena and 'Iolani and Margaret Titcomb, the librarian, and whoever or whatever guided me there. Though I felt the queen's mana *coming off the pages, I did not yet know how valuable her manuscripts are. I know now how many of our most important songwriters were women, like the queen, and Helen Desha Beamer, and Irmgard Aluli, and Kawena. I know now that Lili'uokalani was the first of our composers to write down her melodies. Those pages made a kind of bridge from the ancient time to our time. They show us the way her mind worked, the way she used Hawaiian in the old poetic style. And yet she is also writing it down, which for a composer in her day was something brand new.*

Queen Lili'uokalani (1838–1917), circa 1902.

opposite
Her handwritten manuscript for "Tutu." The word "comic" probably notes how she meant it to be sung, in a lighthearted way.

Iulu. Comic

1st Aia i Kaalaaloa — These live
Kaa wahi kupunawahine — Our dear
Ua nui kona maa la — The
Oka noho ana ike ao nei — She lived
Kana hana i kakahiaka — Her daily
Oka wehe ika Iuke nei — Was to ope
Kii aku la ina maka aniani — She
A pau i a kau ai — And thus, e

(Seizing the a) Oh yes
Chorus E aloha kakou iaia — We must
E malama kakou ia Iulie — We must
E hoano kakou iaia — We must all
Ko kakou kupunawahine. — For she is

2nd A kau mai ke ahiahi — As the shades
Hoomakaukau e Jule — She retires for
Kii aku la ina maka aniani — And
Auwe! ua nalowale — Oh dear! the
Hia ka ika lae — But now where
Ika lae kahi ku ai — She had plac
Iluna ika lae — The high buff
Iku lae kahi kau ai — Way high up

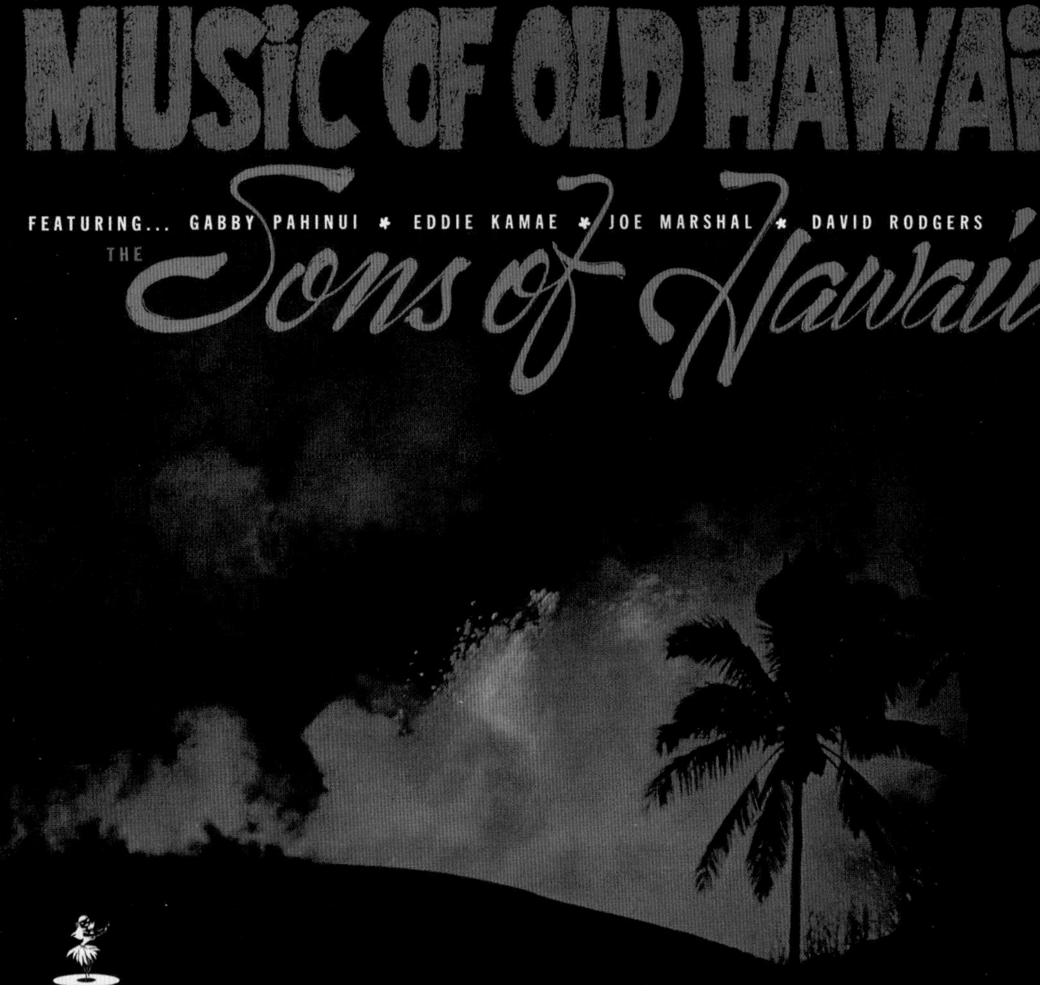

STEREO
MUSIC OF OLD HAWAII
FEATURING... GABBY PAHINUI * EDDIE KAMAE * JOE MARSHAL * DAVID RODGERS
THE Sons of Hawaii
RECORDED IN HAWAII
KOMO MAI • HONESAKALA • HE'EIA • PAUOA LIKO KA LEHUA • 'AMA'AMA • PUA KUKUI
SANOE • MOKU KIA KAHI • KAUA'I • HE NOHEA 'OE I KU'U MAKA • LIHOLIHO • MAILE LAU LI'ILI'

The Sons' second album cover offered a bold image for 1964, linking traditional Hawaiian music with the earth's ancestral power.

4

An Open Sound

on McDiarmid, Jr., wanted to cut a second album, hoping to ride the wave. So did Eddie. He knew they had the songs. The sudden success had fueled his belief in the sound they'd created and the appeal of the music they were bringing back to life.

"Only thing is," he told McDiarmid, "Feet's not here."

"What happened to Feet?"

"He's on a ship somewhere. He joined the Merchant Marine."

"I thought he was a musician."

"He's a sailor too."

"So how long will he be gone?"

Eddie shrugged. "Maybe a month. Maybe a year."

He didn't know for sure. But they both knew the heartful ring of Feet's steel was essential. Without him, it wouldn't be The Sons.

"I guess that means we'll have to wait."

"Good," said Eddie. "When he's back on shore, we'll get the boys together."

Feet had begun to live a restless double life. He loved the steel guitar. He also loved the sea. Like the music, it was in his blood, the age-old legacy of an island people. After the Sandbox gig he stayed in town long enough for the recording sessions, then shipped out on a voyage that would take him around the world.

Listened to throughout the islands, The Sons of Hawaii had a following now, but with Feet gone they didn't quite have a band. Not for the time being. Waiting for Feet, they picked up casual gigs where they could, sometimes together, sometimes singly. Joe was married, with two boys at home. He held on to his day job as a shipping checker down at the waterfront. Gabby was up at dawn each day, reporting for work with the county road crew. ("I don't need no alarm clock," he once said. "Out Waimānalo I got about one hundred chickens.") Whenever they could—free nights, weekends—he and Eddie kept getting together to jam and talk about the songs Eddie was uncovering.

There is one old love song in particular that Eddie recalls from those days in the early 1960s, "Komo Mai" (Welcome, Join Me):

E komo mai i loko e hānai iā 'oe
E 'ai nō ā kena i ka pu'u kē moni.

I do invite love's sweet embrace,
to share the gentle hospitality of my heart.

Eddie heard an elderly aunt singing this song, and the sweet melody caught his ear. He wrote it out, along with the lyrics, and brought it to one of their sessions. "You should sing this," he said.

Gabby looked it over and shook his head. "If you like it, son, then you sing this one."

Eddie knew Gabby didn't have much patience with musical notation; he trusted his ears, not his eyes. So Eddie put the sheet away and played the song. "Just listen," he said, "it's really beautiful."

Gabby listened awhile and smiled his enormous smile. "You're right. We should do it. But not me. You think it's beautiful, you should sing it."

Eddie's hands began to sweat. He'd been singing harmony from time to time, but never had he tried what Gabby was pressing him to do.

"I was a shy guy in those days," he says. "The first time through, my voice was wobbling. Gabby says to me, 'Just sing it, son! Just sing it!' The way he said it gave me more confidence, so we tried it again, and this time it felt really good, doing something I never thought I could do. Gabby said, 'You know what, son? We're gonna record this. When braddah Feet comes back, we'll put this song on the record, with you doing the singing.'"

Eddie wasn't sure he could go along with this idea. It

appealed to him, surprisingly, but it frightened him, too. His voice worried him, and so did his Hawaiian pronunciation. If he sang this song, he had to be sure about his delivery. He felt the responsibility that comes with putting a piece of musical tradition out into the world. Until now he'd never had to think much about this, about actually delivering the words. The next time he called on Pīlahi Pākī, he brought along "Komo Mai."

"The way words look on the page or on the songsheet," she told him, "don't always tell us what we need to know. We have to listen to how the *kūpuna* speak. That is where the music comes from."

Consonants are easy, she explained, eight in the Hawaiian language, and pronounced pretty much the way they look. But the vowels are trickier. You can find three or four vowel sounds in a row. "Look here in this first stanza," she said. "'E hānai i 'ai e hewa e ka waha' [May I share love's happiness and hospitality]. English doesn't do that. Sometimes the glottal stop will break up two vowels. But not always." In her stately and professorial way Pīlahi gave him a simple rule of thumb. "Many times the vowel sounds are side by side. Then you slur them, Eddie, you let one slide into the next. You don't sing *hānai,* then *i,* then *'ai.* That's too stiff. You sing *ha-nai-yai."*

Her hands moved through the air like a dancer's hands, and for Eddie something clicked. He heard again the voices of his mother and father speaking softly in the predawn kitchen of his boyhood, and he understood how their words and sounds had flowed together, how the music of the spoken language worked.

It was what he needed to hear that day. The rest was practice, and bringing those old family voices back to the surface where he could hear them all the time.

In early 1963 Feet's ship finally eased up to one of the loading wharfs in Honolulu harbor. Two days later they were back at the KPOI studio, crammed in there with the mikes and Feet's pancake steel, Gabby's guitar, Eddie's uke, and Joe's big bass across his knees. ("That's how quick Feet was on the uptake," Eddie recalls. "He never said much of anything. But two days rehearsal, after all that time away, he had the arrangements in his head and he was ready to go.") They recorded a dozen new songs, all in Hawaiian, with "Komo Mai" leading off the album. In its modest way this song launched Eddie's long career as a singer whose one-of-a-kind voice would later be hailed for its depth of feeling and authentic Hawaiian character.

"For that I thank Gabby," he says now. "He sort of gave me that chance, like he did for a lot of musicians in that time—help them get out of their shell and open up in a new direction."

As usual, working with Gabby was a mixed blessing. Side by side with his great generosity of spirit lived the heedlessness that would one day catch up with him.

In Eddie's view, one small exchange during these recording sessions typified the situation. After the band had rehearsed for two days, Eddie called Don McDiarmid to tell him he thought they were ready. "Okay," Don said, "let's meet at the studio tomorrow night. We'll be set up. But just one thing, Eddie."

"What's that?"

"I want you to bring Gabby in sober."

"Gabby will do what he wants to do, Don. That's up to him. I can't control it. Neither can you."

By process of elimination Eddie had begun to handle the band's business. On stage he let Joe and Gabby do the talking. Behind the scenes his soft-spoken, no-nonsense manner had proved effective for navigating among the owners and producers and union officials. But Eddie knew better than to tell Gabby when or what to drink. The truth was, Gabby seemed to need a few drinks under his belt to release his best performance. One night at the Sandbox, before they took the stage, he had announced that drinking during the gig had become a problem for the whole band. The others instantly agreed, taking temporary vows of abstinence. But by the end of the second song Gabby was holding his own throat, with eyes bulged out, as if choking to death or dying of thirst, staring around at the others as if they'd ganged up to punish him. Unamused, Joe Marshall said, "Gabby, don't give us the stink eye. You made the rule. You want to drink, just go get a drink!"

Before meeting Don to record the second album, they gathered at Feet's house in Kalihi for one last run-through. By the time they met Don and his sound engineer at the studio, the others had had a couple of beers, but Gabby had been drinking most of the day. He took his guitar out of its case, sat down in front of one of the mikes, strummed a big chord, and called out, "Okay, Don. We're ready. Take one."

From the sound booth McDiarmid said, "Wait a minute."

He stepped out into the studio. "Before we can start anything, Gabby, you'd better tune up."

"Tune up?" said Gabby, with a boyish grin.

"The guitar sounds out of tune."

Gabby pulled his hand across his face and laughed. "Okay, Don. Whatever you say."

As Eddie recalls those early days, it was always like that. "Gabby just jumps in there," he says, "not thinking. It's whatever happens when he is ready for it to happen. Because that's how Gabby is. A few drinks and he is in a mellow mood, so anything goes. And that time we were lucky. Nothing else went wrong. As soon as he tuned up, we did the session, and it was fine."

It was more than fine. *The Music of Old Hawaii* was another milestone. The arrangements were tighter, and their sound had matured. Eddie calls it their "open sound," a singular mix of rhythmic technique and innovative tuning. "It's the tuning," he says now, "that sets the whole tone for The Sons of Hawaii, the motion and the excitement."

The open sound depended in large part on open strings, like the bass strings of a slack-key guitar, which are lowered—slacked—so they hum continually inside the chords. Gabby's favorite tuning, called "Maunaloa," was in the key of C. So Joe Marshall retuned his upright bass, removing the lowest E string, then adding a high string he tuned up to C, which meant in that key he, too, had more resonating, open strings. As for Eddie, he shopped around and found some high-gauge strings that let him tune down a few steps, which gave more body to the lower notes and gave his uke a deeper ring. If Gabby happened to play in another key, Eddie had a second uke that he could retune. In this way he was always playing in C positions, giving him open strings more of the time.

"I had enough *'ukulele* with me," he says. "I could move

overleaf
The Sons of Hawaii recorded their first album at the KPOI studio in Honolulu, 1961. Left to right: Joe Marshall, David "Feet" Rogers, Gabby Pahinui, and Eddie Kamae.

around to do that, and tune my box. So sometimes Gabby is playing in F on the slack-key guitar. And I'm playing chords that look like C. And Feet, he's got the Rogers family D tuning, so it looks like he's playing in E. But it all fits together, because we all want to hear one sound, that simple, sweet, round sound that affects your voice so you can work with it. We need this thing to set the whole rhythm for the band, this open sound rhythm."

Around this ingenious string work, the package itself announced that here was a new kind of Hawaiian album. On the back, Hawaiian lyrics ran side by side with English translations. There were notes on the stories behind the songs, along with a tribute to respected elder and *kūpuna* Pīlahi Pākī, acknowledging "her instructions in the letter and her interpretations of the spirit of this music." On the front, under the red letters, SONS OF HAWAII, a black palm tree stands silhouetted against crimson smoke billowing around a curtain of fiery lava, a photo from the Big Island's volcano country.

All in all it was a bold design for 1964. Album covers from Hawai'i, like the song sheets, tended to feature smiling performers wearing *lei,* or one of the familiar settings, a lagoon, a tropical beach, a grove of coco palms. Why this seething fire wall? What does molten lava rising into a night sky have to do with music?

In most parts of the United States, not much. But in Hawai'i, it goes right to the heart of the matter. According to long held beliefs, this island terrain is both deity and ancestor. In the world's most active volcanic region, moving lava provides a constant reminder of the deepest sources of creative power. Having built each island, lava is the mother of all these inspirational Hawaiian places. The islands, meanwhile, have nurtured the voices of singers like Gabby and Eddie, voices that carry haunting echoes of a centuries-old chant tradition. In this way certain singers of the 1960s, in the very sound they delivered, began to speak what would become the guiding call of the renaissance: *aloha 'āina,* "affection for the land," love for the earth's ancestral power.

Before the second album was released, Eddie had lined up a gig above the windward town of Kāne'ohe. It seemed like the ideal job, one that could reestablish the band in the live music circuit and keep them all working for quite some time. It was also a step up from the rough industrial district on Sand Island Road. Ha'ikū Gardens was a brand-new club, where they would play outdoors, with greenery all around and the lush Ko'olau range rising in the distance.

Opening night was almost upon them, when Feet stood up in the middle of a rehearsal and quietly announced, "I have something to say."

Eddie asked, "What?"

"I'm shipping out again."

"When?"

"Pretty soon. Tomorrow."

"How come you didn't tell us before we signed the contract?"

"I just got the okay from the union."

It was a blow, and it was a dilemma. They didn't want to open without Feet, but breaking the contract would cost them some money. It was Gabby's idea to approach George Rogers, who readily agreed to step in. After George got the feel for their arrangements and repertoire, it was almost as good as having Feet among them, since the father had taught Feet the family tuning and so much of what he knew. George was around sixty then, and in manner much like his son—with one small exception. Though he seldom spoke, he would hum along above the notes when he took his solos, a habit Gabby found amusing. "What was that, George?" Gabby would ask, in the middle of a number. "Did you say something?"

The word spread quickly that The Sons were back. Fans were driving in from all around the island, calling out to hear a favorite tune. Again they were playing "'Ūlili Ē" two and three times a night. "And the same thing happening all over again," Joe Marshall would recall, "lines of people trying to get in. Just like we had at the Sandbox, only prettier, with so many plants around, the kind of place young folks come to get married, people coming early in the parking lot so they can get a good space."

Everyone wanted the gig to last. But Ha'ikū Gardens was fated to close soon after it opened—a bit too far out of town, a bit hard to find. In spite of the music's wide appeal, the club never quite got into the black. Before long the band was once again out of work.

Though they couldn't have foreseen it, that's how things were going to go for several years, as gigs came and went, as clubs opened and closed, as a club owner's enthusiasm for the music waxed and waned, as the boys drifted apart, came together again, or recombined with other musicians, as Feet shipped out on voyages short and long, east to San Francisco, west across the Pacific to Nagoya or Hong Kong.

In 1965 Hula released a third album, this one without Gabby. Called *Eddie Kamae and the Sons of Hawaii,* it featured Feet, Joe, vocalist Bobby Larrison, and the great slack-key artist Atta Isaacs on guitar. Eddie did most of the singing, and you could hear a new confidence in his voice. The album got plenty of air time, the sales were good, and through the years its reputation would steadily grow. (Six years later Rep. Spark Matsunaga would name this album in the U.S. *Congressional Record* as "the best representative of traditional Hawaiian music.")

But as of the fall of 1965, Eddie found himself at loose ends. While the albums were keeping the band alive, the band itself had fallen apart. After a loud argument one night during a date at a somewhat unappetizing club in Waikīkī, he and Gabby had gone their separate ways. When Feet took off on another voyage, Eddie envied his passion for the seafarer's world and his easy access to this second path. At thirty-eight Eddie was no longer sure where his music was going, or where his life was going.

That Christmas he flew to Maui to visit his mother. Widowed now, and seventy-five years old, she was living with his sister in Lahaina. Like those summertime trips when he was young, it was a return to the homestead, to his grandmother's island, and Pīlahi Pākī's island too. Maui was an anchorage, an old touchpoint for the soul, the place where his father had met the love of his life.

His mother happened to be in the hospital recovering from some minor surgery. Eddie spent an afternoon with her, playing music and talking. In those days he had a roommate, the guitarist Raymond Kane, who'd joined him on this outing. After singing for his mother, they stopped at a place called the Broiler to say hello to the manager, Pat Dorian, the fellow who'd first hired The Sons. Pat was closing early and insisted they come along to a gathering at his beach house.

They walked into a swirl of festive chatter. It was cocktail hour on Christmas Day. While Eddie enjoyed parties, he'd always preferred making music to making small talk. He and Raymond grabbed some beers and pushed through the crowd out onto a *lānai* where they found a spot against the rail, to sit and pick a few tunes, Raymond on guitar, Eddie on the concert-size Martin he traveled with. They weren't performing, they were playing for themselves. Partygoers would listen awhile and then move on, all but one young woman who couldn't seem to pry herself away from the doorjamb. After a while Eddie became intensely aware of her rapt attention. So did host Pat Dorian, who stepped in to make introductions.

Her name was Myrna Harmer, originally from Utah, but now on Maui, helping Lee Knight open a new restaurant called Pineapple Hill.

Did Pat say Lee Knight? Eddie took a closer look at this woman, her delicately sculpted Nordic features, her alert brown eyes, her brown hair bleached a shade lighter by the sun. Knight was another colleague from the Sandbox days. He had tended bar there. Like Dorian, he was a Californian who had come to Hawai'i and never left. Myrna had met him and his wife in Honolulu, had actually shared a house with them, and now he'd brought her across to Maui. It struck Eddie as a happy synchronicity, perhaps a sign.

As for Myrna, looking back upon it now, she felt held by something she could not name. "When I walked to the doorway leading outside, I saw two Hawaiians playing this beautiful, soft, gentle music. I had grown up in a family that loved music, and we all had our requisite piano lessons and such, but I'd never heard anything like this—slack-key guitar, concert *'ukulele.* Until that afternoon I'd never paid much attention to Hawaiian music. Their instrumentation was just incredible. Raymond was there because Eddie had told him why he was flying to Maui and Raymond said he'd like to come along and play too. It's a very Hawaiian way to share your feeling. Years later Raymond would get invited to Washington, D.C., to get the National Heritage Award from the Smithsonian for his contributions to American folk music. But at the time I had no idea who either of these guys were. I just stood there, for maybe half an hour. I couldn't move. I had to listen. Then right after Pat introduced us, I had to leave for work, not thinking I would ever see either one of them again."

Pineapple Hill was in Kapalua, a few miles up the coast. A long, green, ranch-style building, it once had been the home of a plantation manager, with a spectacular view across sloping pineapple fields toward the nearby island of Moloka'i. A quarter mile of stately Norfolk pines lined the access road. When Eddie stepped through the double doors, about two hours later, he was there, he claimed, as a favor to his old pal Lee. He would liven up the place with some holiday songs, "Deck The Halls," "Mele Kalikimaka." He had dropped Ray Kane at the airport and picked up another musical partner, a Maui cousin who brought along an autoharp. They strolled among the tables serenading the delighted customers, while he and Myrna exchanged glances across the room. At closing time, when he learned that she was heading back toward Lahaina by motorscooter, he offered her a ride.

They dropped off the cousin, picked up a bottle of Chianti, and returned to the Broiler, now closed and empty. A low wall of lava rock separated its outdoor patio from the beach. They climbed over the wall. Behind the bar they found glasses and some breadsticks to munch. From behind the West Maui mountains a full moon had risen to light the sand and the water and the island of Lāna'i. They chose a table with a clear view across the channel and began to sip Chianti and talk about their lives. They had it all to themselves, one of those balmy and luminous Hawaiian nights that no one can resist.

They spent the next day together, roaming around Lahaina, still talking—about what had brought them both to this place at this particular time, and the strange coincidence that the fellow who once tended bar at the Sandbox should now be Myrna's boss. Eddie learned that she had grown up in a small town called Mapleton, fifty miles south of Salt Lake City, where her father raised corn, hay, and sugar beets. She, four brothers, and a sister had all lived close to the land, in a region where her Mormon great-grandfather had settled back in the 1870s. One grandmother had come to Utah from Iceland.

All Eddie knew of her part of the world was what he'd seen from the window of Ray Kinney's touring bus, snow-capped peaks and frosty mountain passes. To his ears it was still a far-off and exotic realm, as exotic as Hawai'i had seemed to Myrna when she took some time out from the University of Utah to visit a friend who had moved to Honolulu. Planning to stay a month, she stayed a year. When she finally returned to Utah and rejoined the clan at Mapleton, she figured she was there for good. But as much as she loved her homeland—a high-altitude valley with views east toward the spectacular Wasatch Range—Myrna was something of a renegade and restless spirit. A few months later she found herself back in the islands. Now she was falling for Eddie. And Eddie was falling for her.

That night she had the dinner shift again, while he had to return to Honolulu. But not for long. In the early weeks of 1966, he was on the plane to Maui every chance he could get. It was "research," he told his friends in town. And there were "family matters" to attend to.

In the spring he took Myrna to meet his mother. They were talking about getting married. Eddie wanted to be sure he had her blessing. While cross-cultural relationships in Hawai'i are commonplace, in Eddie's family it was uncommon to choose a *haole*. Most of his brothers and sisters had married Chinese and Japanese and other Hawaiians.

Outside Lahaina they turned off the main road and followed a dirt driveway to a clearing underneath some mango trees. For Myrna, who had been waiting tables in Waikīkī and Kapalua, this little turn off the round-the-island highway was a first step from one Hawai'i into another, from the world-famous resort and recreation zone into the world of Hawaiians Eddie inhabited. He showed her the view across cane fields toward Pu'u Kukui and the lush mountains that had framed his boyhood summers. He showed her the grave of his grandmother, Kauhai Likua, a raised rectangular mound, bordered with stones of

The house of Eddie's grandmother, in Lahaina, Maui.

black lava. It was an ancestral shrine, right in front of the weathered frame house.

"This way," Eddie said, "she is always with us."

His mother had heard the car and now stepped out onto her porch, frail and white-haired, eyes shining with pleasure. She was not surprised that her son from Honolulu would show up unannounced, since Eddie never called ahead. Nor did she seem surprised when he presented Myrna.

"I could tell," he says now, "that she liked Myrna right away. Brown skin. White skin. That had nothing to do with it. My mother never judged people by their skin. She knew how to read your eyes and feel your heart. Later on she told me that on that very day she knew Myrna would be the right woman for me. I see now I should have taken my first wife to meet her. It could have saved me a lot of trouble."

Eddie had been married once before, a few years earlier, but it didn't last long. The things that went wrong the first time made it ever clearer what was "right" about Myrna. That spring she quit her job at Pineapple Hill and moved back to O'ahu to be closer to Eddie. In August they were married, in a small private ceremony. A few months later they had a chance to fly to Utah to meet Myrna's parents, a new experience for all concerned. In her family she was the first to cross an ethnic border of any kind.

Just as Eddie had shown her the Maui mountains, she showed him her favorite peak, six-thousand-foot Sierra Bonita. And just as Eddie's mother had welcomed Myrna, so did her family welcome Eddie and take him in. It turned out that being a Pacific Islander was actually an advantage in that part of Utah. Mormon missionary work in the South Pacific had brought numerous Tongans and Sāmoans into Brigham Young University, seven miles away. In towns like Mapleton and Springville, Polynesian faces were not at all unusual. Polynesian voices were often heard in touring choral groups, and as visitors in local congregations. What's more, one of Myrna's brothers had been, since high school, an avid *'ukulele* player. He was eager to meet the master. Once he and Eddie started trading songs, the ice was broken.

Newlyweds Eddie and Myrna, in Utah, fall 1966.

Soon after they returned to the islands, Eddie took Myrna to meet Kawena Pukui. He was, of course, hoping she, too, would approve of their marriage. He wasn't prepared for her reaction.

It was mid-morning. In the cool front room of Kawena's house they talked for a while about a song Eddie had recently discovered, and how to translate some verses Kawena began to recall as soon as she heard him sing a few lines. Sitting crosslegged on the rug, Myrna had opened a looseleaf pad, taking notes on their conversation. After a while Kawena, who did most of the talking, looked at her, then looked at Eddie and said pointedly, "Any *pilikia,* any trouble, between you and your wife, you will be the one who is wrong."

opposite
Eddie and Myrna on Maui, mid-1970s.

She let this sink in. He knew from her look, both benevolent and unswerving, that it wasn't a remark he was expected to challenge or even comment upon.

"She is going to help you," Kawena continued, "in all the things you will be doing to help us understand the Hawaiian spirit and the inner beauty within us and around us."

As she let this too sink in, Eddie knew it was a blessing, as well as a wise and truthful prophecy. In choosing Eddie, Myrna had also chosen Hawai'i, and he was beginning to understand what this meant. At the same time, in the weeks to come, he would begin to ponder another part of Kawena's prediction: "all the things you will be doing." The albums of music, his work in the archives, playing in clubs—was that what she meant? Kawena spoke simply, but her words were always loaded and layered. Was there something else coming toward him, something more than he could yet understand?

A JOURNEY *Right after we were married, I flew over to Kaua'i. There was a certain kind of* lei *I wanted to get for Myrna, a very rare* lei *you hardly ever see. All I knew was that it came from Ni'ihau, which is very famous for its shell* lei*. Ni'ihau is a real small island and reserved for Hawaiians. I love to look at it from the leeward side of Kaua'i, on a clear day with the sea sparkling all around. It's a bluish hump about fifteen miles offshore. But you can't just get in the helicopter and go over there and go into the village and shop around, not even if you're another Hawaiian, unless you have relatives there or some real reason to go.*

So to find this particular lei*, which they call Kahelelani, I went to Kaua'i. If Ni'ihau people leave, that's usually the island they move to, so they can still be close to their relatives across the way. I landed at Līhu'e and started asking around in the shops here and there, and finally an old man told me try the public library. I said, "How come the library?" And he said, "You ask for a woman there."*

Well, it was only a couple of blocks away, a small local library. I said to the woman at the information desk, "Who can I contact about making a Kahelelani lei*?" She was a big Hawaiian woman with a sweet face. She smiled at me and said, "I am the one. Tell me what you want."*

I wanted a lei *that would be very full. Eight strands, I told her, and each strand thirty-seven inches long. And she said to me, "I can do that."*

"Good," I said. "When can I pick them up?"

"It will be one year."

I didn't know what to say. This was supposed to be like a wedding present. "One year to make a lei*?" I said.*

"Come back then, and I will have it for you."

So I said okay. One year later I flew back to Kaua'i and went into the library, and she had it ready, and then I understood why it would take that long. This lei*, you see, is named for the Kahelelani shell, a very tiny purple shell found mainly on Ni'ihau, the most treasured shell on that island. It takes a long, long time and a lot of patience* *to gather enough to make eight strands a yard around, because they are so small and so hard to find.*

This shell, you know, gets its name from a famous chief of Ni'ihau, and the name gives another reason why the lei *has such value.* Kahele *means "to be decorated for a journey."* Lani *means "sky," or "the heavens," or "to be from the heavens," but can also mean "chiefly" or "royal" or "of high importance."*

So when I took this lei *back to Honolulu, I put the long strands of tiny purple shells around Myrna's neck, to mark the first year of our journey together.*

Part Two

No Puna ke ʻala, I hali ʻia mai
Noho I ka wailele aʻo Hiʻilawe

The fragrance is wafted from Puna
and lives at Hiʻilawe waterfall

From the song "Hiʻilawe"

In Waipiʻo Valley, taro has been grown for centuries,
food for both the body and the spirit.

At Huelo, first light silhouettes one of the nineteenth-century chapels strung along Maui's windward coastline.

5

Out There

Eddie had a partner now, a full-time companion, a beautiful woman who loved him and believed in him. Soon she would take over the typing and filing of his findings. To get closer to his work she would enroll at the University of Hawai'i and begin a study of the Hawaiian language that would continue for years. Life for Eddie had never been better. And yet Kawena's words kept coming back to him: "all the things you will be doing . . ." On the day he decided to mention this again, she told him something that was, in its way, more difficult to grasp.

Going into museums and libraries was necessary work, Kawena said, but in the end this would not take him to "the heart of things." When he asked what she meant, she said, "It's out there, Eddie."

"Out where?"

Her arm made a wide swath through the living room. "In the valleys, in the small towns, in the back country . . . all those places we have come from. That's where you will find it, when you are ready to go looking."

Then past seventy, she was sharing the hard-won wisdom of a lifetime. Though she'd spent twenty-five years on the Bishop Museum staff, Kawena's deep knowledge of language and lore, which began with her own childhood training, had come to depend more and more on numerous trips to the outer islands. She had traveled from Kaua'i to Moloka'i, from Lāna'i to the Big Island, seeking out the elders, many of whom had seldom traveled anywhere, listening to their stories and songs, taking notes on how they saw themselves and saw the world.

From these years of trips and interviews and tapings had come her landmark studies of Hawaiian cultural history, among them *The Polynesian Family System in Ka'ū, Hawai'i; Nānā I Ke Kumu (Look to the Source);* and the monumental compilation of proverbs and poetical sayings, *'Ōlelo No'eau.*[1]

For Kawena, the foremost Hawaiian scholar of the twentieth century, the most important lessons had been learned not in the library but "out there." For Eddie, the working musician, this was not a message he could fully comprehend. Not at first. Not on the day he heard her say the words. His whole career had been tied to Honolulu, where the money was, the clubs and the owners, and where the records were cut. What did "out there" have to do with all the familiar habits of his profession—practice, rehearsal, arrangement, performance?

Around this same time, for example, he was playing at the Holiday Inn, in a group that included Atta Isaacs and veteran slack-key stylist Sonny Chillingworth, known as "The Waimea Cowboy," after his 1965 album by that name became a statewide hit. One night as they were tuning up, Sonny told Eddie he'd heard about a new room soon to open on the top floor of the Kuhio Hotel in Waikīkī. The next day Eddie stopped by to see the manager. They talked awhile, and he got the job. He brought Sonny along, with Joe Marshall on bass and the talented young vocalist Palani Vaughan, all musicians who could deliver the sound that had come to be expected of a band led by Eddie Kamae—traditional songs and lyrics, stringed instruments, inspired musicianship, and a spirit of innovation. They not only opened the Maluna Lounge, they drew such crowds that reviewers and business managers began to speculate that Hawaiian music might be ready to come back to Waikīkī in a big way. When Gabby Pahinui started sitting in from time to time, word quickly spread that The Sons were together again and sounding better than ever. The crowds grew, and the gig would last for over a year.

But meanwhile the world "out there" had already begun to call. The island of Maui had begun to call, though it was not the family side this time, not the Lahaina side. It was the opposite shore, the region around Hāna, on Maui's eastern edge, below the dormant crater of Haleakalā. A longtime friend, Carl Lindquist, had taken an interest in some elderly Hawaiian churches strung along that remote coastline. Lindquist had grown up in Honolulu and was among those fans who'd followed Eddie's music since the Sandbox days. Now the publisher of a journal for the construction trades, he wanted to photograph and film these unique chapels that had lasted a century and more, made of lava rock and coral, each set against the lush vegetation of the rain-drenched windward side, and linked in those days by the still unpaved Hāna Road.

One weekend Eddie joined Carl and cameraman Steve Moore as they crept along the fifty miles of potholes and switchbacks, to visit sites from Huelo southward to Ke'anae peninsula, Nāhiku, Hāna town, and Kīpahulu (where Charles Lindbergh would be buried in 1974). Their final stop was Kaupō, the last village, at the foot of a broad gap in the crater rim that once channeled lava from the old volcano toward the sea. They had lunch on the grounds of a local church called Huialoha (Congregation of Love), which sat by itself above the water, on a point east of town. Built in 1859, at the height of the missionary period, when some fifty thousand people still lived along that coastline, it was a classic structure of its era, with walls of white coral, peaked roof, and square steeple. Like the others in that string of Maui churches, Huialoha was a time-capsule of overlooked history.

Carl's film project came into clear focus that day, while Eddie was awakened to a region he would return to time and time again. He liked it there, with the crater's slopes soaring behind him, and thirty miles away across the channel the massive shield cones of the Big Island looming, Mauna Kea, Mauna Loa, Hualālai. It was a rare place, with its own quiet drama and holding power.

Bring Wood, Build a House turned out to be a half-hour documentary, shot in 16 mm. Later that year it was shown as a primetime Christmas special on Honolulu television and then made available to Hawai'i's schools as a cultural resource tool. Working with Gabby and Atta Isaacs, Eddie produced the soundtrack and, to his own surprise, came away with his first film credit, as musical director.

Before the filming was completed, Carl Lindquist had caught Eddie's attention with another idea—as if sent to feed him reasons to step where he hadn't stepped before. On a recent trip to the West Coast Carl had spent a weekend at the Monterey Jazz Festival. It occurred to him that this side of Maui might be the place to mount another kind of festival, one devoted not to jazz but to the rebirth of Hawaiian music.

In Eddie's mind a light went on. Yes! Of course! This hadn't been done, and it needed to be done—an event that would showcase the full abundance of what performers were doing and what was coming back to life. And what better place than Hāna, far outside the city. It was hard to get to, but that's why it still had its own serene, soul-soothing energy, the kind of spot that could provide a perfect setting and bring out the best in all of us. The Hawaiian word for celebration is *ho'olaule'a.* That's what they would call it.

Co-produced by Carl and Eddie, it took six months to plan, and a huge amount of work. "But music opens the door for you," Eddie recalls. "Everyone becomes helpful because they understand the cultural concern and what you are doing. We had to see the owner of the Hāna Ranch, to get permission to use this open field. We had to go to the business sector, the police sector, the bank for funding, the doctor so there would be an ambulance around, just in case. We had to have security. The whole community at Hāna worked to make this project happen, and other folks all over Maui. Carl had contacts through his publishing company, so he took care of the business and logistics stuff, and my job was to line up the performers, the *hula* troupes, the bands."

In a front-page story the *Honolulu Advertiser* would call it "Hawaii's answer to Woodstock" and "the first World Series of Hawaiian music." It was August 1970. Hawaiian Airlines, a co-sponsor, chartered flights to bring performers in to Hāna's airstrip from all parts of the island chain. Over fifty were on the program, among them Hawai'i's premier dancer, 'Iolani Luahine; the revered Maui *hula* master, Emma Farden Sharpe; the Kalima Brothers with The Hilo Hawaiians; Sonny Chillingworth; Palani Vaughan; *'ukulele* sensation Moe Keale; and Gabby Pahinui, who by this time had reunited with Eddie and Joe Marshall. George Rogers was there, elder statesman of the steel guitar (once again sitting in for Feet), and Ka'upena Wong, leading voice in a new generation of chanters.[2]

In ritual white, and wearing a head *lei* of ferns and flowers, Wong opened the event in the Hawaiian way, with a long chant to the place itself, the spirit and history of the point of land where they'd gathered. It was the name chant of Queen Ka'ahumanu, wife of King Kamehameha I; she had been born two centuries past in a cave shelter on Ka'uiki hill, just up the slope from the low stage he stood upon, roofed with palm fronds. A silence fell over the crowd as Wong's voice swelled, guttural and plaintive, sounding much older than he looked, as if an ancient voice spoke through him, as if some old vibration of the earth rose through his throat to quiver in the Maui air. His invocation set the tone for a day of inspired *hula*, drumming, chanting, and song, a festive and joyful day, yet anchored in the mystique and ancestry of this long meadow spread between a surf-fringed sea and the once volcanic eastern slope of the "House of the Sun," Haleakalā.

The Maui projects gave Eddie a larger sense for the outer islands and for some of the less traveled places Kawena told him to seek out. The music he loved to play seemed to have another layer of meaning now. He wanted to see more, to know more, to dig deeper, and he wouldn't have to wait for long.

During the Ho'olaule'a Kawena told him she'd be flying on to the Big Island to meet some friends, perhaps to revisit the places of her childhood, down near South Point, in the lower end of the district called Ka'ū. When she suggested Eddie should come along, he jumped at the chance. Somehow he knew this was a lesson she believed he was ready for.

They met at Nā'ālehu, which takes pride in being the southernmost town in the United States (well below the Tropic of Cancer, at about the latitude of Guadalajara). At the Hilo airport Eddie and Myrna had picked up a jeep. Kawena was with Eleanor Williamson, the traveling secretary who for thirty years and more had taken copious notes on all Kawena saw and thought and talked about on outings such as this. These four set out behind a much dustier and battle-scarred jeep that carried a local ranch manager and Kawena's friend Willie Meinecke, the descendant of a longtime Ka'ū ranching family.

From Nā'ālehu they left the belt road and followed a rutted dirt track south across rugged country, sparsely settled, stopping every mile or so to pass through a cattle gate. Out that way you see no swaying palms, no turquoise pools beside the condo. "From the top of the hill down to the coast it's a mean drop," Eddie remembers. "So I just took my time. It's dry down there, lots of cactus. From time to time Asa Yamamoto, the ranch manager, was pointing out waterholes and the different things they're used for. One place we stopped, Kawena said, 'Over there is another hole, with good water for drinking.' And Asa, he looked at her amazed. She grew up out there, you see, maybe thirty-five years before Asa was born. 'I been on this ranch all my life,' he says, 'first time I heard about that waterhole.'"

At a spot called Puhi'ula Kawena pointed out a large cave where she had sometimes slept as a girl, recalling that they would ride from home on a mule, carrying food, and stay overnight in this remnant of an old lava tube.

They were near the coast, in a district called Waikapuna (meaning "source of fresh water"), when she ordered Eddie to stop. Pointing toward an open rise, Kawena said this had been the site of her grandparents' ranch and her childhood home. She called it Pu'u Makani, which means "windy hill." And that's about all that remained, the steady wind off the ocean, and the treeless slopes. She got out of the car to look around.

This was the home region of her mother, Mary Ke-ali'i-kanaka-'ole, daughter of a chiefly family from Ka'ū. It was also the adopted region of her father, Henry Wiggin, a sugar plantation manager, originally from Salem, Massachusetts, and descended from the early New England poet, Anne Bradstreet. In keeping with the practice called *hānai,* Kawena had been given to her maternal grandmother, a revered *kahuna pule* (master of the praying chant) and a living archive of cultural lore. As the first-born, Kawena was the one chosen to receive her grandmother's vast knowledge. This provided the foundation for her lifetime study of traditional chant and dance.

clockwise from top left
Eddie and Kawena; a Big Island rancher, Kawena, Ele Williamson; Myrna, Kawena, Willie Meinecke, Eddie. In Ka'ū, August 1970.

left
Uncle Willie gathering Hawaiian salt near a cove Kawena visited as a girl.

On the spot where her long training had begun, Kawena now offered a chant of greeting to voice her respect for this place and for the generations that had lived there. While the others listened, while their necks and arms prickled with "chickenskin," her strong voice cut through the wind around her former homestead, with the bright sea surging behind them, and in the far distance the long hump of Mauna Loa, the great shield cone that built this half of her island.

Farther on they stopped at another wind-blown site, where some family friends had once lived. Again she took a few moments to chant her *aloha,* her salute to times gone by and to the lives lived at that place. Then they turned around and climbed up the slope to Nāʻālehu town, cutting across to another road that fingers southward, this one paved and longer, taking them all the way down to the final lookout, which Hawaiians call Ka Lae (The Point), the last edge of the broad, descending plain, where dark cliffs jut into restless water intensely blue.

For Kawena, on this trip to the point, the most important stop was a famous waterhole called Palahemo, a deep rock pool fed by underground streams, a source of fresh water in terrain where no rivers flow and rainfall is sparse. The old waterhole is named in songs and chants and local sayings, one of which Kawena spoke aloud: "I ʻike ʻoe iā Kaʻū ā puni, a ʻike ʻole ʻoe iā Palahemo, ʻaʻole ʻoe i ʻike iā Kaʻū" (If you have seen all Kaʻū, but have not seen Palahemo, you have not seen Kaʻū).

She let these words hang in the air, as they took in the view, not only the look of the rocky pool but all that surrounds and contains it. To left and right, miles of black-edged shoreline angles off toward Kona, toward Puna, while behind you there is nothing but open ocean, from South Point to Tahiti, a thousand miles below the equator. In the history and mythology of Hawaiʻi this is a place of profound arrivals and departures. Some of the earliest Polynesians to reach these shores, traveling by canoe from distant archipelagoes, touched at one of these black-sand coves.

From Palahemo looking north, you see the sprawling scale of the island, the shape of it, as well as the source of its shape, the faraway volcano, thirteen thousand feet high and often capped with snow. This is the youngest Hawaiian island, still being formed, and Ka'ū is the most rugged of its districts, rough-hewn and lava-laced. From Palahemo you can feel the old flows pushing, spreading, probing to make this last triangular leaf of land. In the windy silence you begin to know what it means to be descended from Pele and how someone coming of age in such a place would claim a lineage from the deity of fire. Whatever forces shaped this land had surely shaped Kawena and her ancestors for untold generations.

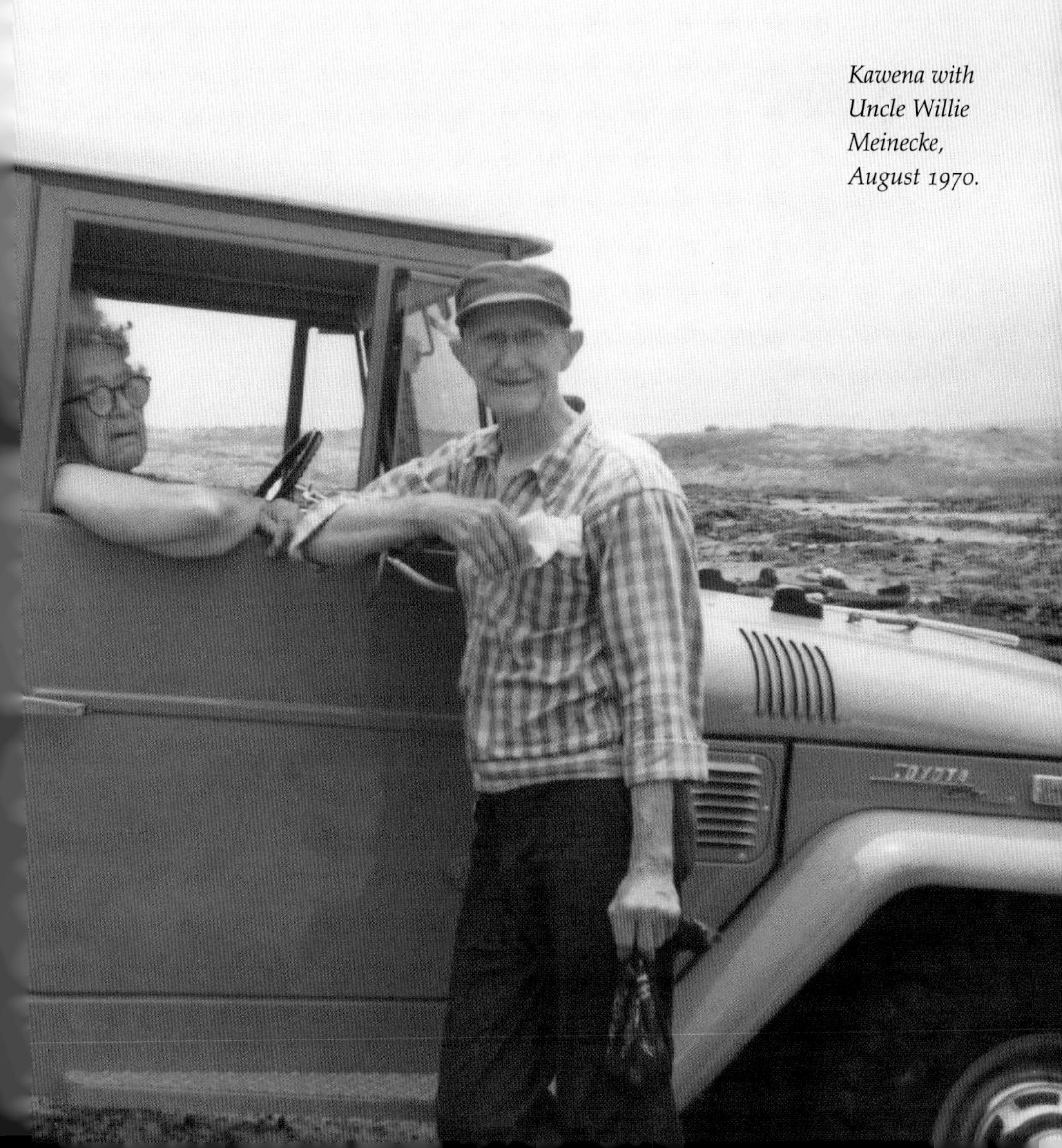

Kawena with Uncle Willie Meinecke, August 1970.

In the jeep, with Eddie driving, they followed Asa back the way they'd come. As they caravanned up the long slope toward the belt road, Kawena was in a festive mood, glad she'd seen all the places they came to see. She wanted to mark the occasion by writing a song about the day and the trip. She and Eddie would write it together, she said. At Willie Meinecke's house, in the town of Wai'ōhinu, where they all relaxed and shared a meal, she began to make notes.

"It was no problem for her," Eddie says now. "By that time she had written over a hundred and fifty songs. Always in Hawaiian, of course. She could write a song in fifteen minutes. That afternoon she recorded her thoughts. Later on I composed a melody. When we were back in Honolulu, she and Myrna worked out the final version of the verses. Then Kawena fit the words to my melody, and that's how we got 'Ke Ala A Ka Jeep.'"

It celebrates both a place on the map and a place in the heart. It is laced with personal references, ending, for example, at Wai'ōhinu, "i ka hale o ka makamaka" (at the home of our friend). Written in the traditional way, which is to say, as a poem to be sung, the lyrics suggest more than one meaning. The title itself reveals what can be contained in a seemingly simple phrase. The word *ala* means "road, path, or trail." But it can also mean "awaken," as well as "to renew, restore, revive." "Ke Ala A Ka Jeep" (The Way of the Jeep) refers to the actual route they followed, so the various stops are named: Nā'ālehu, Waikapuna, Puhi'ula, Palahemo, Ka Lae. It can also refer to how this trip awakened something, perhaps revived them, helped them all to see anew.

Certainly, this is how the trip affected Eddie. While he was getting his first look at the southernmost district of the Big Island, he was seeing it through Kawena's eyes, as a region layered with names and histories. This was far different from finding a long-lost song sheet in the university library. He began to see the living link between melody and story, between a woman's life and an ancient rock-lined waterhole.

He had also begun to feel the Big Island in a new, a deeper way. Each island has its own character, its own mystique, and this one was not at all like his mother's island, Maui. This was his father's island, and his grandfather's, too, yet Eddie didn't know it well at all, and now he wanted to know. There was something here he needed to get hold of. How to do it? Where to look next?

In recent months he'd been hearing reports of an old songwriter, a *tūtū* man, who lived out near Waipi'o Valley, or had once lived there, on the northern side, past the end of the county road. That's where Sam Kamae had grown up. Maybe that would be another trip worth taking. The fact is, he'd been hearing stories and rumors about this fellow for quite some time, like folktales heard around a dinner table late at night with the lights turned low. Waipi'o was known for its waterfall, Hi'ilawe, which provided the title for Gabby Pahinui's first slack-key hit. Some musicians in Honolulu thought the old man was the original composer of that song, one of dozens he'd written. Others said no, it was the long-dead father, though the son had been a great fiddler in his day. Others said, well, whoever wrote that song, they're probably both dead now, but if we sing it, they won't be forgotten.

A few weeks earlier, Eddie had heard 'Iolani Luahine speak of the old songwriter as if he were still alive. While rounding up performers for the Ho'olaule'a, he'd flown to Kailua, Kona, to ask his friend to dance for them at Hāna. At the time 'Iolani was curator at Hulihe'e Palace, once an outer-island residence for the Hawaiian royal family, now a museum and historic site. While they sat at the old porch railing, looking out across Kailua Bay, catching up on things, Eddie told her he might soon be heading toward Waipi'o to have a look around.

'Iolani turned to him. "Then you must see the *tūtū* man!"

"Is he the one who wrote songs?"

Her eyes were dark, her pupils almost black, yet they suddenly filled with urgent light.

"Tūtū Man Li'a. If you go Waipi'o way, he is the one to see!"

"So he's still there?"

"Just ask," 'Iolani said. "Over that way, everybody knows him."

Two months later, at South Point, he asked Kawena about this fellow and got the same message. It was sometime after lunch when he said, "I wonder if you have heard of Tūtū Man Li'a."

Kawena's eyes opened wide, as if this took her by surprise. "You mean Sam?"

"I think so. Yes."

She nodded, smiling. "I know him. Sam Li'a Kalāinaina. He's a very fine composer, too, one of the best."

"I heard he lives in Waipi'o."

"Pretty close by."

"You think he's someone I should meet?"

"Someday I hope you can meet him . . ." Her eyes held him as she went on. "Yes. I think the time has come for you to meet Sam Li'a. And I can tell you where he lives."

"Should I get in touch with him first?"

She shook her head. "He will be there, and he will be glad to see you. And I will tell you how to find another man, too. Both of them have spent their lives on this island—long, long lives. They know things you can only find here. But Sam . . . he is the one. He is like no one else. He is the last."

Eddie watched her warm eyes fill with moisture and the brightness that comes when joy and grief are intermixed.

"The last what?" he said.

"This man writes in the old way, Eddie. No one knows how many songs, or where they all are. He never cared about recording. He writes in Hawaiian, and he gives it away, with his *aloha.* In our time there is no one else like him."

The intensity in Kawena's eyes told him this was more than information. This came as a message, some kind of directive. He was tempted to change his plans and cross the island that very afternoon. But time was against him. The Big Island is true to its name. It was two hours back to Hilo, and from there another hour up the coast to the remote northern valleys.

The trip would have to wait awhile. Not long. A week. Maybe two. Certain business back in Honolulu had to be taken care of. For one thing, they still played the weekend gig at the Maluna Lounge. For another, he needed to talk with Feet Rogers, whose ship was supposed to be docking any day now. Before Eddie had left town for Hāna, someone had made him a very tempting offer. A new record deal was shaping up—a dream deal—if they could put it all together.

There had actually been two offers, both leading in the same direction. He'd become friendly with a young fellow named Steve Siegfried, the son of an island family, who had been following and collecting Hawaiian music since childhood. Siegfried and two companions, Witt Shingle and Lawrence Brown, were brainstorming about a production company devoted to the work of the best contemporary island performers. They wanted Eddie and The Sons to be part of this. They didn't have much experience, but they were all enthusiastic and well connected. They hoped to call their new company Pānini, after a cactus plant that had surrounded the dorms and classrooms of the private school they'd all attended, Hawai'i Preparatory Academy, in cattle country outside the Big Island town of Waimea.

Around this same time Eddie was approached by Honolulu publisher Bob Goodman, who had come up with a similar idea: a new kind of Hawaiian music album. The time had come, he told Eddie, to showcase Hawai'i's musical revival by bringing together the best talent and the best production equipment available. Goodman wasn't a music producer, but he'd produced some beautiful books, and Eddie liked his work.

Eddie's first producer, Don McDiarmid, Jr., had grown up with the music, an island native. Goodman was an islander by choice, or by osmosis, drawn here by songs he'd heard growing up in Cincinnati, on the banks of the Ohio River. Trained as a photo-journalist, he first came to Hawai'i in 1958, as a twenty-five-year-old photographer. In the dozen years since then he'd fallen in love with the music and the people. While working as a *National Geographic* staffer, he formed Island Heritage Publishing Company, and had recently photographed and produced *The Hawaiians,* an enormously popular tribute to contemporary island culture.[3]

His hope now was to reassemble The Sons of Hawaii, still the pace-setting band of their time. If Eddie could get the boys together, Goodman believed he could raise the money and link up with the right technical people on the West Coast.

Eddie made some calls. He talked with Joe. He talked with Gabby. They all agreed they needed Feet. But when was he coming back to town? And would he hang around long enough to rehearse and cut a record?

"I heard he'll be back next week," Eddie said.

"From where?" asked Gabby.

"Probably San Francisco. It's a cruise ship. The President Line."

"Find out when. We'll have a beer and talk."

Two days after Eddie got home from South Point, Feet came ashore. He always stopped first to say hello to his mother, so Eddie was waiting for him at the Rogers family house. That afternoon they all met up at Pōhaku's Bar in Kalihi. Beers were ordered to celebrate Feet's return, and the talk was animated as they imagined what a new album could be like. Since their second collection (now known to fans as the "Volcano" album), six years had passed. They had gone their separate ways; Eddie had done an album on his own, and so had Gabby (his 1969 release, *Two Slack-Key Guitars,* with Atta Isaacs). The time was ripe for a reunion, to reclaim that early 1960s sound, build on it, bring it into the 1970s. This time, Gabby joked, maybe Joe would have enough room to stand up in the studio.

Joe shook his head in mock protest. "If I stand up, does that mean I gotta wear my good pants?"

As for Feet, he liked the drift of all this, he really did, nodding and grinning in his dark glasses and his seaman's watchcap. Yet when they asked him when he could start rehearsing, he told them he was just in town for one day. That night his ship would be heading out again, bound due west for Hong Kong.

This brought their celebration to a sudden halt. Eddie didn't know what to say. There was no use trying to talk Feet out of something he'd already decided to do. Was this project doomed before it even got started?

As they drove back to Feet's house, Eddie was wondering how he'd explain this to Bob Goodman. It was quiet in the car until Feet finally said, "Pops."

"Yeah."

"I been thinking."

"About what?"

"We're coming back from Hong Kong, you know."

"When?"

"Pretty soon. Next month. This time I think I'm getting off the ship."

"For how long?"

Feet shrugged. "Long enough to do the record. Maybe more."

"More what?"

"Maybe for good. Hard to say. But we got to do this record."

That was all Eddie needed to hear. The next day he told Joe Marshall. He told Gabby. He told Bob Goodman, and he set up a meeting with Steve Siegfried and the Pānini three. With so many minds working toward the same end, Eddie figured, why not bring them all together?

Goodman told him to start thinking about songs. This, he said, could be the best Hawaiian album ever produced. A new studio had opened up in Honolulu, with state-of-the-art equipment. They could remix on the mainland. They could do an insert that would be part of the album, with stories on each musician. Maybe there'd be a book about the music itself. Nothing like this had ever been attempted.

"Good," said Eddie. "I like it. When braddah Feet comes in from Hong Kong, we'll be ready."

HOW MOUNTAINS SING *After the South Point trip I couldn't wait to get back to the Big Island to see those oldtimers she told me to look up. It was always like that with Kawena. All the years I knew her, every time we meet she tells me things that keep me excited for days and weeks.*

It wasn't long before I had my chance. I had the directions she gave me. First I drove to Kalapana, way down south from Hilo, looking for a man called 'Olu. 'Olu Konanui. I ask around, and someone tells me, Go down by the old Queen's Bath swimming hole, and just before you turn in, you will find his house right across the road. So I drive out there, and that is lava country, too, you know, like Ka'ū. The place where I found him, I don't think it's there any more. I think it got covered during those big flows a few years ago. If 'Olu was still alive when the lava came, I know it didn't surprise him. He predicted it. The day I met him, a bulldozer had come in real close to this shack, to tear out some trees and widen the road. 'Olu didn't like the bulldozer or any big equipment like that. He looked at the mess it left behind, and he told me Pele was going to come back again and take this land.

"If you spoil it and misuse it," he said, "she will take it. She is always watching to see what we will do."

The time I'm talking about was back in 1970. He lived all by himself in his wooden shack, somewhere down the coast from Kalapana. Those days he was maybe ninety years old, living with his horse, dog, a few chickens, and still getting around. He wore his jeans and his tee shirt, and his back was straight. He didn't need a cane. Once in a while he still worked as a guide for the rangers from Volcanoes National Park. They would come when they needed somebody to show them how to find a certain location, and 'Olu would take them. He knew all the places out that way, the caves, the lava tubes, the burial places, where the villages used to be, and the names of everything, the old Hawaiian names. He had it all in his head.

'Olu knew a lot of things other people had forgotten. My interest was always music. It seems like my trips always led me to a song, or ended up somewhere in a song, and that's what happened on the day

I talked with 'Olu. I asked him did he remember any songs from around there, from Kalapana or Puna. He thought awhile and looked at me and said, "I know one verse of one song."

"What's the name of the song?"

He said, "Mauna Kea."

I said, "You sing it for me."

"Just one verse, that's all."

"Good. Sing the song for me."

'Olu had a high, raspy voice and he sang a verse that means,

What is happening to Mauna Kea,
a mountain that endures?

It was a beautiful melody, one I didn't know. I hadn't heard it before. You could feel the mystery of that mountain in his voice. Mauna Kea is the highest peak in all of Hawai'i and sacred to the oldtimers. It's like Mount Fuji in Japan. I asked him did he know any more verses, and he shook his head. So I asked him to sing it again, and this time I taped it.

*Later on, back in Honolulu, I took the tape to Kawena and played it for her and told her this was the only verse. She said to me, "*Hīmeni. Sing.*" So I got my* 'ukulele *and sang the verse while she started writing on a notepad. Before I knew it, she had written down seven more verses. Each one was like the first one, two lines long, the way an old* hula mele *would be composed. It turned out to be a song about the mountains and craters of the Big Island: Mauna Kea, Mauna Loa, Kīlauea, Halema'uma'u, the firepit that is Pele's home, and then about the region called Puna, where 'Olu lived. It's a song about volcano country, she told me. Years past she heard it somewhere and it was all in her head.*

What an amazing day that was for me—to hear an old song come back to life because of two minds, 'Olu in his shack in Kalapana, Kawena in her living room in Honolulu. She handed her notepad to me and said, "Now it's finished. Now you sing it."

Sam Li'a Kalainaina (1881–1975), the Songwriter of Waipi'o Valley.

Where the Songwriter Lives

Heading north from Hilo, Eddie and Myrna followed the Hāmākua coast. A two-lane road hugs the shoreline, crossing countless streams that lace the rain-watered slopes of Mauna Kea. For several miles a muddy cane truck slowed them down, until it swung off onto a plantation trail, rumbling inland.

They passed through Honoka'a, the main town out that way, a plantation town where porches tilted under darkly rusted sheets of metal roofing. From there the round-the-island belt road bore left toward Waimea, Parker Ranch, and the leeward side, but Eddie continued north along the coastline, passing the village of Kapulena, where a two-wheel track climbed away to the left toward the tract of land where his father had been born eighty years earlier. As they passed the turn-off, he told Myrna how he'd come out here once before, in search of the site, and how he'd met a Chinese woman who said she had known his father.

"'I have a picture of him in uniform,' she told me, and that made me stop and think. 'You sure it's my father?' I said. 'He was never in the service.'" Then the Chinese woman showed Eddie the picture, and it was a smiling, handsome Hawaiian youngster in the uniform they used to require all the boys to wear at Lahainaluna School, on Maui, right after the turn of the century.

Two more miles, and they came to Kukuihaele, the last community before the coast road ends. Eddie slowed down and rechecked Kawena's directions. A grocery store would be on the right, she'd said, and across from the store would be the social hall, and next to the social hall he would see Sam's house. "You won't have any trouble finding it," she'd said. And she was right. It was a wooden cottage raised off the ground for ventilation, with a long roof sloping out over the porch.

Eddie parked his jeep and walked across the grass. As he neared the steps, he saw an old man sitting in a straight-backed chair. Through tinted spectacles he was watching Eddie approach. His face was lean and brown, capped with thick white hair. A white crescent moustache shaped his mouth. The glasses gave him a scholarly look. He wore a white shirt and a necktie and a black suit with the coat buttoned, as if on his way to church or to a wedding.

Eddie said, "Sam Li'a."

The old man nodded.

"My name is Eddie Kamae."

"I know," he said in Hawaiian. "I've been expecting you."

Eddie felt his scalp tingle. He had not called ahead or sent a message.

"I didn't know how he knew," Eddie says now, "but he was waiting for me that day, in his best suit. He was very erect and dignified, and he had a notepad in his lap. Eighty-nine years old, and he was working on a song. Right then I felt like I had met this man before. His house was familiar to me. It could have been my father's house. I felt like I had known Sam all my life. And I know now that he felt the same thing about me, though he didn't say it at the time. Later on he would say, 'You remind me of me when I was a younger man.'"

Sam invited them to sit with him on the porch, and they began to talk, first about Kawena, who had looked up Sam, back in the days when she herself was still roaming around "out there" in search of songs and stories. When Eddie told him about 'Olu Konanui, Sam remembered that they had met many years earlier, on a road somewhere down near Hilo. 'Olu was on horseback, and they talked in Hawaiian for quite some time. "When I got back home," Sam said, "I wrote him a letter and put six dollars in there. It was all I had that day, but I wanted to send him something. I wanted to thank him for being a friend."

Eddie had brought along an old songbook published in Hawaiian soon after Sam was born. *Ka Buke O Na Leo Mele*

Hawaii (A Book of Hawaiian Songs) was bound in worn leather, its pages dappled brown with age.[1] The first Hawaiian songbook to be published in the islands, it was a rare collection of early lyrics, but with no musical notation. One song in particular had been on Eddie's mind. The *Buke* called it "Waimanalo." While he liked the words, he had almost given up finding anyone who might remember its melody. But on the day they met, Sam Li'a remembered. He recognized the composer's name, "Figgs," a whimsical pseudonym sometimes used by King Kalākaua. Sam knew these lyrics by an alternate title, "Na Ke Aloha," a romantic ballad composed by the king in the late nineteenth century. Sam's long memory gave the song new life, just as 'Olu Konanui had helped Eddie to reclaim "Mauna Kea."

Eddie thanked him and said this was why he had come to visit, to meet a fellow musician who could help him learn more about the music, the history of the songs, and also how they were played and composed in Sam's day.

The old man thought about this, then said, "You got a car?"

"I got a jeep."

"Good. Let's go for a ride."

Sam took off his coat, put on his hat—a porkpie with a narrow brim—and grabbed his cane. They drove the last mile of the coast road and parked where the pavement ends, on a high bluff with an observation railing. Overhead the sky was blue, but offshore a rain squall spilled from gray overhang. A cool, wet wind blew in off the water. They stood in the wind and gazed down into a broad valley. Sheer, verdant cliffs made it a tropical amphitheater. Below them, square taro ponds glistened among palms and groves of wild banana. Leaning on his cane, Sam gestured with his free arm, as if offering them all this, and said in a graveled, commanding voice, "Waipi'o."

The word means "curving water." Through the bottomland, a stream curved toward the beach and a narrow, surf-rimmed bay. Across the valley, a furrowed headland met the sea with blunt finality. Up the farther cliff a climbing zigzag line marked a trail to the next valley, one you could only reach by horse or boat and now uninhabited. With his arm flung outward Sam reverently spoke its name. "Over that way . . . Waimanu."

In Eddie's jeep they descended, plunging down a rutted track. As cliffs rose around them, the wind dropped off. The air grew still and sultry. The valley floor was laced with little tributary streams that crossed the muddy road. After they had forded a few of these, Sam told Eddie to pull over in front of what looked to be an abandoned farmhouse, set back from the road. A wild tangle of vines and greenery had begun to repossess it.

They got out of the jeep and looked around. Under a rainforest canopy that blocked the sun, some fragments of lava rock fencing lined the roadside. Off to the south, at the far end of a secondary canyon, a twin-ribboned falls dropped a hundred yards down a shadowy cliff face.

"Hi'ilawe," Sam said.

Then he said the name of the place where they were standing.

"Nā-pō'o-po'o."

His low, grainy voice made each of these names a kind of incantation.

Pointing toward an open space in the grove behind them, Sam said that's where he was born, back in 1881, when this was still a village and when hundreds of Hawaiian families still lived in this valley, farming and fishing. There had been a schoolhouse here, he said, and a store and a church and a *poi* factory. Now all that remained in Nāpō'opo'o was Mock Chew's empty house. Hardly anyone lives in Waipi'o now, he said, not since the great tsunami of 1946, when thirty feet of water poured inland for two miles, burying fields and trees and houses and graveyards. Sam remembered that day. He was in his sixties then. He pointed to the top of an ironwood tree to show how high the water had risen, and Eddie could feel the ghost of that flood still alive and floating through the valley air. Nowadays the farmers who work the taro live up above, Sam said, in Kukuihaele or Honoka'a and come down the road in the morning and go back home at night, heading for higher ground.

They drove toward the falls to get a closer look and to hear the rush of spilling water, then turned and moved farther back into the valley, past the rows of taro, where broad leaves gleamed in their shallow ponds, the *lo'i*, some of them laid out centuries ago, Sam told them, along with irrigation systems that were still in use.

When heavy growth finally stopped them, they looped back toward the beach, where they spread out a picnic lunch Eddie and Myrna had brought along. Right behind the beach, Sam said, had been the site of an important temple, erected hundreds of years back by Waipi'o's legendary chief, 'Umi-a-Līloa, in the days when this valley was a community of many thousands and one of the most influential regions in all of Hawai'i. Great chiefs had their houses here, near the beach, he said, and a wrestling court where they practiced their combat skills, and a sacred house where the bones of the chiefly ancestors were stored, and a temple with stone walls thirty feet high. When Sam was a boy some of those walls still stood—and he spoke the name of the site that will always be a sacred place.

"Paka'alana."

The way the Hawaiian islands are laid out, there is nothing north of Waipi'o until you reach the Gulf of Alaska. Swells roll in uninterrupted, cracking over one by one in the blue water of the bay. After lunch they sat and listened to the waves and felt the gathered energy of this old habitat, supremely tropical, almost empty now, yet still filled with the spirits of the lives come and gone.

When they climbed back into the jeep, Sam was in a good mood. He loved his valley and all the layers of it. The time they'd spent together was as meaningful for him as for Eddie and Myrna. Sam wanted to commemorate the occasion and so proposed that they make a song. Eddie would do the music, and Sam would write the lyrics. It would give Eddie a reason to come again. More important, as Eddie would realize when he later heard the old man's verses, this little pilgrimage had been Sam's first lesson: to know his music, you must first learn about his valley.

On Eddie's next visit Sam would show him a song made of twelve short verses, each one naming a stop on their journey, or one of the places they'd seen—the lookout point, the stretch of shoreline, the rush of distant water pouring down a canyon wall, the dark sea in front of Paka'alana, the long gone temple of the royal ones. "Let the refrain be told," the last verse says, "The mind has seen Waipi'o."

It was the kind of song Eddie had written with Kawena. But this was different. This time he felt he was somehow *inside* the music in a new way. Sam's place was also an ancestral place for Eddie, the home region of his father, his grandfather, his great-grandfather too, and who knew how much further back it went.

Before heading home to Honolulu, Eddie had one more stop to make. There was one more oldtimer he hoped to meet, another fellow about Sam's age, not a songwriter, but a canoe maker said to have a lifetime of stories he was ready to share. All at once, it seemed, Eddie was hearing about these elders, and each one a treasure. This fellow, David Kaho'okele, lived on the windward side of Maui, in the village of Nāhiku, halfway along the Hāna Road, an area as remote as Waipi'o. Eddie had been there once, to see the nineteenth-century church. Since then a friend who taught at a Maui high school had been urging him to go back and meet the canoe maker.

"I have told him about you," the friend said, "and about your research. He knows of your music. He couldn't come to the Ho'olaule'a, but his relatives told him about it. He has many things to share. He is one of the last in the old tradition, who remembers the training of his youth, a *kahuna kālai wa'a,* a master canoe builder. So come with me, Eddie. Fly to Maui. We will take my car and drive out to Nāhiku and meet this man. You can stay with him for two days, or three days, ask him any question and he will answer. He told me this himself."

While Myrna flew on to Honolulu, Eddie got off the plane at Kahului, Maui, planning to give his friend a call—only to discover, as he opened the local paper, that David Kaho'okele had just passed away, at age ninety-five. The memorial service was scheduled for that very afternoon.

"I never in my life saw so many Hawaiian people in one room," Eddie says. "At the funeral parlor there must have been two hundred. My friend was there, and he said, 'Sit with us, Eddie.' So I sat with them. Then it came time for the final viewing, and I walked up with all the others to pay my respects to this man I had never met. In the coffin he was a very small Hawaiian man. I looked into his face, with his eyes closed now, and I told him, 'I'm sorry I didn't come to see you.'"

Near the casket stood three young fellows in military uniform. One of them recognized Eddie. After they'd exchanged a few words, he said quietly, "My grandfather waited for you."

It was a gentle remark, not meant to judge or find fault, but it cut through Eddie like a sword. He thought of Sam Li'a waiting on his porch in his best suit. He knew the grandson meant that the old man had stayed alive a while longer expecting Eddie's visit and the chance to share his memories.

"As I left the service, I felt empty, like I had lost something of great value I could never get back. Like Sam with his music, David was the last of the oldtime canoe makers. He'd been a politician, too. There was a whole part of the history of Maui, and it died with him."

With the burden of Eddie's grief came a shock of recognition. As he thought of these Hawaiian men in their later years, the two he'd met, and the one he'd missed, he thought of others he'd heard of in recent months, on other islands, at the ends of other roads. With a pang of remorse it came home to him that a generation of irreplaceable elders was passing away, men and women whose lives had linked two centuries, two cultures, two modes of being in the world. The loss of this canoe maker had awakened a new sense of mission and, for Eddie, another way of thinking about his own "work" and how all these things are connected: the music, the memories, the making of canoes, the making of songs, the history of Hawai'i's many places, and the ways these places shape the lives. Maybe Waipi'o had chosen Eddie just as it had chosen Sam. And maybe the *tūtū* man's story was going to take him somewhere he'd been trying for years to reach.

TWO FATHERS *By the time I met Sam, his hands were so gnarled and knobby he couldn't play anymore. But he loved to talk about playing, and he could still laugh about the good times he'd had. He played everything, guitar,* 'ukulele, *piano, organ. Later in life he played organ at the church in Honoka'a. He conducted the choir there too. Of all these instruments, his favorite was the fiddle. The first time he heard one he just fell in love with the sound, the same way I fell in love with the* 'ukulele.

He was about eight, and a band of roaming musicians came to Nāpō'opo'o, the way they used to do, riding down into the valley on horseback, going from place to place to serenade the country folks. There would be a uke, one or two guitars, with a fiddle usually playing lead. This was the 1880s, before the steel guitar. When the steel came in, about twenty years later, it would take over that high melody role from the fiddle. But in Sam's day there were still some great fiddle players in Hawai'i.

So one of these serenading bands played outside Sam's house. When they started to ride away, he begged his father to ask them to stay and play a few more songs. The next day Sam went out into the forest and cut some bamboo and made himself a kind of fiddle so he could start playing. When I asked him what he used for strings, he told me No. 10 thread, with mango wax.

He got his first real fiddle about four years later, when he was visiting his brother-in-law and saw one on the bed. He picked it up and started playing. The brother-in-law heard him and came into the bedroom and listened for a while and said to Sam, "That's beautiful. You keep that violin. It belongs to you."

Sam played that instrument his whole life. He played it way past the time when you would have heard a fiddle in any kind of Hawaiian band in Honolulu. On the day I met Sam, he still had it. He showed it to me, and I thought about the 'ukulele *my older brother found on the bus and brought home for me to play. I was about the same age when that happened. I know what an effect it can have on you.*

That was just one more thing connecting us. The more we talked, the more I understood why I felt so close to this kind man who had welcomed me into his life and treated me like his own son. It really clicked into place when he told me his family had sent him over to Maui to attend Lahainaluna School in the 1890s. That's where my father went, just a few years later, coming from this same area of the Big Island. They grew up in towns just two miles apart, with only about nine years between them. And they were both named Sam!

As young guys going to school on Maui, they both learned printing on the big press there at the school. It was after that, when they followed different paths. My father went on to try his luck in Honolulu and left his childhood home behind. Sam came back to the Big Island and never left. When I saw all that, I knew why I saw him as my spiritual father. I loved them both. But in different ways. Sam's whole life was in touch with the spirit of the place my father came from. All his music came from there, too, the same kind of music my father heard when he was growing up and loved so much and always wanted me to play.

One summer Sam came home from Maui and got a job typesetting with the old Hawaii Herald in Hilo. He was eighteen. He was supposed to go back that fall, but the inter-island steamer got delayed for two weeks with engine trouble, so he missed the start of school. He kept working, and he never went back to Maui. He stayed with the Herald for four years. He might have stayed longer because he liked the work, but he got word that his eighty-year-old father was sick. So Sam walked home to see his father. It took him three or four days. It was about fifty miles up the coast, along the muddy plantation road. After that he never went back to Hilo.

He stayed in the valley taking care of his father, and pretty soon he had written his first song. He wrote it to help out a friend, which is how Sam wrote all his songs. For a certain person. Or to mark some special time—just the way his father wrote "Hi'ilawe" about the beauty of the waterfall, but also about two lovers who meet there secretly. At the time he wrote it, there would be references inside the song to tell everyone in the valley who they were.

Joe Perez was Sam's schoolmate from Lahainaluna who also came back to Waipi'o where his father farmed taro. Joe was getting married, so he fixed up his old family house, repainted it, brought in some new furniture. He did such a good job, his relatives got jealous, especially one brother-in-law. They accused Joe of having a house too fancy for the common man, and this hurt Joe's feelings. He asked Sam to help him out by writing a song of welcome. So Sam did. He put a band together with three other fellows, and they played it outside Joe's house at the wedding on Christmas Day. It praises Joe Perez and the beautiful valley they all shared. Some of the folks who were there could tell from the lyrics that they, too, were in the song. So it brought them all together, and the band had to play several encores.

Sam called it "Heha Waipi'o" (Drowsy Waipi'o). He gave the song to Joe as a wedding present. A few years later one of Joe's sisters who lived in Honolulu showed it to Henry Berger, the famous bandmaster from Germany who had taught Queen Lili'uokalani, and Sam's first song was peformed by the Royal Hawaiian Band. Since then other bands have recorded it, the only song by Sam that ever got recorded in his lifetime.

He wrote "Heha Waipi'o" in 1904, when he was twenty-two. In those years he worked at a lot of different jobs, farming, driving wagons for Parker Ranch, mule-skinning for one of the big sugar plantations. I have seen pictures of Sam from that time, a big husky guy, his moustache thick and black, his hair thick, and his eyes strong, but soft too. I have heard he had a reputation as a ladies' man, and they say he had a taste for the home-brew we call 'ōkolehao. *At least he enjoyed it as much as anyone else in Waipi'o. It was just part of the world he knew. Everybody worked hard in the taro or the sugar, then they got together to play music and talk story and have a good time. They say once you start drinking* 'ōkolehao *you better have a comfortable place to sit, because that's where you will stay. Later on, your head might say, "It's time to go." But your legs will be saying, "We're not going anywhere."*

They brewed it from the root of the ti plant, which had to be washed

Sam Li'a with his wife, Sarah, circa 1920.
(Inset shows the son they lost in 1918.)

first, and sliced, then cooked for a few hours in an earth oven, the imu, *then mashed up soft, to get it ready for the still.*

I heard one story about Sam that I made into a song of my own, called "'Ōkolehao." On his way home from the fields, sometimes Sam would stop to visit a guy who brewed his own at the back end of the valley. One day Sam stayed so long at this guy's house and drank so much, they had to tie him to his horse and point the horse toward home.

I heard another story from my friend Herb Kāne, the artist. His father and grandfather both lived in Waipi'o and knew Sam in the old days and told him about the time he was riding home late one night, feeling no pain, and coming down that steep road at such a gallop his horse just went right over the side and rolled down the cliff. The next morning people saw the horse at the bottom of the cliff and it looked like something terrible had happened to Sam, but they couldn't find his body. They looked all over, feeling so sad they were starting to weep with grief. Then they saw Sam come walking down the pali *road. Just before his horse went over, he had fallen off. He'd passed out up there and slept all night, and now he was wondering, did anybody see his horse?*

Whatever Sam did in those days, he always had a band of traveling serenaders like the ones he'd heard when he was a boy. I met a man in Honolulu, David Makaoi, who was in his late eighties, a retired high school principal who lived in Nu'uanu, and he remembered roaming around in a band like that with Sam when he was fifteen. One day Sam told him to grab his 'ukulele *and join in. Sam was the leader. Someone else played banjo, and there was a guitar. David told me how they would meet with their horses in late afternoon. In those days Sam was always riding a white horse. That was his trademark. He would sit on his white horse and hit a G note on his fiddle. When they were all tuned up, Sam would shout, "Let's go!" and away they went.*

In towns up on top they would play outside the plantation manager's house and the schoolteacher's house, then they rode down into the valley and played outside the farmhouses, taking turns singing.

One time I was curious about the way Sam handled his band, and I asked him, "How did you approach your boys and playing the music?" and Sam told me, "Let each and every one of them share their mana'o, *their intention and feeling, the way they want to play their song, and share the way they want to strum along with you. I let 'em do that," he said, "and all I tell 'em is play it simple, play it sweet, don't forget the rhythm, and don't forget the melody line."*

People would always pay them a little something, or invite them to share some poi *or some pig, whatever they had. David Makaoi remembered getting back to his own house at dawn, when Sam would count out the money they had made and split it four ways. When I talked with David seventy years later, he was still impressed with this.*

"I was so much younger than all the other guys, only fifteen then, and I only knew one song I could take the lead on, but Sam said everybody gets the same."

That's the kind of world it was back then, everybody shared, the world my mother remembered when I was growing up. I saw it with her, the way she called out to everyone she passed. I saw it with Sam Li'a too.

The Folk Music of Hawaii, released in 1971, came to be known as the "Five Faces" album, thanks to inspired drawings by Big Island artist Herb Kāne.

7

"Five Faces"

It was a long trip from Sam's world to the Honolulu world of hotel lounges and recording gigs, much farther than one could measure in air miles or inter-island travel time. And yet there was a way to keep them connected—Eddie saw that now—through songs that carried the lives and loves and journeys and precious places like Waipi'o. This was not something he could have explained with words. But he could sing it. He could play it. He could channel it into the album they'd been talking about, the one Bob Goodman said would be the best Hawaiian album ever produced.

Goodman had asked Eddie to start getting the boys together, and he'd already decided to bring in one more voice. Though the first idea was to reassemble the "original" Sons, Eddie had been listening to a young singer named Moe Keale. During Eddie's months at the Maluna Lounge, Moe was working in the Kuhio Hotel restaurant, two floors below. He started early, playing for the dinner crowd, so Eddie caught Moe's show from time to time, and the more he listened, the more he believed Moe had some qualities that could enrich the vocal blend for this new recording.

He had grown up in Pālolo, a semi-rural valley that cuts deep into the mountain range behind Diamond Head, but Moe had strong family ties to the all-Hawaiian island of Ni'ihau and its self-contained musical tradition. His distinctive voice was similar to Gabby's, with that same full-throated heartfulness, though somehow softer around the edges. Moe was also a gifted *'ukulele* player, first inspired by Eddie's instrumental work on the early albums. He was among those who'd cheered them on at the

Sandbox, back when he was nineteen and just finding his way as a musician. When Eddie approached him about joining a rehearsal session, Moe was flabbergasted.

"I cannot believe these people that I idolized," he said years later, shaking his head with wonder, "asking me to come and play with them. . . . I was just in shock, for the next maybe five or six years. . . . It was such a privilege . . . this younger brother from Pālolo was over there with The Sons of Hawaii."[1]

Moe fit right in. He already knew their songs. He could sing harmony or take the lead. He knew Hawaiian and took pride in correct delivery of the lyrics. Like Gabby and Joe, he had a ready wit and an infectious sense of humor. Before long they were rehearsing at Moe's house (as a married man with a wife expecting, he had a place in Kaimukī and a back room where the band could assemble), trying out new songs, new arrangements, and once again waiting for Feet Rogers's ship to appear on the horizon.

While the musicians worked on content, Bob Goodman and the Pānini three set up their fledgling company and moved ahead on the production side, thinking about everything at once: sound studios and engineers, funding, distribution, marketing, promotion. Packaging was crucial, they all agreed, a design and layout to match the music. To that end, Goodman tracked down Hawaiian artist and writer Herb Kāne, then based in Chicago, four time-zones away.

"I got his number and I called him," Goodman said later. "I told him that we wanted to present Hawaiian music the way mainland artists are presented. The music was so good and so original it deserved to be packaged beautifully, richly, and promoted richly—and would he be kind enough to do the art. And he agreed. Then we had to find a sponsor, because all this cost money. And so it turned out that Schlitz Brewing Company had just bought all rights to the Primo Beer label here in Honolulu, and they were going to be entering this community as an outsider."[2]

When Goodman flew in to Chicago, Kāne met him at the airport. For the next three days, at his studio in suburban Glencoe, they worked on a layout, a rough sketch for the album jacket and for an accompanying booklet. Then they climbed into Kāne's car and drove north along the shore of Lake Michigan to Milwaukee where Schlitz has its main office. Goodman was nervous, with everything riding on whether or not the brewer would come in as a major sponsor. But with Herb Kāne as an ally now, he was in good hands. Kāne knew Ralph Gibson, the marketing director, and he also knew Hawai'i.

Born on the Big Island, Kāne had grown up in his mother's home state of Wisconsin (his father's family name, pronounced "Kah-nay," means "man.") After training at the Art Institute of Chicago he had settled in Glencoe, working as an illustrator and ad designer. But his heart was still in the islands. In recent years he'd become intrigued with the design, construction, and navigational lore of ancient voyaging canoes, a passion that would eventually bring him home to become a founding member (in 1973) of the Polynesian Voyaging Society.

As Kāne recalls those days, "I had set up this meeting. When we walked into Gibson's office, I saw on the sideboard behind his desk a big box of Maui onions. I knew Ralph was a gourmet, the kind of guy who once he had tasted a Maui onion would have them flown in. I saw that box, and I knew we had a winner."[3]

And he was right. Gibson took to their proposal immediately. For decades Primo had been the locally brewed beer of choice in Hawai'i. With a new parent company now located in the far-off Midwest, it would be a good thing to be seen supporting a project designed to elevate the musical tradition. It would be good for the company's image. It would be good for Hawai'i, too.

Thus it came to pass that many lines began to converge to make this album happen. While the band's new singer brought his family lineage from Ni'ihau, the major funding came from Wisconsin. While Feet was crossing the Pacific from Hong Kong, Herb Kāne flew in from Chicago. As soon as Feet came ashore, they both joined the gathering at Moe Keale's house—Kāne with camera and sketchpad, to catch on-site impressions of the boys in rehearsal, and Feet, with his steel, playing as if he'd never been away.

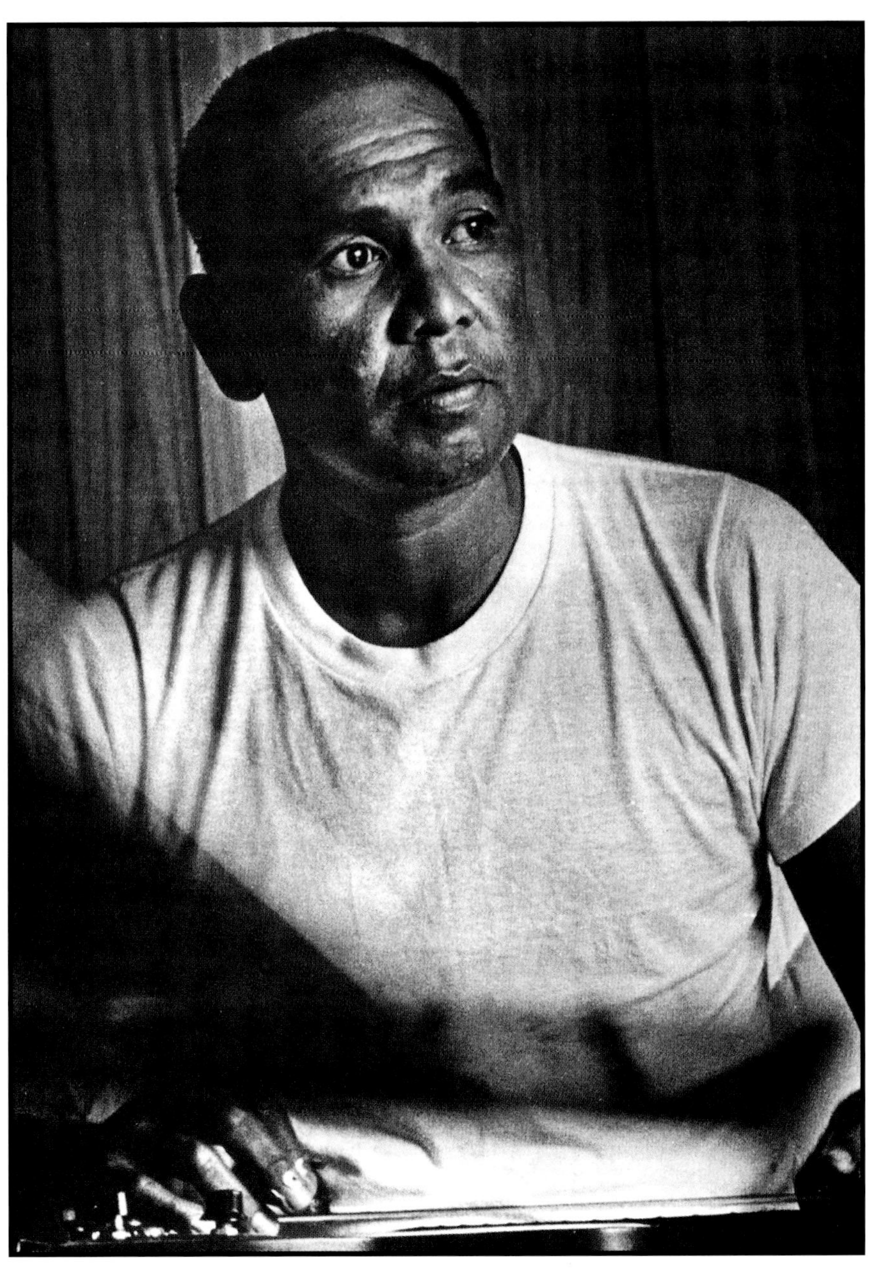

David "Feet" Rogers

The new guy in the band, and the youngest by several years, Moe was astonished at Feet's quick grasp of things.

"The first time I meet him he come in and sit down, and I'm thinking, We've been practicing for three months and this guy just walking in here now? So we start the first song, we went through maybe one verse, and Feet go, 'Okay.' Then the next song, we play maybe two, three lines. Feet go, 'Okay. Got 'em.' And we went through all the music like that. We start singing, and then it's time for the steel solo, and Feet's right in there. I couldn't believe it! Songs Feet never played before in his life!"

With Rogers back, everything seemed at last to be in place. The first recording session was scheduled at the Commercial Studios near Ala Moana Boulevard. Every voice was miked, every instrument. They had a Scully eight-track recorder, a Fairchild eight-track mixing console, Neumann and Sony condenser mikes, RCA ribbon mikes, AKG dynamic mikes to get tight against Gabby's guitar. No Hawaiian band had ever had this much equipment in front of them. It was the chance of a lifetime.

There was only one problem: Gabby Pahinui had been drinking all day. After everyone had tuned up and tested for mike levels, they tried a run-through on the first tune. But Gabby lost his way. He couldn't remember the arrangement. They tried it again, and again he lost his way.

"We did nine takes like that," says Eddie, "then I told Bob and the engineers to cancel the session. There was no use taking up everybody's time. We quit for the day. After we packed up and left, outside the studio Feet got into my car, and he was disgusted. He didn't say one word, but I knew what he was thinking: I come back from Hong Kong and got off the ship for *this?* All of a sudden he look at me and say, 'You know, pops, if not for you, I would have pulled my plug and left that place.'"

But they had to give it one more try. And by the next day Gabby—contrite, and full of apology—had pulled himself together. He had a couple of drinks before the session, not enough to disable him, just enough to lubricate his voice and his fingers. After that the album came together very quickly, fourteen songs in all, some new, some reaching back to the nineteenth century. Eddie had chosen them and devised fresh arrangements.

There was "Manu Kapalulu" (The Quail) by Queen Lili'u-okalani, and "Po'e Koa" (People of Courage), a 1940s Ni'ihau song from Moe Keale's family. There was the standard "Hano-hano Hawai'i" (Majestic Hawai'i), celebrating each island's symbolic flower—*'ilima* for O'ahu, *mokihana* for Kaua'i—and the old Maui tune, "Huelo," about a girl and boy from the Hāna coast, one from Huelo, one from Ke'anae, who boast about the charms of their home regions. There were two original tunes by Pīlahi Pākī, her "Aloha Chant" and the haunting "Mauna 'Alani," inspired by the look of a famous peak in the west Maui mountains as it catches the glow of a rising sun.

Mauna 'Alani's venerable glow was then enhanced by state-of-the-art technology. The master tapes were shipped to Capitol Records in Hollywood for remixing on a brand-new Quad-8 custom console. The lacquer masters were cut at Capitol on a computerized Newmann lathe. During this same time the illustrated background text was being published out of Norfolk Island, Australia, where Goodman's company was based, with the printing and binding done in Kyōtō.

The album was finally released in December 1971, at the height of the Christmas shopping season, with a reception and concert at the Liberty House in Kahala Mall, on the city's east side. The upscale department store chain had never been involved in launching an album (it didn't even have a music section), which somehow added to the event's glitter and rare appeal. Hundreds of fans gathered among the aisles of cosmetics and *aloha* shirts and lingerie to hear the band and buy early signed copies.

Called *The Folk Music of Hawaii,* it would be known ever after as the "Five Faces" album, a tribute to Herb Kāne's striking cover illustration. Original portraits of each musician are set against a backdrop of billowing crimson, which could be smoke or could be flowers. It was a fold-open jacket with a booklet inside called "The Musicians," featuring artful photos by Bob Goodman, along with lyrics to all the songs, and biographical essays on each performer, compiled by Carl Lindquist

(who had co-produced the Hāna festival the previous year). Interspersed were more drawings from Kāne's sketchbook, catching the flow and flavor of a band in rehearsal—with shirts on, shirts off, sometimes barefooted, laughing, strumming, hunched over the fretboard, close up on the hands, or the eyes squeezed shut in concentration.

Herb Kāne's sketches of Moe Keale appeared in "The Musicians," an original booklet packaged with the 1971 "Five Faces" album.

With the album and the booklet came a bound book called *Old Hawaiian Folk Music,* which included historic photos, an essay by *Honolulu Advertiser* columnist Sammy 'Āmalu, and an illustrated memoir by Herb Kāne entitled "Waipi'o." It begins like this: "'To understand the old Hawaiians, you must listen to their music,' my father said. 'I know at least fifty Hawaiian songs about love or the beauty of certain places, but only one song about war.'"[4]

Taken together, the album, the artwork, the pamphlet and bound book, and Liberty House launch comprised what would later be called "the most ambitious marketing and promotional package of Hawaiian music to date."[5] But this was not marketing for its own sake. The aim of it all was to honor the band, their songs, the long tradition they'd helped to revive. And the music inside more than lived up to this investment.

Their instrumental work is better than ever, the vocal work too, with Eddie more prominent, singing at a new level of assurance, while Moe's tender phrasing blends perfectly, often taking the lead. Their "open sound" is bigger, fuller, surpassing what they'd recorded in the early 1960s, due in part to first-rate studio equipment from both sides of the water, in part to the rhythmic energy. Eddie's uke is bigger now, twice the size of the concert Martin he played in the mid-1960s. It's a custom-made baritone box, almost a small guitar, strung like a mandolin, with eight strings in two courses, giving it twice the volume. On this album most of the solo work comes from Feet's steel, his bell notes ringing through the acoustic pulse. Meanwhile Eddie, Gabby, and Moe, all renowned for their solo picking, have set aside melodic inventiveness to keep the rhythm uppermost, giving themselves to a pulsing current that is distinctly and generously Hawaiian.

opposite
"Five Faces" came packaged with Herb Kāne's illustrated booklet, "Waipi'o," remembering the days when bands of serenaders would travel from house to house.

This drawing later appeared as the cover of The Sons' 1978 Christmas album.

By December 1971 it seemed that all the pieces of this visionary puzzle had somehow fallen into place—songs from Huelo and Ni'ihau, money from Milwaukee, lacquer masters from Hollywood, and binding from Japan. With the album out there and getting rave reviews, a series of meetings were held in Honolulu, to finalize the complex contractual arrangements that had evolved as this project moved forward. There was a lot to talk about, a lot to negotiate, since they were also considering how to keep the momentum alive, via radio time, TV spots, concerts, and club dates, maybe a mainland tour.

It was a three-way conversation, with three attorneys sitting in. Eddie and the band were the talent. As publisher of Island Heritage, Bob Goodman had produced the books and raised most of the money. Steve Siegfried, Witt Shingle, and Lawrence Brown had set up Pānini Productions as a separate entity. They held these meetings in the Kuhio Hotel's Maluna Lounge. On the third day, while they discussed royalty shares, Eddie spoke up on Goodman's behalf.

"I'm thinking of all the work Bob has done. I think he deserves ten percent."

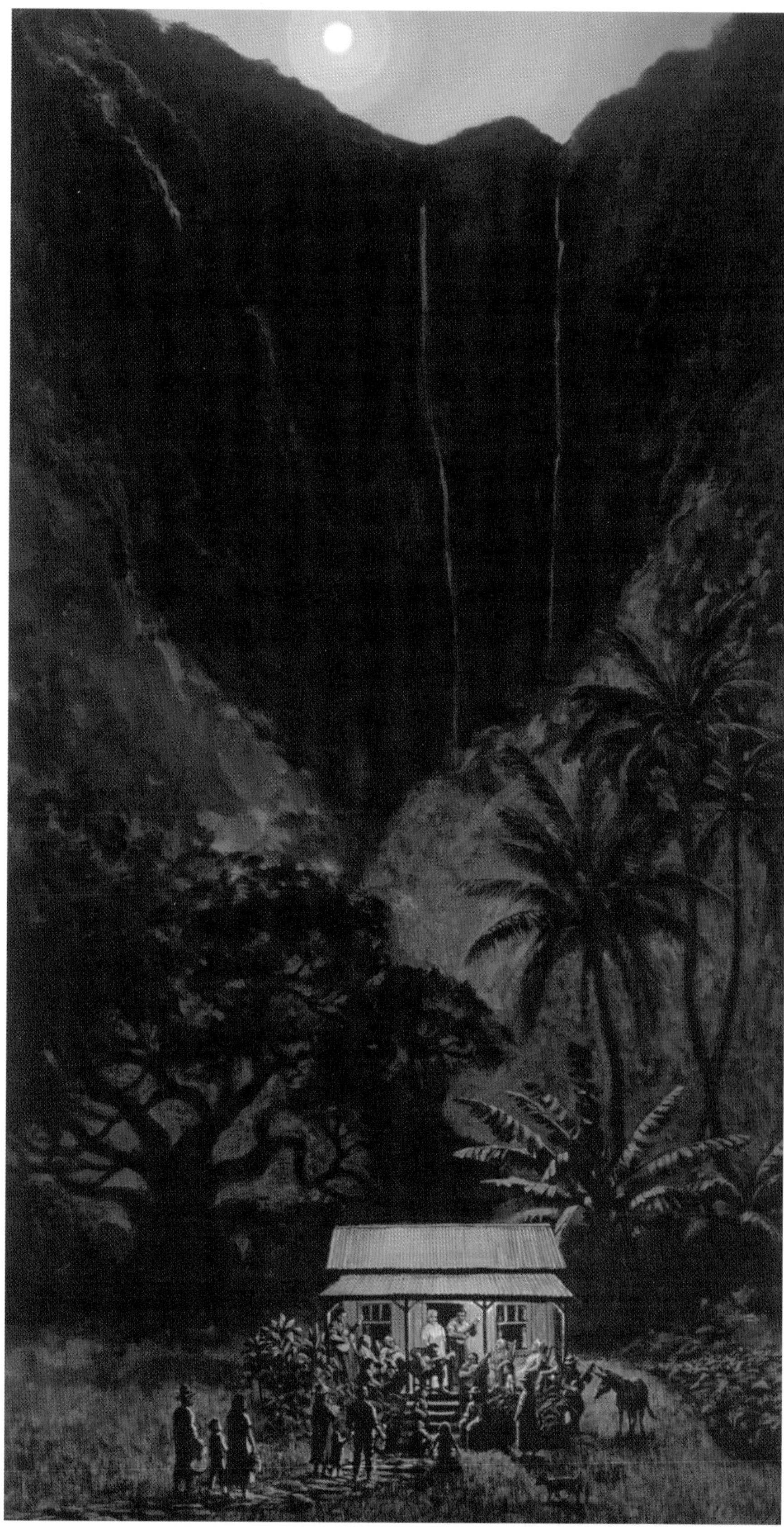

At that point one of the lawyers chimed in, a fellow who thus far had been speaking for Pānini. "In that case, we deserve another ten percent, because we now represent Gabby Pahinui."

Eddie was stunned.

"I thought I was there speaking for the whole band," he says now. "This was the first sign we had that Gabby signed a letter of intent with somebody else who was going to manage him separately from the rest of us. We'd all been running around together promoting, playing gigs, and all that, and we didn't know this because Gabby never told us. Feet was there that day. He just looked at the lawyer and he looked at me, and he didn't say anything."

Eddie couldn't say much either. He didn't know what to say. To this day his voice fills with regret when he talks about that meeting. What had the Pānini three offered to lure Gabby away? Eddie didn't know. He didn't ask. "But after that," he says, "things just came to a standstill. It stopped cold . . ."

By "it," he meant The Sons. After that meeting the band unraveled. As for the album, "Five Faces" already had acquired a life of its own. As its reputation spread through airtime and word of mouth, it continued to sell faster than any other Hawaiian album in recent memory. Over the years it would become one of the most influential albums ever recorded in the islands. As the monthly *Hawaiian News* would note twenty-seven years later, when the long-awaited CD (digitally remastered) was finally released, "Its arrangements, harmonies, superb musicianship, and sensitive use of Hawaiian language set a path which emerging generations of performers continue to emulate."[6]

This gathering of five virtuosos and fourteen songs had capped a decade of musical revival in the islands, a decade that had seen dozens of LPs from fledgling production companies, along with the launching of KCCN, the first all-Hawaiian-music station, the launching of the Merrie Monarch Festival of Hula in Hilo, the historic Ho'olaule'a O Hāna Maui, and the first bilingual anthology of traditional song lyrics, *Na Mele O Hawai'i Nei.*[7]

"Five Faces" also spoke for the decade to come. The timing could not have been better. A readiness was in the air: Hawai'i's cultural awakening. Throughout the 1960s it had been looking for a form, looking for a voice, a local version of what was happening all across the United States. From the late 1950s onward, stirred by the civil rights movement, there had begun a general and widespread redefining of identities and the rekindling of ethnic pride. In Hawai'i its full flowering would come during the 1970s. Five years later, the drama of Hawai'i's cultural history would go public and international, when the Polynesian Voyaging Society sailed the double-hulled *Hōkūle'a* (Star of Gladness), from the Big Island to Tahiti without any nautical instruments, re-creating the legendary voyages of ancient times, and proving once and for all that Pacific islanders had ranked among the world's great navigators.

But in this land where music has always been a key, it is true to the culture that the early voices in the renaissance were not writers or politicians or campus activists; they were dancers and singers, musicians and performers—like The Sons of Hawaii, like The Sunday Mānoa, a younger band that also released an album that December and has since come to share this significant moment in the long story of island music. It was a trio — *'ukulele,* bass, twelve-string guitar—doing traditional lyrics with a contemporary edge. In their early twenties when they brought out *Guava Jam,* Peter Moon and the Cazimero brothers gave a new generation some young heroes to listen to.

Together The Sons and The Sunday Mānoa defined a time and announced a new era. And yet by the end of 1971, while "Five Faces" was breaking sales records, The Sons of Hawaii had once again broken up.

EVERYBODY LOVED FEET *When I think back, it's a miracle "Five Faces" ever got made, considering all the things that happened. You take Feet Rogers. One morning we go in for a recording session, me, Moe, Joe, Gabby, the sound man, Bob Goodman—everybody there but Feet. Fifteen minutes go by. Thirty minutes. We're waiting around. Finally the phone rings. Bob picks it up, then passes it to me, and it's Feet calling from the police station.*

I think to myself, "Oh no! What is it this time?"

Feet, you see, was always getting in and out of trouble. I think it's one of the reasons he shipped out so much. It was a pretty rough part of town, where he grew up. Maybe life was simpler for him out at sea.

"What's the charge?" I ask him.

"Attempted robbery."

"Did you do it?"

"It was a mistake . . ."

"Who's the sergeant on duty there?"

"Guy named Fernandez."

Herb Kāne's sketches of Feet Rogers from the 1971 booklet "The Musicians."

Well, I know this guy a little bit. Maybe he is related to me some way or another, though I couldn't say exactly how. Anyway, he comes on the line and I say, "Joe. It's Eddie Kamae."

"Hey, Eddie. Howzit."

"What happened with my boy Feet?"

"I guess he tried to hold up a liquor store."

"We're in the middle of a recording session down here. We got a new album for The Sons of Hawaii. We gotta have Feet."

One thing I remember about those days—everybody loved Feet, no matter what he did. They loved his music. They loved the way he never tried to show off. They loved to see him smile. I could hear it in the sergeant's voice. I knew it was one of those times when he wished he wasn't a cop.

"I want to help you, Eddie. I got no choice. We got to book him."

"How long will that take?"

"Forty-five minutes."

"I'll be there in half an hour. I'll have some bail money, too."

"Come down, then," he says. "I'll do what I can."

So I drove down there, and they let him out on bail. We had to stop at Feet's house to get his guitar. Then we stopped at a bar for a drink, just to settle our nerves. I didn't ask him why he held up the liquor store. He needed the money for something. But it was none of my business.

The whole time at the station I'm looking at my watch, thinking I told everybody we'd get started again by eleven. And by golly, we did! Feet walked right in the way he always did, sat down and started playing, everything in tune and never missing a note. People coming down to Liberty House standing in line to buy an album never had any idea where Feet was just an hour before we started recording those songs.

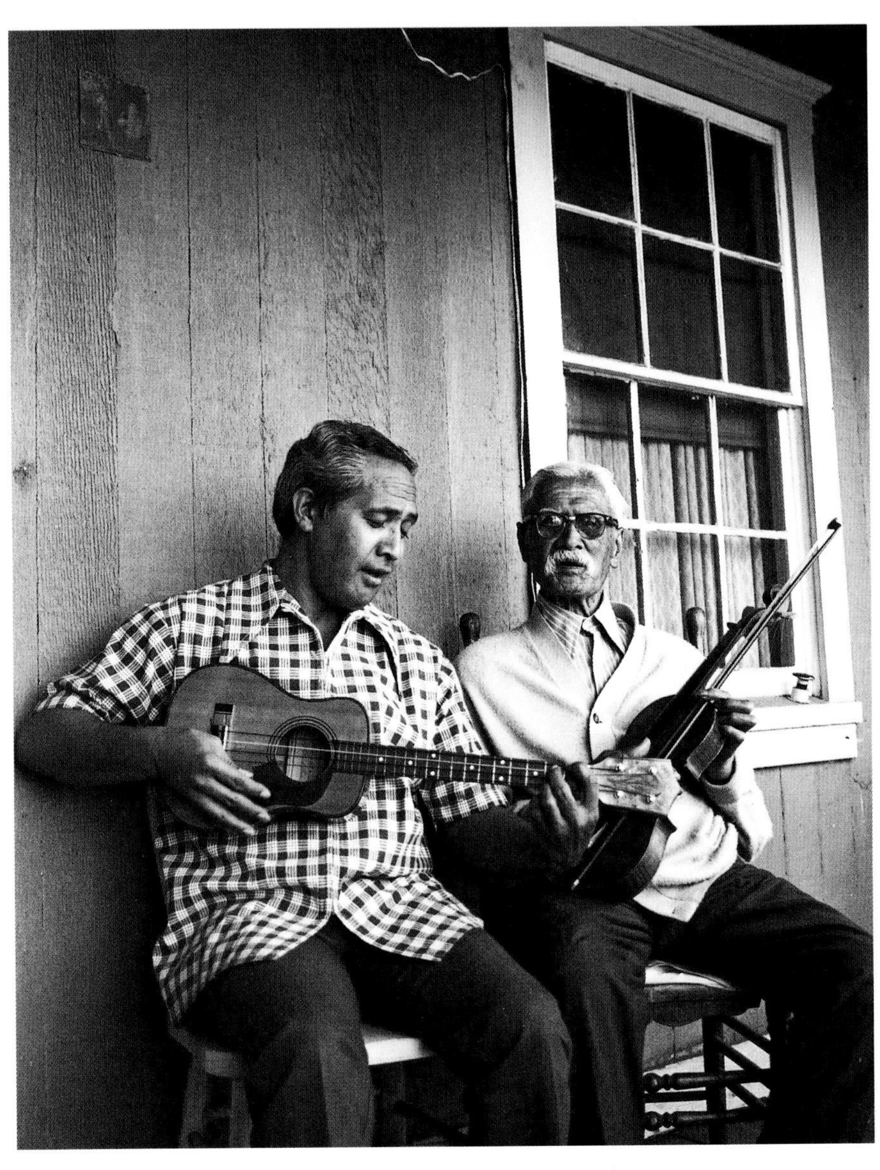

Eddie with Sam Li'a in Kukuihaele, 1972.
"Play it simple," Sam said, "play it sweet."

The Soul Comes Home

At the age of forty-three Eddie once again found himself trying to make sense of his career, and unsure what the next step should be. Sandbagged by Gabby's separate contract with Pānini, he didn't know what to do about the band. Feet felt betrayed, having agreed to remain on shore in order to promote the "Five Faces" album. Now all the promotional gigs had been canceled. The Maluna Lounge job, which had lasted over a year, had ended a few months back. While the lounge itself had stayed in the black, occupancy at the Kuhio Hotel had been hurt by a rash of overbuilding in Waikīkī. To cut costs, management had decided to close the room. Just one more version of the musician's fate, thought Eddie. You're always at the mercy of the hotel manager, or the building contractor, or the attorneys now wrestling for control of the new album and its proceeds.

For all that, the turmoil and uncertainty of the next few months proved a blessing, giving Eddie an excuse, another reason to spend more time "out there," away from the hazards of marketing and contracts. In the best of times he'd never liked the business end of music. He could handle it when he had to, but it could make his stomach knot up. He was glad to have a mentor to return to, a man who'd lived a musical life by entirely different terms, a man for whom the word *career* had little meaning. What a relief, what a gift to know he could fly to Hilo, pick up a car, drive out along the Hāmākua coast to the last town at the end of the road, and the *tūtū* man would be there, with another song or a new memory.

In the year since they'd met, Eddie and Sam Liʻa had become

Soon after they met, Sam told Eddie, "You remind me of me when I was a young man."

more than good friends. Sam had demystified the uncanny surprise of their first encounter. One day he looked at Eddie with a sly smile and said, "I knew you were coming to visit me."

"No," said Eddie. "I didn't tell anybody I was coming out here."

"I knew."

"How did you know?"

"Tūtū Kawena wrote me from Honolulu. So then I knew you would visit me one day."

"You tell me this now? After a year?"

"Yes."

"But you had your suit on, your necktie. And you didn't know what day I would come."

"I knew, Eddie. People tend to wait for the right person to come along. I been waiting for a long, long time."

If Eddie had found a spiritual father, Sam had recognized in him someone he'd been looking for and hoping to meet. It took another musician to appreciate all that Sam knew and what was still in his head. His fingers were too stiff to play it anymore, but Eddie could play it for him.

They spent many hours together on Sam's front porch in Kukuihaele, or in his sitting room, among his song sheets and books and instruments. Eddie always brought along a tape recorder, and Sam would talk, sometimes in English, sometimes in Hawaiian, laughing, singing, chanting, his voice dusted with age, yet still rich with resonance and feeling. Sam's voice itself was like a rare recording preserved from a long gone era, linking the 1880s to the 1970s, a pure channel for the spirit of a place and an earlier time.

In Sam's mind it all turned together, and no one piece of it could be separated from the whole: the past, the present, the lives lived, the words, the music, the ancestral valley. He'd composed songs about every aspect of Waipi'o, and every song came with a story. One afternoon he told Eddie about the song he'd written for Prince Kūhiō, nephew of King Kalākaua.

Sam had lived so long he remembered the days when Hawai'i was still a monarchy. When the king died in San Francisco, in 1891, Sam was already ten years old. When the government led by Kalākaua's sister, Queen Lili'uokalani, was overthrown in 1893, he was twelve. News of such events, of course, took days and weeks to reach the valley people Sam lived among. The lives and politics of the royal family had always seemed far removed —until the day Prince Jonah Kūhiō Kalaniana'ole paid a visit, in the fall of 1918. No one could remember when a man of his rank had come into Waipi'o, perhaps not since the time when the great chiefly families still occupied their thatched compounds along the beachfront.

As the delegate from the Territory of Hawai'i to the U.S. Congress, Kūhiō was touring the outer islands before heading off to the mainland. When his entourage made its slow way down the trail and finally reached the village, Sam happened to be in the social hall. He recalled that before he and his friends could stand up, the prince took a chair, eager to sit with them and talk story. He was down to earth, at ease among country people, and Sam liked that so much he wrote a song on the spot, "'Elele No Hawai'i Aloha I Wakinekona" (Hawai'i's Delegate Is Going to Washington). Before the prince departed, Sam and his band played it for him there in the social hall, a song asking each island to contribute a *lei* made of its favorite flower, to honor this leader as he set out to represent his people.

There was also the story of a song Sam had written for his wife, a woman he still spoke of with deep affection, almost reverence. He didn't marry until he was thirty-three. She was only sixteen at the time, a local girl named Sarah Poepoe Kepela, and her father was not at all pleased to hear she was being courted by a man twice her age. But Sam was crazy about her. Defying the father's wishes, they eloped. In those days Sam traveled everywhere on his famous white horse, tipping his hat to anyone who passed. This time Sarah sat behind him, with her arms around his waist, as they rode together into the back end of the valley and up a winding trail to the ranch-country town of Waimea, where they were married by one of Sam's former Lahainaluna classmates, now a judge.

"After that," he told Eddie, "my father-in-law couldn't do anything about it."

They made their home at Nāpō'opo'o, where Sarah bore him one daughter and a son who died early. They stayed together for almost forty years, until Sarah passed away in 1951. By that time Sam was seventy. For the rest of his life he talked about her and eventually he wrote a song about her, this one from the perspective of an old man thinking back upon his youth. The title, "Hinahina Kū Kahakai" (My Flower by the Sea), refers to a delicate blossom still found along the beach at Waipi'o. This flower, *hinahina,* also refers to Sarah, the wife he longs for. In the song he now has three legs—a way of saying he has to walk with a cane—but he can still savor their good times together and remember all the treasured places where they once made love.

During his ninety years Sam had composed dozens and dozens of songs this way. He couldn't remember them all. But those he remembered, as well as those that would turn up later on, took Eddie somewhere he had not been before. Sam Li'a

In his nineties Sam Li'a was still composing.

Kalāinaina was not only a repository of songs in the style of an older era, he was a composer who wrote in Hawaiian and still *thought* in Hawaiian. When Eddie brought some of Sam's lyrics back to Honolulu to show to Kawena, for translation, she looked at the page for a long time, then removed her glasses and looked at Eddie.

"Nobody writes like this anymore," she said, "in the old poetic way. His choice of words is simple, but the flowery images are full of so much meaning. We are both lucky, Eddie. We have met the last of the true Hawaiian poets."

His melody lines could be deceptive, sometimes echoing American folk tunes he might have heard as a young man. But there was more to it than melody, more to it than the word play with double and triple meanings. A new kind of knowledge began to move through Eddie, like a long glowing beam of light, bringing into full clarity things he'd known in his bones to be true—things he'd known to be truly Hawaiian—ever since those first, long ago jam-session days in Waimānalo. Whatever else may have passed between him and Gabby in these last dozen years, Eddie would always be grateful for what had been opened there. With the lyric power of his singing, Gabby had opened a door. Now Sam Li'a had led Eddie to the source: the essential dialogue between a place and its poet. Sam was a man whose mind was still in harmony with the valley of his birth. In one way or another all his songs were tied to Waipi'o. This valley where he'd spent his life had nourished and inspired him. He in turn gave voice to the beauty and the mystery of the place, in an ongoing dialogue, and each song was part of it, each song a poem made of words and earth.

In these days together during the next several months, something passed from Sam to Eddie. It was much, much more than a collection of songs. The Hawaiian word is *mana,* which in its broadest sense means "power." Not the power to conquer or subdue by force, but the power of the spirit that wells from within. When *mana* passes from a teacher to a pupil, it is a power lodged in the very nature of a tradition or a practice—in this case, music. It gave Eddie a new place to stand, and rekindled his passion for the songs he loved to play. By early 1973 he was ready to bring The Sons of Hawaii back to life.

opposite
Dennis Kamakahi joined The Sons in 1973. This is from the cover of their 1980 album, Grassroots Music.

Left to right: Joe, Dennis, Eddie, and "Feet."

Joe Marshall was still around, working his day job and picking up casuals with other groups. Feet Rogers had shipped out for a few months and recently come ashore. As for Gabby, that old on-again, off-again partnership had reached its end. With another group he'd already cut a second album for Pānini. Moe Keale was available, Eddie knew, with his masterful *'ukulele* and his angel voice. But if there was going to be a band, he needed a new guitar player.

He'd been listening to other groups around town and had singled out a young fellow who was earning praise for his slack-key styling. Like Eddie, Dennis Kamakahi was Hawaiian with some Chinese mixed in, but he was less than half Eddie's age. Also an aspiring writer, Dennis wore owlish aviator glasses that gave him a somewhat scholarly look. A recent graduate of

 Kamehameha School, he was starting to play in local clubs while taking classes in musical composition at Leeward Community College.

"You don't replace someone like Gabby," Eddie says now. "He is one of a kind. We had to do something totally different. What I saw in Dennis was a young, intelligent, aggressive, and creative young musician. And he had a voice, too, a fresh, young voice, so I asked him to come along."

The newly formed Hawaiian Music Foundation had been promoting an all-steel-guitar concert, which would be Hawai'i's first. Feet was featured on the program, with Eddie and Joe providing back-up. They needed a rhythm guitar. It would be an easy way to get acquainted, musically. So they invited Dennis to a rehearsal.

"I was real nervous," he recalls, "only nineteen, and I'm playing with the established legends of Hawaiian music. At that time I had another group. I was the leader, and I was used to rehearsing things over and over to get the arrangements just so, until you really got to not like rehearsing. But this was entirely different. I mean, there was nothing said. The music went and you went with it, and you could feel this whole thing come together. Right away I knew, this is what I want to play. Your mind, your heart, your music—everything moves in one direction."[1]

For Dennis it was a new approach, and yet there was something so familiar he could grasp it intuitively. Like Moe Keale, he had grown up with this influential sound. He remembers that The Sons' first album had been released in the same year his family bought their first stereo system.

"I was seven," he says, "and my grandfather brought the album home, and he would play it over and over again. Prior to that I guess all I knew about Hawaiian music was what you call chang-a-lang-a-lang, all the *hapa-haole* stuff. When I heard this, even at seven I had the feeling, here was a whole new dimension."

Like Moe, Dennis fit right in. On twelve-string slack-key guitar, he could push the rhythm along or pick a tender solo. As a vocalist, he could harmonize with ease, or take the lead.

After the steel guitar concert he continued sitting in. By the time their next big gig came along, he was part of the band.

The Territorial Tavern in downtown Honolulu had recently become a favorite showcase for the rising wave of Hawaiian music, featuring performers such as Keola and Kapono Beamer, Jerry Santos and Olomana, Peter Moon, the Cazimero Brothers. It was a corner building on Bishop Street. Inside its stone façade there was a bar, a bandstand, a wide staircase leading to a wrap-around balcony with railside tables. When the reconstituted Sons of Hawaii opened there in mid-1973, they took the place by storm. It was a five-piece band again—steel, bass, twelve-string guitar, and two *'ukulele,* one of them dwarfed by the huge frame of Moe Keale, who in those days was pushing three hundred pounds. Every weekend they delivered the famous "open sound" local listeners were hungry for, but with a fresh voice now in the mix. There was a new vigor, a new energy, a new look. Instead of *aloha* shirts—standard musician's garb for decades—The Sons came in wearing short-sleeved *palaka* shirts, which had a very different kind of history.

Palaka is a checkered pattern—sometimes red, sometimes blue, sometimes black—that traces its origins to a nineteenth-century workshirt often seen around the pineapple and sugar plantations. In the early 1970s it still suggested some personal tie to the land, and by tradition it was a shirt to be worn only by someone with local roots. In those days, while people all across the nation were being politicized by the turmoil in Vietnam, there had emerged a widespread yearning to reconnect and get regrounded. In Hawai'i it gave new urgency to the phrase *aloha 'āina* (love the land). When The Sons took the stage in *palaka* shirts and denim overalls, they caught the spirit of those times. The outfit itself said "songs of the people," and "music of the earth." And the shirts somehow fit the proud announcement that now opened and closed every show: "We are The Sons of Hawaii! And we *are* Hawaiian!"

Their Sunday jam sessions at the Territorial Tavern were like the early days at the Sandbox, only more so. Fans lined up along Bishop Street waiting to get in, while overflow crowds filled the inside staircase and the balcony above. Listeners came from every sector of island life, Hawaiian, Sāmoan, Asian, *haole*: lawyers, beach boys, fishermen, cabbies, insurance salesmen, and other musicians and off-duty cops. With Moe just past thirty and Dennis at twenty, it was a more youthful band, and this had its own kind of appeal. Joining fans from the late 1950s came new generations of high school kids and college students drawn to the sight of a fellow their own age playing side by side with Eddie and Joe and Feet.

"That place on Sunday was crazy," Moe Keale recalls. "You had everybody, the good guys and the bad guys, the slick guys, and the guys who weren't cool. You had the politicians and the gangsters, too. One group of gangsters at this table, another group over there, and upstairs was the vice squad looking down on everybody, checking around. But the thing about The Sons of Hawaii, wherever they played, nobody made trouble. They came for listen. If you guys were enemies, at the end of the night you going be hugging and kissing each other. That's the kind of place the Territorial Tavern was. That's what The Sons did to people. It all came out in the music."

Jackie Kaho'okele Burke is a Honolulu businesswoman with longtime family ties to Maui's Hāna coast. She remembers those Sundays with more than nostalgia. Then in her early twenties, she followed the band the way mainland listeners had followed Creedence Clearwater and Joan Baez. She speaks for many of her peers when she says, "Their music gave me an anchor, told me where I came from. I felt like my soul came home."[2]

Some of what was being played that year can be heard on two albums from the mid-1970s. The first, *Music of Hawai'i* (1974), was part of the prestigious "Sounds of the World" series being developed by the National Geographic Society. The Sons were still regarded as an emblematic band of that era, and Eddie had been enlisted by producer John Lavery as a production consultant. Eddie gathered the performers, advising Lavery on the selection of sixteen songs and chants that would convey the vocal and melodic richness of a long legacy. The album opens with the skin-prickling throb of two voices backed by a single gourd drum—'Iolani Luahine and her niece Hoakalei Kamau'u

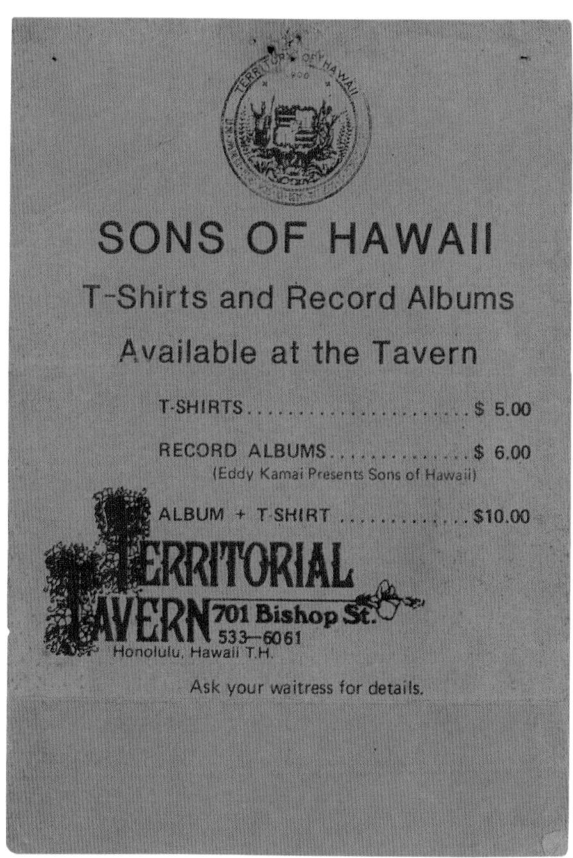

speaking the ancient name-chant, "Maika'i Kaua'i" (Beautiful Is Kaua'i)—and ends with The Sons' rendition of "Aloha Oe," Queen Lili'uokalani's century-old ballad of farewell.

One of eight albums in the National Geographic series (with an estimated sale of two hundred thousand copies), *The Music of Hawai'i* went into households and libraries across the country and around the world. It included ten cuts by the re-formed Sons, as well as some fine guitar, singing, and drumming by the multitalented Beamer brothers, then in their early twenties, and an emotionally powerful voyaging chant by master chanter Ka'upena Wong. We hear Eddie come back to "Komo Mai," the first song he sang on record, enriched now by ten years

of performance. On the traditional love song, "Loa'a Kō Puni Kauoha" (Grant Me a Solemn Promise), we hear young Dennis Kamakahi take his first recorded instrumental chorus. (Two decades later he would be touring Europe and Japan, after the release of *Pua'ena* [Glow Brightly], his hit solo album in Dancing Cat's "Hawaiian Slack Key Masters" series.)

The full range of this mid-1970s band was heard the following year on *Eddie Kamae Presents The Sons of Hawaii.* The album cover shows the five of them sitting on lava rocks beside one of the "Seven Sacred Pools" near Hāna, Maui, all barefoot, wearing what had become their uniform and trademark: denim overalls, the red-checked *palaka* shirts.

For Eddie it was a new beginning, both musically and managerially. This time the label did not say Hula or Pānini. It said Hawaii Sons, Inc. Having learned hard lessons about control and distribution, Eddie had set up his own production company, based in Honolulu. For a performer of Hawaiian ancestry, this was a bold move. In the sixty-year history of recorded island music, there were few precedents. Yet as the musical renaissance had unfolded, this was, you might say, an inevitable next step. In the 1960s he had furthered the reclaiming of songs and lyrics. In the 1970s he was among the first Hawaiian musicians to establish his own recording label.

This album features some exquisite guitar work, as Dennis and Feet trade choruses on slack-key and steel, or share intros made of interweaving notes. As always, thanks to Eddie's ongoing research, there are new arrangements of Hawaiian songs from earlier times—the gospel hymn, "Mai 'Ae I Ka Hewa," sung reverently by Moe; the bawdy and suggestive *hula mele,* "Tomi Tomi," composed at the turn of the century by the prolific David Nape. These mix with songs recorded here for the first time. "Ka 'Ōpae" (The Shrimp) is a playful early piece by Dennis Kamakahi, the first of his songs to be recorded anywhere. It describes a day on Moloka'i when he and some small cousins were walking along a stream.

"We heard laughing and giggling up ahead," he says. "So I went through the brush to see what it was. Well, there in the stream were all these nude hippie women. The kids asked what it was, and I said, 'Nothing for you to worry about. Just some *'ōpae.'"*

Also heard for the first time is the now classic ballad, "Morning Dew," written by Eddie, his wife Myrna, and Larry Kimura of the University of Hawai'i. Moe Keale sings both lead and dubbed-in harmony on this love song, in a rendition that would become one of the most widely replayed tracks of modern times. Within five years of the album's release, "Morning Dew" itself would be picked up by other vocalists and bands, to be recorded more than any other Hawaiian song composed since World War II.

On this album Eddie also introduced songs that had come to him during his Big Island travels, each one marking a personal discovery. It opens with "Ke Ala A Ka Jeep," the one written with Kawena Pukui (also destined to become a Hawaiian standard), telling the story of their journey to South Point. "Mauna Kea" is here, the verse that ninety-year old 'Olu Konanui had remembered, along with the seven more verses remembered by Kawena. There is a song Eddie had co-authored with Pīlahi Pākī, an upbeat and satiric piece aimed at the acrid smell that greets you near Lahaina, from the residue of burnt sugarcane fields after harvesting. Called "Kela Mea Whiffa" (The Thing That Smells), the song is whimsically subtitled "The Breath of Love."

During these first years of partnership with Eddie, Dennis Kamakahi was actively writing songs. Only one or two had yet been recorded. But the folders of pages were piling up in his front room, and the more Eddie heard, the more he liked what Dennis was doing. In an era when most musicians his age were captivated by rock and roll, Dennis was looking for ways to bring Hawaiian songwriting into his own time. Eddie wanted to take him to the Big Island to meet Sam Li'a.

He was still flying over to see the old man whenever he had the chance. During one of their visits Sam had mentioned that he hoped one day to hear Eddie's band. "I've met your wife," Sam said, "and some of your other friends, but I still haven't met your boys. Next time you come, bring them, and we can talk about this beautiful music of ours."

From Eddie's stories Dennis already knew something about the *tūtū* man. Now he got busy and finished a song he'd started, a tribute to this legendary composer he had yet to meet. He called it "Kanaka Waiolina" (Violin Man). One day he brought it to rehearsal, and everyone got excited. On the spot they put together an arrangement they would play for Sam. They would surprise him with a little world premiere for an audience of one. They added a few of Sam's tunes, too, to make it a private concert.

Soon after the album was released they made the trip: Eddie, Joe, Feet, Dennis. They flew into Hilo, rented a van big enough to carry the four of them and all their instruments, and drove out to Kukuihaele, singing along the coast road, practicing their harmonies.

When Sam expected someone he usually sat on the porch. Today as they pulled up next to his yard, the porch was empty. With the engine off, the yard and cottage seemed strangely silent. Under heavy cloud cover the air was still. Eddie walked across the grass and stood by the stairs, listening. He leaned down and drew a finger along the topmost step. The stairs and porch were layered with dust. No one had walked there for several days. He didn't have to knock or call out. He knew the place was empty. Eddie was sure he'd told Sam they'd be coming. Maybe the old man had forgotten. Or maybe he was off on a trip. Once or twice a year he went to Hilo.

Eddie checked with a neighbor and learned that Sam had gone into the hospital in Honoka'a and was now in intensive care. It wasn't a place you could take a band. Only immediate relatives were allowed to visit. Their concert would have to wait. After Sam came home, they all agreed, they would plan another trip.

"We'll come back next time," said Eddie, "when he's feeling better."

But there would be no next time. Though Sam had been vigorously healthy for most of his life, in recent years he'd been troubled with diabetes, and finally it caught up with him. Doctors had told his family they'd have to amputate a foot. As Eddie says now, "I think he decided it was time to go. The old Hawaiians had a phrase for this. 'Nā kānaka ku'u wale aku i ka 'uhane' (The people dismissed their souls freely and died). Sam didn't want to come out of the hospital and be a burden on anyone. He was ninety-four, and he'd lived a good long life."

When Eddie got the news, a week later, that Sam had passed away, it hit him hard. Yet it wasn't like the loss of the Maui canoe maker who had postponed his own death waiting for Eddie to come. He would always carry a lingering regret that he missed hearing the voice of David Kaho'okele. In Sam's case, a mentor was gone, and the grief ran deep. But on tape and in his head he had Sam's voice, a bridge of words from that long gone time. He had Sam's stories and songs, some old ones, some new ones. They'd written songs together. Even young Dennis, though he never met the *tūtū* man in person, had somehow received his *mana* by osmosis. You could hear it in "Kanaka Waiolina," the song he wrote for Sam, and in others he and Eddie were already planning to record, songs in Hawaiian, with an ear for the poetry, composed in the same spirit that gave birth to the song Eddie and Sam wrote on the day they met, back in 1970.

On the album that had just come out, "Waipi'o Valley Song" is the final cut on side one—melody by Eddie, words by Sam Li'a Kalāinaina, composed in the two-line stanzas of a *hula mele.* One of the last Sam wrote, it is only the second of his many songs to be recorded anywhere. In Eddie's voice there is both celebration and sorrow as he sings it to the rolling lilt of Dennis Kamakahi's slack-key rhythm. Naming the places they touched that day, he honors Sam and all his mentors and the centuries-old songmaking tradition they had helped to keep alive. "Turn and gaze at the dark sea," goes the English translation, "the beauty of Paka'alana has vanished . . ."

The beautiful temple of the royal ones,
of 'Umi-a-Līloa, passed on.

Let the refrain be told:
The mind has seen Waipi'o.

SO MUCH ALOHA *Before we left the Territorial Tavern, Feet got in trouble again. It was worse this time because he'd tried to hold up a bank. Not a big bank. Just a local branch. You want to know why he didn't get away with it? He forgot to cover his face. Somebody looking at the surveillance tape recognized him from the front of the "Five Faces" album, which was in everybody's house all over Honolulu. The branch manager happened to be a guy Feet went to high school with. When he heard what happened, his feelings were hurt. He says, "Hey Feet. How come you hold up* my *bank? Why don't you hit one of the Japanese banks?"*

Feet shrugged and told him he was sorry, said he didn't know that guy got promoted up to manager.

Anyway, I called my friend Alvin Shim, who is a lawyer here in town, and asked him could we come talk with him. He said, "Eddie, you know you can come over anytime." So we went to his office, me and Feet, and Alvin came out and said to his secretary, "No calls for an hour."

We went in and sat down, and I told him what happened and how there's a court-appointed lawyer to represent Feet. Alvin says no, it's better to let him handle it, because he knows all the guys involved, the bank manager, and the judge, too. Alvin always played poker with the judge one night a week. So he would handle this, he says, and donate his services, too. Alvin was like everybody else, you see. He loved Feet's music and wanted to help him out.

Every Sunday Alvin used to come in to hear us play. His apartment was in a building right across the street from the Territorial Tavern. I knew his favorite song was "Moloka'i Nui A Hina," which means 'Great Moloka'i of Hina.' It's an old song from the turn of the century that celebrates the island and the goddess Hina, who is the island's mother. So the next Sunday when I saw Alvin come in, we played it. Joe Marshall always sang it. He had the perfect voice for that song. Later on, when we took a break, I went over to Alvin's table, and he wants to tell me something.

"Eddie," he says, "I am sitting here and you guys play my favorite

 song, and all of a sudden, right in the middle of it, Mukhtananda comes to me, like he is talking to me, and I start writing down the whole idea of how I am going to defend Feet at the hearing."

Right here I have to tell you something about Alvin. He was fifty then, and well known as a labor lawyer with a big heart, always willing to help people out. Up in his apartment, on the wall, he had a poster of Swami Mukhtananda, who used to have an ashram here. One time Alvin took me to this retreat, and we listened to a woman give a lecture on the principles of life. The guru was there. When people started making offerings to him, some of them urged me to go up and play something. I brought along my box, you see. So I sat down and started playing for the crowd. But Alvin signaled me to turn around and play for the guru. When I did, Mukhtananda began to talk to me. He called me "Musician." He told me my whole life. From listening to my music he knew everything about me.

Music can do that. Music did that for Alvin. Listening to "Moloka'i Nui A Hina" he saw Feet's life. While he was sitting in the Territorial Tavern, he wrote down his ideas on this napkin he gave me. I still have it. One look at what he jotted down, you can see what was on his mind:

- *More than just one more Hawaiian statistic*
- *A human being who needs and craves assistance*
- *Kick habit*
- *Find himself*
- *Respect himself*
- *Meditation*
- *Not hurt others*
- *Background: poor neighborhood—limited formal education*
- *Many share his music, his sensitivity of what it means to be a friend*

While Alvin was showing me the napkin, Feet came over and sat down with us. When he read what Alvin wrote, he couldn't talk. Tears started coming down his face.

You see, Alvin was a local guy who loved Feet and understood where he came from. As a young guy growing up in Kalihi, Feet got into some things. I was lucky to get away from that element when I did. But here was Feet, almost forty, and now drugs were taking him down. I never knew him to use drugs on the job. He didn't do that. But whenever he got into trouble, drugs had something to do with it. Alvin saw the whole picture, how easy it is to grow up Hawaiian in these islands and not respect yourself for who you are, so you get on some kind of negative path. Alvin knew Feet had to find the love inside himself that was already coming out through his music. He told me that was what he was going to tell the judge at the hearing. And by golly, that's what he did!

It didn't take long. Alvin went in there and started talking, and pretty soon the judge told him to keep it short. Alvin knew why. Just the night before, the judge had lost a lot of money in a poker game. He wasn't in a mood to spend all day in court. Maybe Alvin had already talked with him about Feet. I brought along some bail money in case he had to go to jail. But the judge, after he listened to Alvin for a little while, he gave Feet probation.

Now some people in town were shaking their heads, that a guy who is caught red-handed robbing a bank gets off on probation. But here's what happened. After that hearing Feet was a changed man. From one day to the next he just quit using drugs. He cleaned up his life. He never got into any more trouble with the law. It was one night after we finished playing when Alvin came up to him and said, "Feet, I been watching you. You kicked the habit cold turkey. How come?"

Like I told you, Feet never said much. But whenever he talked, you listened. He looked at Alvin. He said, "It was what you wrote down on the napkin. Knowing people are concerned. There was so much aloha . . . *so much* aloha . . ."

That's all Feet could say. His voice cracked. You could see the water filling up his eyes again.

While filming Li'a *in 1986, Dennis Kamakahi and Eddie caught the eye of a Big Island youngster.*

Do It Now

Sam Li'a had recognized something in Eddie and felt the veteran's kinship with a younger musician. Eddie, in turn, had seen some of himself in Dennis Kamakahi's search for his own place as a writer and performer. Eddie made sure he met Kawena Pukui, who welcomed him, much as she'd welcomed Eddie fifteen years earlier. As the band's leader, he watched Dennis's music mature and gave him an increasingly prominent role—first as slack-key soloist, then as a lead singer and as the composer of original songs that would reshape the band's repertoire.

"I came in when Gabby left," Dennis recalls, "and I said, Holy mackerel! Here Gabby left the group, and that's a big hole and a big shoe to fill, but I don't want to be Gabby. He is his own man. So you gotta find an identity. It worked around the composition of music."

In the ongoing search for songs and sources, Eddie and Dennis often traveled together. Sometime in 1975 they were driving a back road on Moloka'i, heading east along the shoreline to look up one of Dennis's cousins who lived in remote Hālawa Valley. As they passed the district called Kamalō, about halfway between the main town of Kaunakakai and the island's easterly cape, Dennis asked Eddie to stop the car.

"We got to look at those mountains!" he exclaimed.

Eddie eased onto the grassy shoulder, and they both climbed out for a clearer look. From the coast, ridges sloped inland toward the island's spine and the five-thousand-foot peak, Kamakou. Far upcountry from where they stood, white spills of water came ribboning down where waterfalls were seldom seen. Soon other cars were lined along the road, as other travelers—visitors and locals alike—stopped to gaze. No one they spoke with had ever seen such a spectacle.

"Even the oldtimers," says Dennis, remembering that day, "they'd never seen that. As much as I visit Moloka'i, this was something special. From that side you just very seldom see the top of that mountain. But you know, ever since I joined The Sons, these things happen to me. Every place I go, something happens."

Eddie had advised Dennis to carry a tape recorder at all times, so that whenever an idea came to him, a melodic phrase or a line of lyrics, he could talk it or sing it right onto the tape. At the rare sight before him, Dennis's head was buzzing. He reached back into the car and found his recorder.

"I remember looking at the mountains, and I could hear this melody coming out. It was singing to me. I remember humming into the recorder. No other song have I ever written where the mountain or the thing or the place was actually singing back to me. This was the only time. I mean, words started flowing. We went on to visit my cousin. But that stop by the side of the road must have been the real reason we went to Moloka'i. When we got back to Honolulu, I felt the same feeling, this melody just coming from that place where we stood, Kamalō, and that's when I finished the song."

Dennis titled it "Wahine 'Ilikea" (Fair Skin Woman). He likens the mist of Mount Kamakou to an enchanting beauty who lingers forever in the mind of the beholder. The song is a spirited call to the woman, to the seductive mist, to the island itself. Along with four other new songs by Dennis, it would be featured on the next Sons of Hawaii album, released in 1976. Now a Hawaiian standard, "Wahine 'Ilikea" would establish him as a leading contemporary composer. It would be the first of his songs to become a hit in the islands, and its origins were typical of the dozens he would write and record in the years to come: musical poems inspired by the natural features of his island world.

A year later the band was on Kaua'i, the northern island, to play for the mayor. Someone offered them the chance to spend a night in the high-country forest preserve called Kōke'e, up above Waimea Canyon (the many-colored gorge Mark Twain once dubbed "the Grand Canyon of the Pacific"). The next morning Dennis rose early and drove out to the end of the road, to a famous overlook above a verdant, other-worldly valley somewhat like Waipi'o, but deeper and narrower. Kalalau is a ribbed and rippled notch carved into the steep cliffs along Kaua'i's north shore. Once heavily populated, the valley is now empty, accessible only by treacherous foot trail or by small craft. Dennis's goal was to rise early and see Kalalau in the post-dawn light.

When he arrived at the overlook, the famous bowl was filled with misty, impenetrable clouds. He waited, asking the place to reveal itself to him. Eventually the clouds opened up, and there it was, the green and carpeted valley floor, the channeled walls, the scooped-out gorge dropping, from the precipice where he stood, four thousand feet to the sea. His prayer was answered. He had the place all to himself—until a carload of visitors appeared, early-rising photo bugs bearing cameras and telescopic lenses. As they lined up along the railing, angling for the choicest shots, the clouds re-formed, filling the valley. They grumbled awhile, but with nothing to photograph they were soon on their way to the next site. Once again Dennis waited and prayed, and once again the clouds parted. The stirring vista was revealed anew, as if a gift for him alone.

"It was such an overwhelming moment," he says now. "And I remembered something Tūtū Kawena told me. Write about your time, she said, write about what's happening now, in your time, because once that's written it becomes the past for someone else, but they can tell what you felt when you wrote it. So I started writing the song that same day. The melody just started flowing. We were staying that night down at Po'ipū. I kept working on it after we got back to the hotel."

A bilingual song, mixing Hawaiian and English lyrics, "Kōke'e" is also a place song, a *mele pana.* It celebrates Kalalau as seen from above, and Waimea, the sea-level town you pass through to reach the forestlands, as well as Po'ipū, on the southern shore, where the band stayed and where Dennis finished the writing. After its first release, by The Sons of Hawaii, "Kōke'e" became a standard, widely recorded by other bands, and also a local anthem for those who live on the Waimea side of Kaua'i:

Kalalau Valley, on Kaua'i's rugged north coast.

ʻO Kalalau he ʻaina laʻa
I ka ua liʻiliʻi
ʻO Waimea kuʻu lei aloha
Nevermore to say goodbye.

Kalalau is a sacred land
In the drizzling rain.
Waimea is my beloved wreath,
Nevermore to say goodbye.[1]

These were fertile years for Dennis. Every trip produced a song. On another day, on another island, while driving south toward the fishing village of Miloliʻi, another melody came flowing through his mind, and he began to write "Hualālai" (1977), named for the massive shield-cone rising from the Kona coast. A few months later, on a trip to Seattle, he was missing his sweetheart back in Honolulu and wrote "Pua Hone" (Honey Flower), which turned out to be their engagement song, as well as another island favorite in the years to come. He phoned her that same night and sang it long distance, and then he proposed.

"I could see this flower blooming in the snow," he says, recalling what came to him while he was up there in the cool latitudes at the edge of Puget Sound. "This flower grows right up through the snow, in the center of everything. . . . This flower represents the love in someone's heart."[2]

Knowing a band of first-rate musicians were ready to record what he was writing gave Dennis that much more reason to write, and his songs, as they flowed forth, gave the band fresh life. Eddie and Myrna were composing, too, still working with Kawena. In the next five years The Sons would cut five more albums. Tunes from the older repertoire intermingled with these new songs arising from the same tradition. And there was no more haggling with producers: Eddie was producing now, and the company was always Hawaii Sons.

Eventually Moe Keale moved on to form his own trio. After that, guest artists sat in from time to time: Sonny Chillingworth on a couple of albums, and the Big Island singer, Diana Aki. But in fact it was a four-piece band again—Eddie, Feet, Joe, and Dennis. With an album coming every year, they were among the most sought-after groups in the islands, playing long engagements at clubs such as the Sty in Honolulu, the Oceana Restaurant, and the Outrigger Hotel's Blue Dolphin Room in mid-Waikīkī, where visitors from Canada and Illinois mixed with the multilayered local crowd that followed The Sons wherever they went.

One such fan was Tony Good, an investment banker, originally from California, and a close friend of Feet Rogers. He traveled with the band one Christmas when they played two nights at Maui's Kula Lodge, halfway up the long slope of Haleakalā. Tony and his family and the band members all stayed at the lodge, and one of his memories catches the spirit and general good times of that era.

On the first night, after the gig, they all sat around drinking and talking story, all but Joe Marshall, who had gone to bed early. The others turned in around 2 A.M.

"Feet was rooming with Joe," Tony recalls, "and we went to the room, and the door was locked. Feet banged on the door a bunch of times and called, 'Eh, Marshall! Come on! Open up the door!' But there was no response, so he banged some more, and finally Feet said, 'Okay, if you don't open the door, Tony and me going to sing "The Hawaiian Wedding Song," and he's going to do the falsetto part.' Joe was such a stickler for singing songs the right way, Feet was sure this would get his attention. But still there was no response. So we start singing. You know, 'This . . . is the moment . . . I've waited for . . .' I mean, this goofy thing outside the door at two o'clock in the morning. I remember there was a big moon and a red poinsettia bush, and Feet put a poinsettia behind his ear, and we keep singing, until all of a sudden Joe can't stand it anymore. The door flies open. He is in his shorts. He says, 'You guys knock that off! Just stop! Okay? You win! You win.' So finally Feet is able to get inside his room and go to bed."[3]

In between gigs there would sooner or later be an annual trip to Hāna, where they'd found an ideal rehearsal spot. At a shoreside inn they would rent a large, airy apartment that looked out across the beach and a palm-lined cove, a secluded spot where they could immerse themselves in the making of another album.

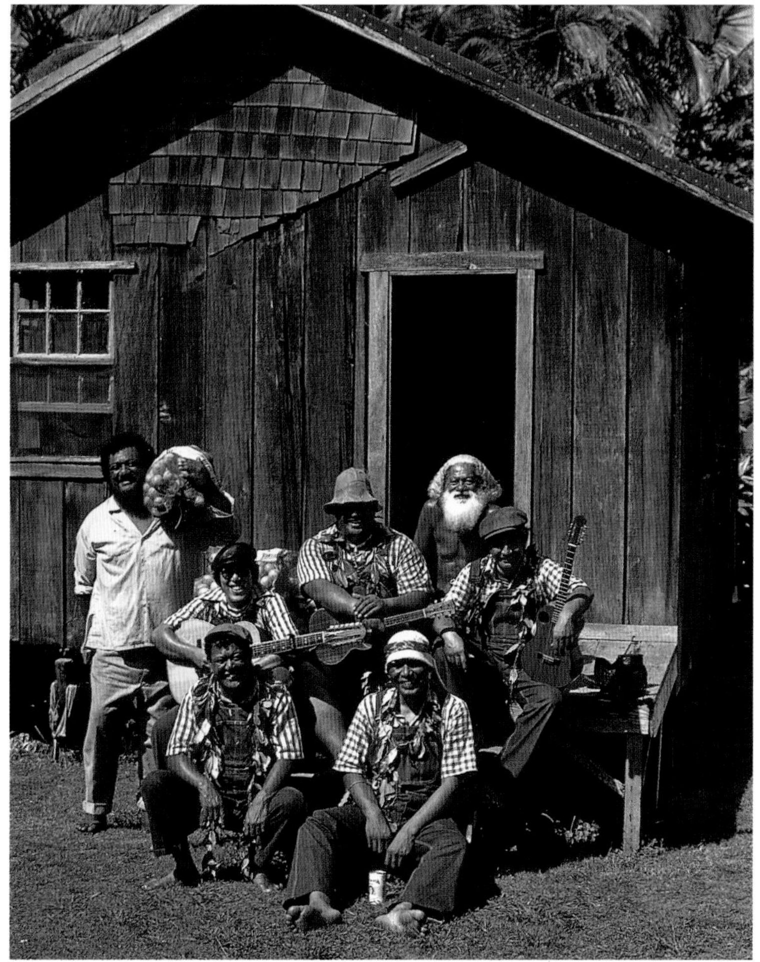

After rehearsals for the 1976 album at Hāna, Maui, two locals joined The Sons for this cover photo—Uncle Sol Ho'opi'i (in the doorway) and Tiny Malaikini (standing).

The band (clockwise from top): Moe Keale, Eddie, Feet, Joe, Dennis.

"I remember when we went there to rehearse the first time," Dennis says. "We spent one week with no TV, no telephone. Joe Marshall was the cook . . . and we learned what it is to be in our music, in a place where we can express our music and nobody to bother you, out of respect. Then the night before we leave to go back to Honolulu to record, we tell everyone around Hāna the rehearsal was over, and the whole community come out, party with us, partake of . . . you know, the food that's there and share that *mana'o* and *aloha.*"

Throughout the late 1970s The Sons were on a roll. Dennis was hot. Feet was clean and staying put. The band's sound was right where they wanted it. Hawaiian music was on a roll, too, with its twenty-year revival now in high gear. And 1978 turned out to be the biggest year so far, a banner year, the year the University of Hawai'i Press brought out *Hawaiian Music and Musicians: An Illustrated History.* A project of the Hawaiian Music Foundation, and edited by George Kanahele, this encyclopedic labor of love still stands as the most detailed, ambitious, and informative look at the subject ever undertaken. That spring the foundation also launched what would become Hawai'i's equivalent of the Grammy Awards—Nā Hōkū Hanohano (Stars of Distinction), an annual gala to honor island artists and their recorded work. There was more to honor, it seemed, than ever before. Record production peaked in 1978, with one hundred ten albums locally produced.[4]

Among them was *Christmas Time with Eddie Kamae and The Sons of Hawaii.* Its December release was tied to a television special by the same title, first shown on Honolulu's KHON. This half-hour celebration of Christmas Hawaiian-style had been Eddie's idea, and he co-produced the show, working closely with a young local director, Hawai'i-born Dennis Mahaffay. They filmed it all on Maui, backing seasonal songs with footage from the spectacular shoreline around Hāna and Kaupō, such as the white-walled Hui Aloha chapel, built in the 1850s and still perched on its own point of land. This film featured the celestial voices of the Honolulu Boy Choir, some original drawings by Herb Kāne, and original songs by Dennis and by Eddie and Myrna, with some help on one of them from Kawena Pukui. A huge success in the islands, *Christmas Time* was later screened at the New York International Film Festival, where it received a Bronze Award, and went on to win a 1979 IRIS Award from the National Association of Television Program Executives for excellence among locally produced musicals.

Ten years after *Bring Wood, Build a House,* when he and Gabby had cut the soundtrack, Eddie had taken his second step into the world of filmmaking. It was a foretaste of things soon to come, as his Hawaiian eye began looking for scenes to match what he had so long been hearing with his Hawaiian ear. Midway through *Christmas Time,* for example, we see two elderly, bearded men sitting on a rock wall in Hāna, speaking intimately in Hawaiian. For Eddie, this soft and flowing, back-country sound is as much a part of the holiday season as a church's steeple or the giving of gifts.

Co-producing this film had awakened him to some new possibilities. Since Sam Li'a's death, Eddie had been looking for a way to say more about his mentor. Sam, he believed, was not a man we could afford to forget. His songs were being played, of course; his influence could be heard in everything Dennis Kamakahi wrote, in all the songs The Sons performed. But Eddie wanted people in the islands to know more about the man himself, his life, and what he'd stood for. Now he was thinking a film might be the way, a film full of songs and memories and Sam's Big Island places. Eddie started testing his idea on people he could trust. He mentioned it to Pīlahi Pākī, among others, and her keen interest was soon to move him one step further along this path.

The year 1979 turned out to be full of awards. The Sons' next album, *Ho'omau* (Continue!), introduced nine compositions by Dennis; one of these was a Nā Hōkū Hanohano selection as the year's best new song. At age twenty-six, five years after his first recording, Dennis was coming into his own. "E Hihiwai" (Pouring Water) was another song from Moloka'i, an island he was drawn to by old ancestral ties (a great-grandfather had come from there, bringing with him the family name). This one was inspired by the windward side, where legendary valleys have been chiseled into the world's highest, steepest shoreline cliffs. In the final verse the singer and his beloved and the natural spectacle all speak as one:

'O makani ku'u leo;
'O ke kai ku'u pu'uwai;
'O ka 'āina uluwehi ku'u nui kino.

The wind is my voice;
The sea is my heart;
The lush land is my whole body.[5]

After three decades of pioneering work, Eddie was twice recognized for his lifetime musical achievement. The first came from the Hawai'i state legislature in a resolution put forward by Sen. Jean King. Soon afterward the Honpa Hongwanji Mission named him a "Living Treasure of Hawai'i." This Mahayana Buddhist enclave had been a mainstay in the Honolulu community since its founding in 1889. Stirred by the cultural revival, the mission had established these annual citations, modeled loosely after Japan's practice of honoring artists and master craftsmen. When he was named in 1979, Eddie joined a select company that included 'Iolani Luahine, Mary Kawena Pukui, Gabby Pahinui, composer and guitar stylist Alice Nāmakelua, and the Big Island chanter and *kumu hula* Auntie Edith Kanaka'ole.

Eddie is never at ease with such honors, or with the cermonies that surround them. While composing a song is one of his greatest pleasures, the task of composing an acceptance speech makes his mouth go dry. In general he keeps his distance from formal occasions and will avoid a banquet if it means he might have to wear a jacket. When he heard that the Hongwanji Mission was hosting a "Living Treasures Luncheon," his first reaction was to tell them he'd be out of town. But when he learned it was to be at the Willows, a popular dining spot in midtown Honolulu, he changed his mind, knowing the food would be good and the tropical atmosphere congenial and relaxed.

He arranged to seat himself next to Pīlahi Pākī, who'd also been recently honored. These two had some catching up to do. They were waiting for the coffee and dessert when she leaned in close and said, "Eddie, tell me—how is this work of yours coming along?"

He knew she referred to the film about Sam, and he told her he'd been thinking about it more and more, talking with Dennis Mahaffay, who'd directed *Christmas Time,* and with Myrna, and with the boys in the band. He'd found some more of Sam's relatives, he told her, and he was trying to make time to develop his ideas, though all the gigs and studio work had kept him pretty busy.

While he talked, Pīlahi watched him closely, holding him with a look he hadn't seen before, so fixed and penetrating he stopped in mid-sentence. Her face was stern, her eyes unblinking. She was then near eighty, and still had her regal bearing, her white hair coiffed and luminous. Her black eyes seemed ancient, as old as Hawai'i, and her voice seemed to drop an octave as she said, for his ears only, "Don't wait any longer, Eddie. Do it now! For there will be no more."

He knew exactly what she was talking about. Like all the best teachers, Pīlahi had reminded him of what he already knew in his heart to be true. "No more" meant no more like Sam. It also meant the ones who'd known Sam while he was living and could help Eddie get his story told: they won't be with us too much longer, she was saying. She meant there is a world of memory and lives lived that soon will slip past us and be gone, just as the old canoe maker had slipped past Eddie nine years earlier. He felt a rush of chickenskin, as if a hundred voices had gathered around them inside the Willows to echo her prophecy, her warning, and her command.

For Eddie it was a loaded moment, full of challenge, full of questions. Her words came as a kind of validation, giving him permission to move out along the path that had been calling him. Yet even as he nodded in agreement, he knew how much he did not know. He was far from being a filmmaker. He was a musician. He'd seen the crews gathered around with mikes and wires and lights and lenses. He knew it took money, more than he'd ever make playing gigs. On *Christmas Time* he'd picked the sites and the songs, and rehearsed the band, and later on monitored the soundtrack and the mixing. But cameras were still mysterious to him, and editing was an unknown world. If he somehow managed to do this, he wanted it to be a Hawaiian film, in the way that Sam's music was Hawaiian music. But what did that mean? Were there other Hawaiians he could talk with about it? At the time Eddie did not yet know that the answer was, hardly any. Though a thousand films had been shot in the islands—from dramatic features and documentaries to travelogues and TV specials—no person of Hawaiian ancestry had ever directed or produced one. Hawaiians had performed in many films, but someone else had always been in charge.

THE POWER OF WORDS *Pīlahi Pākī believed every word has power. That was the foundation of her teaching. Whether you're talking or singing, she would say, you speak clearly, you show respect for the language, you enunciate, and you choose your words with care, because they have an effect far beyond what you can hear.*

I remember a talk she gave once about all the layers of meaning in just one word. I tell you it brought tears to people's eyes. It was one of those times when everybody was waiting for a certain thing to be said, not knowing what it would be or who would say it, but waiting and listening and wishing someone would stand up and tell them what they needed to hear.

This was a few years back, a big gathering at the Kennedy Theatre up at the East-West Center on the university campus, where the governor was hosting a four-day conference called "Hawai'i 2000." The idea was to look ahead and imagine some future vision for the state. Experts from different fields sat on panels and gave lectures on everything—politics, tourism, hotels, schools, crops, and highways.

On the last day, after one of these panels, there was a question-and-answer period. Some people in the crowd got into a long discussion about "the aloha *spirit" and how it fit into our future. One guy thought we should have a special budget to mention "*aloha*" in more of the travel ads. Somebody else thought every visitor should get a free* lei *at the airport. They were going around and around. Finally, in the middle of the theater, Pīlahi stands up and waits until one of the guys with a microphone comes to where she is standing.*

She takes the mike and waits a little longer. She was a tall, solid woman, you know, with that look of command about her. That day she is wearing a beautiful red-and-white flowered mu'umu'u *that catches everybody's eye.*

"I would like you all to understand," she says, "that aloha *spirit is a coordination of mind and heart."*

The place is packed, because this is the finale of the four-day conference, and now it gets real still in there. Her voice is strong and deep, a real wise Hawaiian voice, and she takes her time, practicing what she preaches, weighing each word.

I guess that gave the reporter time to write down everything she said, because it all came out the next day on the front page of the Honolulu Advertiser *with a big picture of Pīlahi.*

*"It is within the individual," she says, "it brings you down to yourself. You must think and emote good feelings to others. Permit me to offer a translation of the word '*Aloha,*' letter by letter.*

"A stands for akaḥai, *meaning 'kindness,' to be expressed with tenderness.*

"L stands for lōkahi, *meaning 'unity,' to be expressed with harmony.*

"O stands for 'olu'olu, *meaning 'agreeable,' to be expressed with pleasantness.*

"H stands for ha'aha'a, *meaning 'humility,' to be expressed with modesty.*

"A stands for ahonui, *meaning 'patience,' to be expressed with perseverance.*

"These are the traits of character that express the charm, warmth, and sincerity of Hawaiians. It was the working philosophy of my ancestors."

As she hands the mike back to the attendant, there is a long moment of silence like the quiet in the ocean while a big wave is getting ready to break. Then the whole theater explodes with applause, everybody jumping up to give her a standing ovation!

Everybody who was there that day trying to figure out the future of Hawai'i, they knew what Pīlahi had done. She had that kind of gift. With one word she could take us all back to the root, back to the most essential thing.

Part Three

Ka leo o ka maka
Let the eyes speak

A family saying from Clyde Sproat of Kohala

10

A Way of Seeing

opposite
John K. ("J. P.") Purdy, seated, and John Holi Mae, longtime friends of Sam Li'a, shared their memories during the making of Li'a.

Sam Li'a had been many things to many people: composer, performer, chanter, teacher, choirmaster, father, grandfather, community patriarch. But how to turn his century of life into a film? Eddie knew his first task was to track down anyone who'd known Sam or knew about him. On his next trip to the Big Island he heard of a relative who lived somewhere up around Waimea, a retired man who might have a good story to tell. On another trip he heard about a family who cherished a song Sam had given them in years past, composed as a Christmas present. Other families claimed to have birthday songs or anniversary songs written by the grand old man.

Eddie made inquiries, tried to arrange meetings. But meetings like these weren't always simple to arrange. You had to take your time. When you're dealing with country people, everything takes time. You can't just walk into a yard and start asking questions. It's best if someone paves the way with an introduction, as Kawena had paved the way, back in 1970. You meet. You eat. You talk story. You might have to come twice or three times and talk about other songs, maybe sing a few together, before you got around to the song Sam gave the family. Or maybe you never got around to it.

"When you call on *tūtū* folks," Eddie says, "give them one hour. Then they get tired. You sit with them. You wait. If they say, 'What can I do for you?' then you ask. If they don't ask, you don't ask."

As for bringing in a camera to capture that song or story on film—well, who knew how long it might take to build up that kind of trust? The oldtimers in particular, they're never sure about cameras. It was too soon, of course, to worry about that part. Take one thing at a time. First, find the people. Find the stories and the songs. Then, find the funding, and find a crew. When it came to film work, doing it now was easier said than done.

In the meantime Eddie still had his hands full keeping up with all the business that pulled him back toward Honolulu: the recording dates, the gigs that seemed too good to turn down. In 1980 The Sons cut another album, called *Grassroots Music,* with nine new songs by Dennis Kamakahi, who just couldn't stop writing. This album included "Kōke'e," recorded for the first time, along with another tribute to the northern island (and also destined to become a standard), "Kaua'i O Mano." A year later came *The Best of The Sons of Hawaii,* a round-up of top tunes from all the albums they'd cut since the Territorial Tavern days, island-wide favorites like "Morning Dew," "Mauna Kea," "E Hihiwai," "Wahine 'Ilikea," and their popular version of Lili'uokalani's love song to Hawaii's native birds, "Hanakeoki."

A spread of red-checkered *palaka* cloth fills the jacket cover of this album, and on it rests Eddie's two-holed *koa*-wood *'ukulele* surrounded by white plumeria blossoms and music sheets that name the famous songs. The "Five Faces" album had capped the first decade of their music. *The Best of The Sons of Hawaii* capped their second decade. At the time no one could have foreseen that it would be their last release.

With seven albums in seven years—studded with hit songs and much imitated arrangements—The Sons were among the most sought-after bands in the islands. They were at the peak of their popularity, playing one night at a club in Kaka'ako called Our Place, when Feet Rogers passed out in the middle of a song. It wasn't drugs. It wasn't drink. He just keeled over, swooning with dizziness, and fell off his chair.

The next day he went for a checkup, which led to a series of tests. A week later the shocking diagnosis came back: it was a brain tumor, and fairly well advanced. In the weeks that followed, his decline was alarmingly swift. For a while Feet kept showing up for gigs, but he knew his sense of timing had slipped. Before long he had quit playing, to spend his days at home, as his new wife Jeannie nursed him through the chemotherapy treatments.

They'd only been married for six months. By all accounts these had been the happiest months Feet had known, which only doubled the blow. Always a free spirit, he had finally, at age forty-seven, found the love of his life. Jeannie felt the same about him. A *haole* woman of about his age, originally from southern California, she'd lived in the islands for many years. She was also a born-again Christian whose strong faith got both of them through this ordeal. Before his collapse Feet had started studying the Bible, and for the first time began to contemplate matters of the spirit and his personal relationship to a higher power.

Eddie remembers what he calls "the final jam session," when he, Joe, and Dennis brought their instruments to the apartment. Feet had lost a lot of weight and a lot of energy, but when they gathered around him, tuning up, his eyes brightened and the big smile lit his face.

"Feet liked to eat half-dry aku," Eddie says, "a kind of savory fish, like tuna, so we brought him some of that. Then we put the steel in his lap, and we just played all our favorite songs, so we had good times right up until the end, you see. He took solos on every one of them, until all of a sudden he couldn't move his fingers any more. We went back to his bedroom where he could lie down. We noticed he had an open Bible on the table by his bed. Dennis was always kind of a religious guy and interested in Bible things. He said to Feet, 'I see you reading passages.'"

"Oh yeah," said Feet, reaching out a hand to touch the pages. "You know, all my life I always looked for answers and never could find 'em. Now I think I found all the answers in this book right here."

Dennis thought about that and said, "You know, Feet, this is a great book, the Bible. But don't forget about your music. That gave you answers too. God gave you that ability, and it was your way, you see, to give something back. You can find important answers in this book. But it was in your music too. Every time you play, you express your soul."

Later on Dennis would recall that day. "For all the years I

 knew Feet, I never seen him serious about spiritual things. But I guess I figured music was his religion, because of how he played. I'm not sure if he always saw it that way. But I wanted him to be at peace with his life and not pass away regretting how he had lived. After we talked that day, I could see it put him at ease. He was quiet for a while, then he told us he was going home, he was ready to go home. And that was the last time we talked."

Not long afterward Feet went into a coma and never came out of it. He was buried in Kāne'ohe, on O'ahu's windward side, with one last gesture from his fellow musicians. It was an open-casket service. An overflow crowd had filled the mortuary, among them numerous dignitaries such as Henry Peters, Speaker of the House of Representatives, and Lt. Gov. John Waihe'e. After all the testimonials had been heard, after Joe Marshall had spoken on behalf of the band, after everyone else had passed by to pay their last respects, Eddie and Dennis walked together toward the pulpit carrying Feet's steel guitar. They placed it in the casket, and the lid was closed.

"We said *aloha* to our brother," Eddie recalls, "and he got his final wish. The guitar went with him."

The band had bookings lined up for weeks and months to come. And they continued to perform, with other musicians invited to sit in. But in Eddie's heart something had shifted. Feet's untimely passing was another blow. He'd lost a close friend, a confidant, a longtime musical ally. And Feet took with him a sound that only he could produce. Its loss would change how Eddie thought about his band. Though Eddie could not yet talk of this out loud, he already knew their recording days had ended. Without Feet's singular styling, his bell notes to punctuate the phrasing, the sound could never again be what it had been for a quarter of a century. Though he and Dennis and Joe continued to play clubs and concerts, working with new musicians and listening for the best mix of voices and strings, Eddie found himself putting more and more attention on Sam Li'a and the film he'd been dreaming about. Feet's death was the final prod, urging him to push this project to the forefront.

In his mind it had been turning like a wheel, a moving collage of sounds and images, faces and scenes. How and when it would all fall into place and find its sequences—a beginning, a middle, an end—he was not yet sure. He had photos of Sam and sheets of music in the old man's hand, along with tapes of him singing and chanting and remembering. On Eddie's inner screen he saw Sam's house, the coastal towns, the places they'd visited together. Waipi'o was part of this movie, too, a big part. If he could capture that—the valley as a place that had shaped Sam's life—this could make it a truly Hawaiian film: the role of the valley, along with Sam's role in the lives of the island people he had touched. Eddie needed more time to travel to the outer islands, to go seek them out in earnest, and now he gave himself that time.

In Waipi'o he found a woman who once studied *hula* with Sam. "Which style?" Eddie asked. "*'Auwana,* or *kahiko*? Modern, or ancient?"

"Both," she said with a grin. "Sam knew it all."

He tracked down a woman who'd learned to sing in Sam's Sunday school class when she was a girl. "He likes children," she told Eddie, "that's why we gather around him. Those days, you know, he still had his wife. He used to call us, 'Come to the house and enjoy.' And then we used to tell him, 'Uncle, teach us how to sing.' And he used to sing for us and play his violin!"[1]

In her eighties when Eddie met her, this small and feisty woman with the calculating eye of a watchful seabird was known to everyone as Auntie Ruth. She'd spent most of her life in and around Waipi'o, where she'd raised seventeen children. She'd known Sam in the early days and thus had intimate knowledge of his world, that remote community of fishermen and taro farmers. She could also talk about it both in English and in fluent Hawaiian, which she'd learned as a first language. The sound of voices like Auntie Ruth's would be as important to Eddie's film as any of the songs he'd gathered along the way.

In Hāna, Maui, he located a carpenter who'd worked on the restoration of a church in Honoka'a at a time when Sam was the organist and choirmaster there. A huge man called "Tiny,"

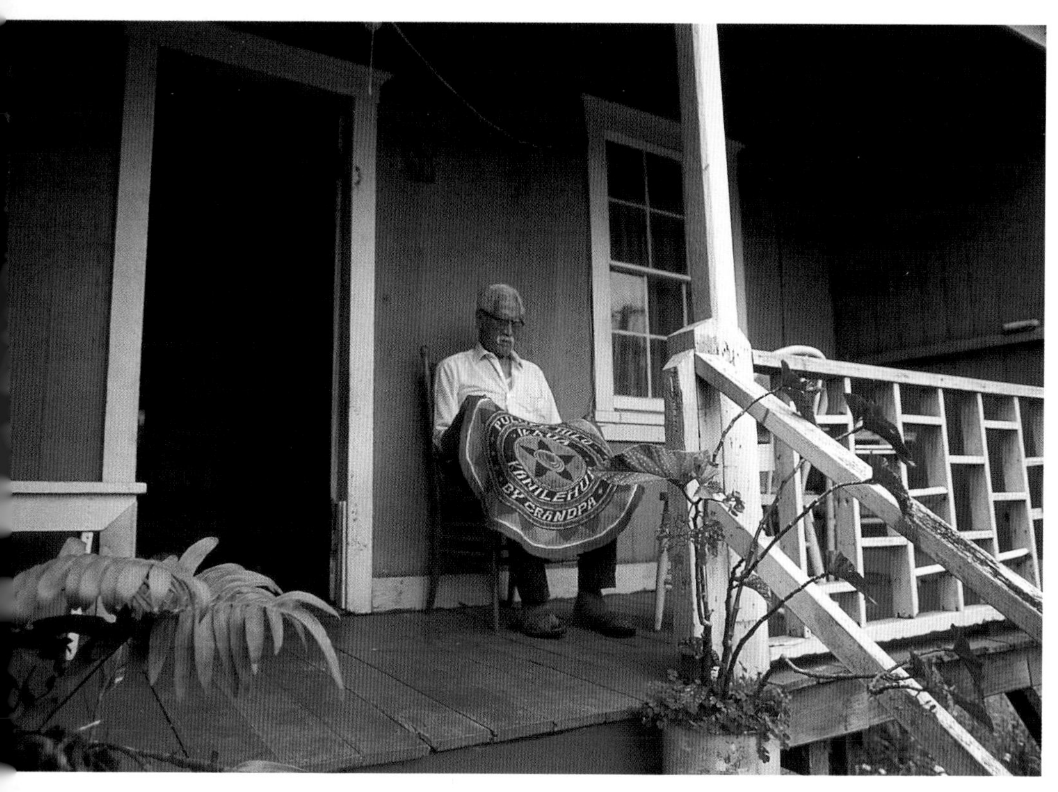

While filming Hawaiian Voices, *Eddie and Auntie Ruth Makaila Kaholoa'a (1905–2002) visited Waimanu valley, near Waipi'o, where she spent several of her childhood years.*

As a pastime, Sam Li'a wove colorful yarn rugs and wall hangings which he gave away, as he gave away his songs, to loved ones and to community centers.

he had bunked in the basement of the church, and his face glowed with pleasure as he told Eddie how Sam would pump the organ on a Sunday morning, while the voices of the congregation swelled out the windows to be heard all around the old plantation town. Tiny's warm and open Hawaiian face joined the images flowing through Eddie's mind, and the organ's swell was added to the inner sound track.

In Honolulu he found David Maka'oi, the elderly musician and retired school principal who'd played *'ukulele* in one of Sam's horseback bands. And around this same time Eddie heard of someone named Luther, who might also have played with Sam, a Hawaiian man said to be in his nineties and still active—so active he was hard to pin down. While Eddie's search for this elusive fellow would be typical of his outings, it was also unique for what it gave him, a defining piece in the telling of Sam's story.

"From what I'd heard," Eddie says, "I knew he was somewhere on the Big Island. Every time I went over there I would ask around. People told me, 'Yeah, Luther was here last week.' Or, 'Yeah, he was there last week.' He was always getting in trouble with the cops, you see, even in his nineties. Finally I heard that he hangs out in Pāhoa, south of Hilo. So the next time I fly to Hilo I rent a car and drive out to Pāhoa early in the morning and find a woman in a bar who tells me, 'You looking for Luther? Go down 'Ōpihikao, that's where he lives.' So I drive to 'Ōpihikao, all the way down there by the south shore, and stop at a house, and a woman comes to the door. 'I'm looking for a man named Luther Makekau,' I tell her. And she says, 'Go down the road along the water and turn left and you'll see his clothes hanging up on the tree.'"

'Ōpihikao was not a town. It was a rural district at the bottom of a road that followed ten miles of sloping terrain, old broken-down lava flow, arable here and there. Eddie passed a few more farmhouses, set back among the trees, with their rain-rusted roofing. He swung left onto the narrow coast road and soon came upon a small point of tree-covered lava jutting into acutely blue water, a cobalt blue stretching away to the south. He parked and got out of his car. Cartons and jugs were scattered under the trees. Up-ended boxes seemed to serve as tables. There was a weathered black car seat, a hammock slung between two trunks, a rope that might have been a clothesline, though nothing hung from it. The air was balmy. The only sound was water lapping at the black lava, from time to time a white surge of surf.

"If this is Luther's camp, " Eddie thought, "he picked a pretty good spot for himself."

But from the look of things no one had been there for a while. So he drove back up the road to Hilo, where he had one more lead to check out. A friend in Honolulu who knew of Eddie's project had told him any time he needed to find something on the Big Island, he could call on the director of the local historical museum. At the museum Eddie found what he was looking for, but not from the director. As he walked into the entry room, he told a receptionist what he was telling everyone he met.

"I'm looking for a man named Luther Makekau."

Immediately she said, "Oh sure. I think the girl upstairs knows him. She comes from 'Ōpihikao."

On the second floor, in the photo archive, he found a young Hawaiian woman who said yes, she knew Luther, and some of his family, too, and if Eddie could wait she'd make a call. Five minutes later she came back with a phone number and a Hilo street address printed on a memo page. "He's over there," she said.

"For how long?"

With a cryptic smile, she shrugged. "Who knows? Better go now."

It was only a mile away, in a neighborhood of wooden bungalows, low palms, bougainvillea. Eddie walked across the grass and up onto the porch. When he knocked, he heard a raspy voice say, "Hey. Hey, somebody at the front door."

A stocky Hawaiian appeared in front of him, wearing a tee shirt and shorts, a fellow Eddie recognized.

"I knew this guy," he says now. "Bill was his name. I knew him for years. But I never knew he was Luther's nephew because we never talked about Luther. Little by little I would find out he had other relatives I already knew from somewhere along

the way. Luther had lots and lots of relatives. He had dozens of children, you know. He had lived so long he was a kind of legend, but an invisible legend nobody talked about unless you asked them. And now I finally found him. He was sitting there in the front room, on the sofa, in the shadows, waving his arm."

"Come in," Luther said. "Come in."

"I'm Eddie Kamae . . ."

"I know. Come. Sit. Sit here."

He was a wiry man, very alert, wearing jeans and a long-sleeve white shirt. Luther had worked ranches on the Big Island for much of his life and still had the long, rangy build of a cowboy. He had a full head of thick white hair. His dark face was stubbled with white whiskers. There was a piece of notepaper on the low table in front of him. He pushed it toward Eddie.

"Here. Look. Just this morning I wrote your name."

Eddie glanced down. There it was.

Watching him, Luther's eyes were shrewd, playful, touched with wonder. Eddie waited. In a scratchy, ragged voice Luther said, "You been looking for me. How come?"

The hairs prickled on Eddie's neck and arms. This took him by surprise. And yet it didn't. Wasn't this how things always came to him, with the way somehow prepared ahead of time?

He got right to the point. He'd brought along an envelope with an old photograph of five musicians, members of a band back around 1910. They wore hats and black jackets. Sam Li'a was one of them, somewhere in his twenties. Luther recognized him, and all the others, too. He knew them by name. He knew which instrument each man had played, and the songs each one was known for.

"I sing with them myself," he told Eddie, "in old times. When I had my voice. Sam played his violin while I used to sing falsetto."

Again Eddie waited, and eventually Luther began to talk, answering questions Eddie didn't need to ask, as if eager to dredge up these memories. And in truth, he was. As Eddie would soon learn, others had pursued Luther in recent years, as an elder with rare stories to tell, hoping to garner whatever they could. Until now he'd put everyone off, kept his distance,

opposite
Luther Kahekili Makekau (1890–1988), still a warrior cowboy at age ninety-five.

 played hard to get, hard to find. Luther would later reveal that even before this meeting he knew Eddie would be the right one to talk to.

"In church," Luther went on, "we always get together, too, and sing songs, you know, as a choir. He played songs the old folks know very well, and he make 'em cry. The violin cry. And the old folks cry. Right now, my memories come back to me. My tears falling down. My tears, my memories come back. My baby days."

The old photos had moved Luther deeply, because these two had been more than fellow musicians. They had shared a close bond as friends and as Hawaiian men of the same era, who'd witnessed and survived the same decades of tumultuous change. Before this first meeting ended, Luther revealed that Sam had once given him a song, with the understanding that he wouldn't sing it until after Sam had passed away.

"When he's gone I can sing this song. Otherwise it is a promissory note between him and me, Sam Li'a Kalāinaina and Luther Kahekili Makekau. And until today I do not sing it."

"You still remember it?"

"Sure. Every word."

"What's it called?"

"Ka Pua o Ka Lehua."

"The Flower of the *Lehua* Tree."

"Yes, " said Luther, beginning to recite the words. "'Auhea wale ana 'oe, pua ka lehua . . . When she buds, you see the beauty of the flower . . . and then the clouds reflect the heat of Kīlauea while she is erupting . . ."

It was a rare song for Sam, unlike any of the others Eddie had heard. While most were inspired by Waipi'o, this one came from the island's southern corner where the lava flows. It also tells of a clandestine love affair, perhaps involving Sam himself, which may have been why he'd instructed Luther not to sing it until he was gone. Kīlauea is the great skillet-shaped caldera where Pele is said to make her home. When it erupts, the fiery glow sends brilliant color to tint the clouds, the same color you see in the vein-red *lehua* blossoms. They bud from a rugged tree that flourishes in volcano country and seems to feed on lava rock. In Hawaiian poetry the vivid, anemone-like *lehua* has numerous meanings: as the flower of the Big Island, it is Pele's flower; it can be a beloved friend, or relative, or sweetheart. In this case it refers to a loose woman who goes with every man who pleases her.

"For Eddie Kamae I will sing it," Luther told him. "Only for you. Sam's song. The one he gives me, from seventy years ago."

Back in Honolulu Eddie had secured some preliminary funding from the first of several local backers who knew his music and had faith in this new venture. All along he'd imagined he would shoot in 16 mm. But after a heart-to-heart talk with an experienced independent filmmaker from the mainland, who filled him in on the hard facts of production costs, Eddie decided to work in video. It would be cheaper to do that and have it transferred to film when the time came.

"Some things you have to learn by trial and error," Eddie says. "I had a lot to learn. With video it doesn't cost so much, so it's easier to change your mind. There's a monitor on the camera that tells you what you shot. You can try things different ways and afford to make mistakes. Every day, you know, whatever I'm doing, I give myself a quota. I give myself five mistakes. If something goes wrong, I tell myself, Hey, you still got four to go."

His wife Myrna, now developing resource films and study guides with the state Department of Education, would handle the budget and take on the producer's role. Their three-room apartment would become the production office (and when cassettes of footage began to accumulate, it would become the archive, too). One by one they chose the people they would work with. Big Island photographer Boone Morrison was a longtime friend with a deep knowledge of Hawai'i's cultural history. Gene Kois and Rodney Ohtani were cameramen with years of experience in local television. Jim Walters was a gifted sound engineer with an abiding affection for Hawaiian music. Before moving to Honolulu, freelance editor Ralph Biesmeyer had worked in New York, Los Angeles, and San Francisco.

As a novice documentarian, Eddie would need their technical advice at every level. But the key to this project, as with all the films to follow, was his own internal radar, his Hawaiian ear, his Hawaiian eye. To speak the voice-over narration, Eddie would choose premier chanter Ka'upena Wong, and in his voice we hear the flavor of contemporary island idiom blend with the richness and tonal range of an ancient tradition.

On location Eddie would always look for pictures that could take you inside the world Sam had known. There was the day, for example, when they finally made their way to Waipi'o, hoping for an early morning shot of Hi'ilawe Falls, an image central to this story. The sky was dark. A squall was moving in from the sea. Soon the valley would be drowning in downpour. As they stood at the overlook, the camera crew figured there was no point in going any farther: the day was lost. But Eddie said, "No, we're going down!"

Once they reached the falls, the gorge was filled with fog and mist, obscuring the famous double ribbon of spilling white. The crew now figured they'd have to wait out the weather, hoping for a clearer shot, perhaps some blue sky to sharpen the high, green ridge. But Eddie told them, "Don't wait! Shoot it now! I want that mist!"

It was exactly what he'd asked for and prayed for as they drove north from Hilo. The result was not a scenic shot, but a haunting and mysterious moment, so that early in the film we see this foggy mist and then, as if rising into it, we hear the graveled spirit-voice of Sam Li'a chanting. And *then* the mist opens up a bit to reveal the falls in muted morning light.

What we get, on screen, is something other than Hawai'i as spectacular and photogenic terrain. In shot after shot we get a Hawaiian's way of seeing. It is revealed, as well, in the eyes and faces of those Eddie calls upon to tell their stories. Whenever the crew went out on location, to the backyards and front porches and living rooms and taro ponds, Eddie stayed off-camera, but he was always there. When the islanders remember and talk and share their memories of the *tūtū* man, they are talking with another Hawaiian, and a rare kind of window is opened. A cultural border dissolves.

In the case of Luther Makekau, Eddie was the only one he'd allow to interview him. Toward the end of the film, when we see Luther sing "Ka Pua o Ka Lehua"—about the flower that flames in volcano country—he is not only singing it for the first time since he and Sam were young men; it comes in the form of another gift, this time for Eddie, whom Luther trusts to honor it as part of Sam's Hawaiian legacy.

The *tūtū* man's songs are heard throughout the film, sometimes sung by those who have stories to tell, sometimes performed by The Sons of Hawaii, who brought to the task their own respect and reverence for a role model and musical ancestor. By this time Joe, Eddie, and Dennis had been joined by two new musicians. George Kuo was an up-and-coming slack-key talent whose first solo album, *Nahe-Nahe,* had appeared in 1980. "Braddah" Hoapili Smith, regarded by many as the best rhythm guitarist in the islands, was a nephew of Gabby Pahinui, with a penetrating vocal style that brought some of his uncle's flavor back into the band.

These five had been playing some prestigious gigs. At the annual Merrie Monarch Hula Festival in Hilo, they accompanied the award-winning dance troupe led by *kumu hula* Johnny Lum Ho. In 1984 they were guest artists with the Honolulu Symphony, playing to sold-out crowds at Blaisdell Concert Hall in downtown Honolulu. In 1985, when Garrison Keillor brought his weekly *Prairie Home Companion* from Minnesota to Hawai'i, The Sons were invited to join the show, and their songs were heard across the land over National Public Radio. Now it was 1987, and they had a new role, performing on- and off-camera, as they played the songs that marked the chapters in Sam Li'a's long life, songs such as "Hi'ilawe," composed by his father; "Heha Waipi'o," the song Sam gave to Joe Perez in 1904; "Hinahina Kū Kahakai," the one he wrote for his wife, Sarah; and "Kanaka Waiolina," the song Dennis Kamakahi wrote for Sam.

When it was all put together, early in 1988, the finished film was one hour long. Eddie and Myrna had titled it *Li'a: The Legacy of a Hawaiian Man,* and they submitted it to the Hawaii International Film Festival, hoping it might find a place in the annual documentary series. Then in its eighth year, the festival was drawing wide attention in the film world for its ongoing theme, "When Strangers Meet," and for its emphasis on works from around the Asia/Pacific region, films that in one way or another enhanced cross-cultural understanding or opened doors of recognition.

The members of the selection committee were so impressed they decided that *Li'a* should not only be screened, it should open the week of screenings, followed by a gala reception at the Hyatt Regency in Waikīkī, where the festival would be headquartered. They had films coming from India, China, Japan, Korea, Vietnam, the Philippines, Australia, New Zealand, and Canada, as well as from other parts of the United States. But what better way to open than with a film made right here in the islands, and one that spoke so directly to the festival's theme? They would bill it as a world premiere.

This was a lot more than Eddie and Myrna had hoped for, an unexpected honor. Yet they could only accept with the understanding that the true premiere would be happening somewhere else. For years they'd been telling themselves that if this film were ever completed, it would show first in Kukuihaele, out there at the end of the coast road, the last stop before you reach Waipi'o Valley. It was Sam's film, after all, and this was Sam's town. If he was going to be there in spirit, he wouldn't have to travel very far. And a lot of the Big Island folks who would never come to Honolulu, they would be sure to show up at the Kukuihaele Social Hall.

"So that's where he had the first premiere," says Eddie with a huge and satisfied smile, "in the town where I first met Sam in 1970. I came over with the boys in the band—Joe, Dennis, Smitty, George Kuo. Clyde Sproat was there from the Kohala side with his *'ukulele,* because he was in the film taking the part of one of the serenaders in Sam's horseback band. We played music. There was food all over the place, *lū'au* style, *poi, kālua* pig, *laulau,* barbecue, teriyaki chicken, you name it. We invited all the folks who were in the film, and the relatives, and the old-timers from out that way. That night inside the social hall we set up a screen. It was still on video. Everybody loved it. The old folks sat there clapping their hands every time they saw somebody they knew."

A month later, at the Hyatt Regency in Waikīkī, it was a very

To tell Sam's story, Eddie filmed the making of 'ōkolehao, *Hawaiian home-brew, from steamed and fermented ti root.*

Left to right: Charlie Mahi, Harry Nihau, and his son John.

different event, yet equally infused with the islanders' welcoming generosity. The Hawaii International Film Festival had a style that drew upon its mid-Pacific location. It had been called "the festival with a conscience." Roger Ebert once dubbed it "the festival with a heart." Much of this was due to the vision of its founding director. The ongoing cross-cultural theme had been Jeannette Paulson's idea, as well as the policy that screenings would be free of charge, to ensure the widest range of community involvement. A native of Oregon, she possessed a charismatic enthusiasm for film as a trans-oceanic messenger. During her ten years in Honolulu she had studied Hawaiian language and history, and now looked to locals for guidance, for ways to bring hospitality and joyfulness into the festival mix, and a bit of traditional ritual, too.

At the Hyatt a double-size conference room had been layered with foliage and flowers, stalks of torch ginger, clusters of ti leaf for blessing, hundreds of *lei.* The Sons were there, setting a pattern Eddie would follow for years to come. Where else but in Hawai'i would you find a filmmaker who also led a working

band? From *Li'a* onward, he would use them whenever possible to warm up a screening with close harmony, Hawaiian lyrics, the humming lilt of slack-key guitar, the driving rhythm of his own *'ukulele.*

The film was introduced by John Waihe'e, the state's new governor, the first person of Hawaiian ancestry ever elected to the post. He spoke fondly of his own family ties to the Big Island. "As a boy," he said, "I spent a lot of time in Waipi'o Valley," noting that one of those interviewed for the film was in fact a relative, a onetime cowboy from Sam's era named J. P. Purdy.

opposite
Rev. Roy Toko (left) and Eddie Thomas (right), Sam's hānai *(adopted) son, escorted Eddie around Waipi'o during the filming of* Li'a. *Famous Hi'ilawe falls are in the background.*

As Governor Waihe'e stepped off the low stage, the sound of a *pū* filled the room, the trumpeting call of the helmet shell, the triton conch, to announce a series of welcoming chants. The *pū*'s long note fell away, and Ka'upena Wong walked onto the stage, in ceremonial white robe. His throbbing voice began to cast its spell. He recited a Ke Welina (Greeting of Affection) that dated back to the fourteenth century, composed in the time of Kiha-nui-lūlū-moku, a ruler of Waipi'o Valley and grandfather of its famous chief, 'Umi-a-Līloa.

Next came the rumble of a *pahu,* the round temple drum, a carved and hollowed coconut log stretched with sharkskin. Its tattoo announced a Mele Ho'ohanohano (Glorification Chant), another chant from Sam's home region, a poetic tribute to Waipi'o. Ka'upena, whose voice would soon be heard as the film's narrator, had been joined by three young Hawaiian men wearing *palaka* shirts. In the combined pulse of their voices the valley's legend vibrated through the conference room and out into the corridors of the Hyatt Regency:

Aia Waipi'o o Paka'alana
Paepae kapu ia o Līloa . . .

In beautiful Waipi'o stands Paka'alana,
sacred shrine of the ruling chief, Līloa

As their chant subsided, the trumpet note of the conch was heard once more, this time to announce the film. The ancestors had been invoked, the gathering had been blessed, the room lights dimmed . . .

SIGNS *All the time we're making this film, things keep telling me we're on the right path. When we first start setting up shots, I go to a meeting of the Waipi'o Valley Association, the farmers and local people who live down there now. I tell them about my project and how we need a helicopter to fly in early one morning, but I respect their peace and quiet, and so I come to ask their permission.*

*The president tells me, "*Mahalo*, Eddie, thank you, we'll take it up at our next meeting."*

But then a young Hawaiian calls out, "Why not now?"

The president looks at him, and the fellow stands up and says, "Every day I hear the helicopter go right over my place, making all kind noise. This the first time anybody ever come to ask my permission. So mahalo *for that, braddah Eddie, and I will vote yes right now!"*

The president took a count, and everybody else including him raise their hands, yes. So, you see, you show respect, then there's good feeling all the way around.

After that we go up to Waimea, me and my friend, Boone Morrison, the photographer, where he knows somebody who will rent us a helicopter. And from there we fly down toward the ocean. I never did this before, hire a guy to fly us around with a camera. It's costing me a lot of money, and I'm supposed to be the director telling everybody else what to do.

We got close to the beach, and Boone says, "Okay, Eddie, what'll it be?" Well, I still needed some time to think. I said, "Let's go out over the water," while I start silently asking my spirit-friend, "Now what shall I do?"

When we're offshore I tell the pilot to go low and come into the valley right above the river mouth. I tell Boone to get the beach and the flow of the river and the taro patches. Then out of nowhere, a white horse appeared right below us at the edge of a field. A horse with no rider. I couldn't believe it! A white horse just like the one Sam used to ride! I shouted, "Boone! Did you get it?" He said he did, and I knew then this was the right place to be.

That happened on the day we started filming. When it was all over, we saw the horse one more time. This was after we had the screening at Kukuihaele. Me and Myrna wanted to take some lei *to Sam's grave. So we drove over by ourselves and parked the car. Just as we started to walk across the grass, we saw him on the far side of the cemetery, a white horse, standing by the sugar cane, looking at us. He watched us for a while, then turned and loped away along the cane field road. After we put the* lei *on the grave and said our* aloha *to Sam, we got back in the car and drove down the road a ways trying to see the horse again. It was gone. Disappeared. But we both figured it was a sign that Sam was right there with us that day.*

It makes me think of something else that happened. This was back in 1986, after Tūtū Kawena passed away. She was ninety when she died. We went to her funeral over at the cemetery in Kāne'ohe. It's a big sloping lawn with a view toward the ocean. A crowd was there, hundreds of people. We waited till everyone else had gone up to the casket to pay their respects or lay a flower or whatever. Then I went up with Myrna, and we put our hands on the casket, and I thanked Kawena for all she gave me and for her guidance in all the things that I knew. While we were standing there, the casket started moving. Right underneath our hands we felt it roll back and forth. We looked at each other and wondered what this meant. We just looked and waited until it was still.

Later on I was talking with my friend David Ka'alakea from Maui, who was a minister, in his seventies then, and a very wise Hawaiian man. I said, "Kāwika, can you explain to me this motion of the coffin?"

He looked at me and told me exactly what Kawena had told me all during the twenty-five years I knew her.

"Ho'omau, *Eddie," Kāwika said,* "ho'omau."

That means "continue." I knew then she was still speaking to me, telling me what to do right to the end. Finish the work. That's what she was saying. Finish it.

Pualani Kanaka'ole Kanahele and Nalani Kanaka'ole Zane,
of Hilo's Hālau o Kekuhi.

11

It All Connects

Now blown up to 16 mm, the film traveled with a dozen other festival selections to the outer islands, Kaua'i, Maui, Moloka'i, Hawai'i. After showings on statewide television, *Li'a* was featured at festivals in Seattle, Santa Cruz, and Palm Springs, the first film by a director of Hawaiian ancestry to be exhibited outside Hawai'i. In 1990 it would be named among the ten best documentaries shown during the Honolulu festival's first ten years.

The music Eddie and The Sons revived in the late 1950s had empowered a generation of performers and listeners. Now something similar was happening on the screen. By looking to his elders, listening to their songs, honoring the power of place and the role of language, he had found a filmic voice that speaks from deep inside his own island world. And for these very features, the film was being recognized and honored. In an essay for the 1988 festival program, selection committee member John Charlot called *Li'a* "a visual song, in which music, place and people find their original harmony. . . . the extension of an ethnic sensibility into a new art form."[1]

By the late 1980s Eddie was not alone in what he was trying to do. But the reception of his film, due in part to his position as a leading voice in Hawai'i's cultural renaissance, served to point a way, to validate work being taken on by younger filmmakers, opening new doors of possibility. The work itself made a persuasive statement: film can be another means for the authentic expression of our cultural values, another way to tell people who we are, how we see and feel, where we have come from.

The making of *Li'a* had opened new doors for Eddie, too.

While seeking out those who knew Sam, he'd come across others—like Luther Makekau—who had their own stories to tell. After that early preview screening at the Kukuihaele Social Hall, Eddie stopped in Hilo to show the film to Luther, since the old man had been unable to make the two-hour drive up the coast.

"By this time he was ninety-eight," Eddie says. "He was in the hospital. He went for a check-up, and they kept him there for more tests. Old age was finally catching up with him. But Luther, he just winked at me and said he was in there 'resting,' and keeping an eye on one of the nurses who he said was falling in love with him."

Eddie had a VCR wheeled in. Luther sat up to watch himself and all the others talking about his longlost friend, singing his songs. He cried. He laughed. When it was over, he applauded as if they were in a theater.

Wiping his eyes, he said, "But Eddie, you know you're not finished."

"Sure, I'm finished. This is the final edit. We're all done."

Now Luther was smiling his rascal smile, his charmer's smile. "No, Eddie. You have one more film to do. And that's mine!"

Eddie hadn't thought about this. But as soon as heard the words, he knew Luther was right. From this dark and grizzled face they came as another command, another commission. Eddie had been picking up bits and pieces of gossip and lore. He'd discovered that the mention of Luther's name could cause one person to burst out laughing, the next person to utter a curse. He'd heard enough to know that Luther, like Sam, had been many things to many people; yet he was not at all like Sam. He was, in fact, a completely different type of Hawaiian man.

Eddie didn't waste any time. The next day he came back with permission forms. One was for the hospital administrator, who at first said flatly, no, they couldn't allow any filming. It would be too disruptive for the other patients and the staff.

"They had him in the mental ward, you see," Eddie says. "Not because Luther had a mental problem. The hospital was just too crowded. It seemed like the administrator had forgotten why they'd put him there. I had to explain who Luther was and why it was important to get his memories recorded. Then he said okay, but Luther would have to sign a release form, too, to free the hospital from any liability and all that."

Luther arrived in a wheelchair. After Eddie explained that there were two forms to sign—one for the hospital, and one granting permission to use any footage they filmed—Luther said in his gruff, forthright way, "Let me see it!"

Eddie handed him the paperwork, and Luther sat up a bit straighter, flipping through the pages, reading each one with care. Finally he announced, "Okay. Give me a pen."

"He signed in front of everybody," Eddie recalls, "then he said to the administrator, 'Now you sign it!' Which he did. Because Luther, you see, had caught him off guard and taken charge of the room. He thought Luther was just a feeble old Hawaiian man in the mental ward. But here he had read through six pages without glasses, and signed in a good strong hand. Next he told the head nurse, 'You too! You sign!' So they all signed it. They could see his mind was still sharp, his eyes were good, you could read his writing. When I shook his hand that day, I tell you, he was ninety-eight years old and he still had a grip like a steel vise."

After he'd talked with Luther awhile longer, Eddie flew to Honolulu, planning to return the day after Thanksgiving, as soon as he could pull his crew together. But Luther didn't last that long. Less than forty-eight hours later a nurse called Eddie—it was the morning of Thanksgiving Day—to tell him Luther had passed away.

It was another loss and seemed at first to be another opportunity that had too soon slipped past him. Even so, Eddie felt grateful that he'd met Luther when he did. He had his face and voice and vitality on film, the only existing footage of this rare Hawaiian character. His commission from the hospital bed—"You have one more to do!"—was another kind of promissory note, this one between Luther and Eddie. And he knew he would honor it. He also knew it would be trickier than telling Sam's story, require more ingenuity on Eddie's part. Luther had not been so universally revered. One person might call him a living treasure, the next might call him a scoundrel who should have been punished for his sins.

In the months and years to come, Eddie would locate dozens of people who'd known Luther or had stories to tell. At a reunion of the Makekau clan he would learn that Luther might have fathered more than fifty children. He would meet former wives who still bore grudges. Then he would find old cowboys who described legendary feats of daring horsemanship. On the outer wall of a bar in Pāhoa town he found a larger-than-life mural of Luther standing by his white horse, painted by a local admirer. On Maui he met a *kapa* maker who told him Luther knew things about turning bark into cloth that everyone else had forgotten.

Luther had been the prodigal son of a large Hawaiian family, the fifth of seven children born to a Big Island judge who'd spent several terms in the state legislature. He attended St. Louis College in Honolulu, went on to study law at the University of California at Berkeley, then dropped out after two years and spent some time roaming the mainland from coast to coast. In the decades to follow, he'd lived and worked on every Hawaiian island, consumed by a restless energy. He'd been a horsebreaker and a cattle rustler, a choir leader, an amateur lawyer and a part-time engineer, a sheriff's deputy and a frequent overnight tenant at the county jail. To some he was a rough-riding, hard-fighting renegade. Yet those closest to Luther knew that within him there burned an older flame. And this is what had captivated Eddie from the moment they met.

He was descended from generations of *ali'i nui,* warrior chiefs of Maui and Hawai'i. His full name was Luther Kahekilinui'ahumanu Keali'imakekau o Nu'uanu. He had been named for his eighteenth-century ancestor, Kahekili Nui 'Ahumanu, a fierce battle chief and the blood father of Kamehameha I. Among Hawaiians a name itself has power. It connects you to the spirit of whoever carried that name before you. As Eddie would discover, Luther had always been aware of this, proud to bear a name with such a history.

"I think he was born a hundred years too late," says Eddie now. A wild and untamed spirit, he had carried a kind of warrior's fire that had nowhere to express itself in the changing picture of the twentieth century. Part philosopher, part outlaw, he was a promiscuous rebel and another storehouse of cultural detail. When Eddie fulfulled his promissory note and finally got this film made, he would call it *Luther Kahekili Makekau: A One Kine Hawaiian Man,* a tribute to a warrior cowboy from an older time who had lived into our own time.

But that was almost a decade away. In the months right after *Li'a* was released, Luther's story was becoming part of a tapestry of stories finding form in Eddie's mind, one of several interlocking projects that would keep him busy for the next ten years. As he continued his transition from music to film, Eddie would begin to document a broadening range of cultural expression.

He had been finding stories everywhere he went, stories that cried out to be recorded and shared. Here and there his reputation as a performer had helped to pave the way. Throughout the islands there were elders and *kūpuna* willing to talk with him while a camera was rolling, just as they had agreed to talk with him in the early days when the tape recorder was spinning. Ideas for documentaries were hatching, turning in his mind like kaleidoscopes of sound and scene—lyrics, legends, faces, fern grottoes, *hula* troupes, bright rivers of pouring lava . . .

The first to get made was *Listen to the Forest,* a film that speaks to the widespread concern about rainforest preservation. Eddie is not an environmental activist. He came to this subject via song and dance, guided by a theme that has run through all his work: the intertwining of culture and nature. In the world so many of us inhabit now, a world ruled by cell phones and satellites and credit cards, culture and nature often seem impossibly far apart. But in Hawaiian tradition, these two can't be separated, any more than Sam's life as a composer could be detached from the valley that nourished and inspired him.

In *Listen to the Forest,* taro provides the symbolic link. From its bulbous, potato-like root comes *poi,* which for many centuries has been a dietary staple. At the same time, taro is regarded as an ancestor. The broad, triangular leaves are lifted by a stem called the *hā,* which is also the word for "breath," so that each stem is an umbilicus, joining the plant world to the human.

As with *Li'a,* the making of *Listen to the Forest* was a looping journey of open-ended searches and fortunate meetings. Eddie was on Kaua'i, for example, when he heard about a man in his seventies named William Kūwalu, whose parents had been musicians early in the twentieth century and had passed on many songs about the island. A small and gentle man, he spoke the kind of soft, flowing Hawaiian Eddie likes to hear. He lived on the leeward side, near the town of Kekaha. After they'd talked awhile, William began to describe a trip he'd taken some sixty years earlier with his father and an uncle, up into the lush forest along the slopes of Mount Wai'ale'ale (famous as the wettest place on earth). It was May, when a certain species of lobelia was in full blossom, a species found only there, in Kaua'i's well-watered high country. They were searching for a specific tree that showed these blossoms to particular advantage and would be filled with the colorful *'ō'ō* and *'i'iwi* birds, the hummingbird-size honeysuckers with their needle-thin beaks.

It was a pilgrimage young William never forgot. The green-purple blossoms were open, clustered at the ends of curving

William Kūwalu of Kekaha, Kaua'i

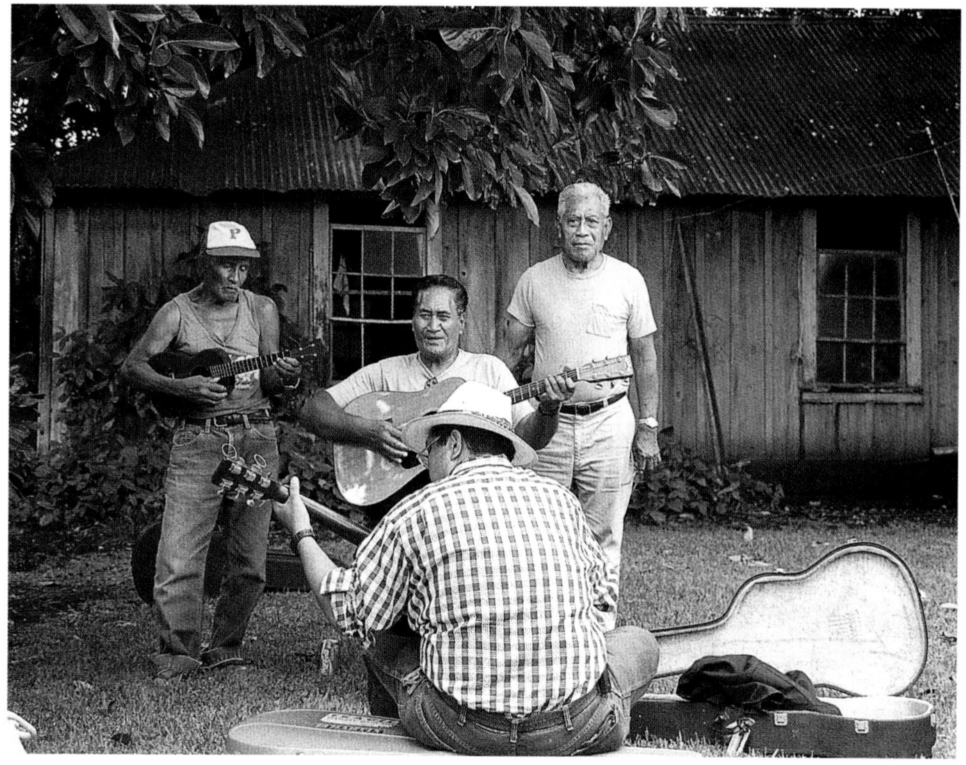

At Kekaha, while filming Listen to the Forest, *Dennis Kamakahi (foreground) made music with, left to right, William Kūwalu, Malaki Kanahele of Ni'ihau, and William's brother, Joseph Kūwalu Ka'ili.*

branches. The reddish orange *'i'iwi* were flitting from branch to branch, pausing to release their full-throated calls. William remembered asking his father, "What is the name of this tree?"

"Hāhā 'ai a ka manu," his father said, the sweet lobelia, food of the birds.

While they sat there, his uncle sang a song by that same name, already an old song back in the 1920s, composed to celebrate one tree, so beloved by local residents, and the forest birds that fed there. It also celebrates Wai'ale'ale, whose seldom-seen peak will sometimes show through laden clouds that hover almost constantly over the center of the island.

On the day William Kūwalu sang this song for Eddie, he said there were other verses he couldn't recall, but he knew a woman who might remember more than he did. Before flying home, Eddie arranged to meet her. She had a library of books on Hawaiian music, but none that mentioned "Hāhā 'Ai A Ka Manu." Eager to help, she called an aunt who lived in Līhu'e, and the aunt said, yes, she knew that song; she had learned it from her grandmother. For Eddie, she sang two verses over the phone. When he asked how he could gain permission to use those verses, she said, "Eh, I learned them from my grandmother twenty-five years ago. She was already eighty-one. This song comes from a long time back. Just go ahead. Sing it!"

Once again he'd uncovered some lyrics that otherwise might have drifted away with time. He'd also found the perfect song to convey how Hawaiians have used music to honor their uniquely populated habitat, a place where countless species of fauna and flora once proliferated free of predators and foreign interference.

The next time Eddie saw his friend Johnny Lum Ho, he asked him to choreograph an original *hula* based upon "Sweet Hāhā 'Ai A Ka Manu." It would become a featured sequence, with music provided by The Sons. And the following spring Eddie made a pilgrimage of his own, out along the slopes of Mount Wai'ale'ale, in search of the famed purple-green lobelia. He brought along his crew, to catch the rare flowering of this singular species and to catch the bird sounds. The tiny *'ō'ō,* alas, is now extinct. But the *'i'iwi* can still be heard. When Eddie says, "Listen to the forest," this is one of the voices he's talking about, the trilling warble of the reddish orange *'i'iwi,* among the last indigenous Hawaiian birds still with us.

To make this film, Eddie relied upon numerous experts, naturalists, field biologists, and elders such as "Papa" Henry 'Auwae, Hawai'i's most respected *kahuna lapa'au,* a master of Hawaiian medicine. Then in his eighties, Papa Henry lived near the Big Island town of Keaukaha, south of Hilo. For him the rainforest was nature's pharmacy, a sacred grove where herbs and leaves and strips of bark held healing powers, if you knew what to look for. As a child he'd been chosen by his great-grandmother to receive the knowledge that had come down to her through many generations. In his view, preserving the forest was essential to preserving the physical and spiritual health of his people.

Eddie with "Papa" Henry 'Auwae, in Keaukaha, 1991.

Eddie has a vivid memory of the day they met. He'd been talking with a friend about healing herbs, and the friend suggested Eddie meet Papa Henry. A phone call was made, and soon Eddie was knocking on his door. Henry was a husky bear of a man, still vigorous, who wore a simple short-sleeve shirt, his silver hair cut close to the scalp.

"He had those eyes that look right into you, and the first thing he said was 'You were chosen to do the work you are doing.' Later on I asked him why he said that, and you know what he told me? 'As soon as you walked in,' he said, 'I could see light around your head. You were giving off light.' That's the way it was with Henry. We never messed around with small talk. He told me, 'Sit down,' and then he said, 'Anything I can give you to help in your work, I will give you. It was the same with me. I was chosen to do this work.' I leaned forward and said to him, 'Can you tell me, what is the purpose of your work?' And he said something then that really affected me. He said, 'To care for the souls of my people.' I had never heard anyone say anything like that, except maybe in church when I was a little kid. As soon as he said it, I saw that for a long time I'd felt the same way about playing music. Not that I was anybody's savior. But there is something healing about music, too. When you're sick, sometimes it's the body. Sometimes it's the soul. Sometimes it is both. Sometimes music can help people make it through, when it's played with *aloha*. So it was important to meet Henry when I did. Talking with him helped me see where my film was going, and how it all connects—music, and healing, and what lives in the forest."

They went for a walk in a nearby grove, pausing every few steps while Henry identified a plant. "This is *'awa,*" he said, touching a shrub with green, pointed stems and heart-shaped leaves. "South Pacific people call it kava. Hawaiians call it *'awa.* It makes a drink you use for ceremonies when dignitaries visit. But it's also important for my medicinal work. I keep some growing right in my yard. It helps with toothache. You put a piece of *'awa* right in the area of decay. I also use the *'awa* to help people with hepatitis."[2]

"We call this one *'ie'ie,*" he said, touching the strand of a woody, branching climber. "It's usually been used to take care of women after they give birth. We make a tea for them to drink to control the flow of blood. We take the shoot out, we split the shoot in half, pound it, boil it in a quart of water . . ."

"This tree we call *lama.* It's a type of ebony. We use the bark. We blend it with the bark of that tree over there, the *'ōpiko,* to treat for heart problems, enlarged heart, or leaking heart."

As they strolled, Henry explained that knowing the plants was but one part of a three-way process. The plant has its power to heal. The healer must have his mind prepared, as he gathers the plant and directs its power toward the one seeking help. The patient meanwhile must bring a belief in both the healer and the medicine.

You don't go out seeking patients, Henry told him. You wait for them to ask. Once a person has come to you, you identify the ailment, then you wait for the right time, the right moon, to enter the forest. Before you leave the house, you pray for guidance and ask forgiveness. You go out early, so that by sunrise you have gathered your medicine. If you're taking bark or breaking off a branch, you take from the shaded side, because the tree's wound will heal faster if not exposed to direct sunlight in the heat of the day. And whatever the medicine, you never take more than is needed to cure this specific patient. Before you depart, you thank the tree or the bush, which is the source of the medicine. You ask it to help the one who came to you. You ask for a blessing, and while you pray you walk backward from the plant or the tree, in humility and gratitude, showing your respect. Finally, you turn and head home to dry the bark or boil the leaves or strip and mash the root to make a poultice.

In his firm, soft-spoken way Henry gave voice to an old ecological wisdom, summed up in the phrase *mālama 'āina,* "care for the earth." It would be at the center of the film-in-progress. When Eddie says, "Listen to the forest," he is also saying listen to what we can learn from our tradition, from a culture long grounded in respectful dialogue with the natural world.

It's a dialogue you hear in songs and stories, and see dramatized in the *hula,* an art form that goes back a thousand years and more. *Hula* began as narrative movement designed to enhance the meaning of the chanted legends, the genealogies, the stories of origin and migration, love and war. In pre-contact times it was a centerpiece of Hawaiian life, just as its twentieth-century revival was central to the renaissance. To open this film, Eddie called upon the prestigious Hilo dance troupe, Hālau O Kekuhi, known for its purity of performance. In the early minutes we see male and female dancers bedecked with ferns. They dance in the older style called *kahiko,* accompanied by a single drum and the vibrant chanting of a single female voice. In this style, moves can be as soft as mist or as startling as a thunderclap. The knees pop, the arms jut skyward, while the hands talk, making rivers, mountains, fluttering leaves.

The chanter is Pualani Kanaka'ole Kanahele, the *kumu hula* (teacher of the dance), a gracious and spirited woman, pure Hawaiian, with an infectious smile, a face both smooth and seasoned. Descended from generations of Big Island chanters and dancers, she comes from a much honored family that traces its lineage back to Pele herself, and the eruptive fires that shaped their island. As with Henry 'Auwae's work, the practice of Pualani's art and sacred calling is intimately connected to the forest.

 Typical of her teachings is the proper way to gather and bless the ferns and vines that decorate a dancer's body.

You go in early, she says, when the ferns are wet and fresh. You take only what you need to make your *lei* for that day, for that particular dance. And you always give thanks for what you take.

For her these plants are much more than lovely sprouts of forest greenery. Her rich, deep voice goes deeper as she says, "It's not just plants. It's part of us. It's Hawaiians. They've lived here all their lives, and they were here before we even got here. So we have to give them their respect of being the elders of the land, not come in and just pull them up because they cannot talk and tell us how to behave. Humans are supposed to have common sense. Some of the common sense we're supposed to have is how to take care of things."[3]

Toward the end of the one-hour documentary, Pualani speaks again, this time surrounded with emerald-green taro leaves. She wears a *kukui* nut necklace, with one white flower against abundant black hair that falls to her shoulders, as she speaks of the snails, insects, and honey-sipping forest birds featured elsewhere in the film, the ingenious variety of small creatures and delicate plants that define the rare ecology of these islands. Her eyes have seen everything, at once tender and generous and grieving and loving and fierce. And her voice, like Sam's and Papa Henry's, seems to speak for the whole island, as habitat, and as an ancestor who must be attended to and honored.

"All these creatures around us, they were here long before us. They are the real Hawaiians. I feel very sad when I look around and find the forest disappearing, because it's the true Hawaiians who came before us who are disappearing. And after they go . . . then we go next . . . we who are humans who call ourselves Hawaiians. The erosion process is happening. But we can stop it. We stop it by teaching our children to be sensitive to the creatures, to the plants around us, to the nature of this land . . . If the creatures live, then we live."

Over a hundred years ago John Muir, founder of the Sierra Club, expressed what would become the environmental movement's guiding idea. Speaking of the natural world, Muir said, "When we try to select out any one thing, we find that it is connected to everything else in the universe." And so it is in the mid-Pacific, though Eddie Kamae, in his second film, defines a distinctly Hawaiian ecology, wherein healing and *hula* and songs and ancestral ties are all part of the mix.

Listen to the Forest premiered at the Hawaii International Film Festival in November 1991. As with *Li'a,* it opened the week of screenings, then toured the outer islands with other recent films from the Asia/Pacific region, and played twice on Honolulu television. After receiving an Award of Recognition from the Hawai'i chapter of The Nature Conservancy, it was invited to the National Film and Video Festival hosted by the Oakland Museum.

That spring Eddie and Myrna also moved into high gear with an ambitious schools program they'd started four years earlier. The children of Hawai'i had long been a personal priority for Eddie. "If they can look at my films," he has said, "and begin to understand the wisdom the oldtimers have to share, then I have succeeded in what I set out to do."

Under the aegis of a newly formed nonprofit foundation, they donated 350 video cassettes to elementary, middle, and high schools throughout the islands—a contribution that would continue, from film to film, for years to come. They prepared a study guide that explores the links between song, dance, science, and ecology. Thirty-five hundred of these went to libraries, resource centers, and every school district office in the state. With support from the Department of Education's "Artists in the Schools" program, Eddie and various band members toured for three months, performing free of charge in auditoriums and cafeterias from Kaua'i to the Big Island, playing songs from the film and talking with kids about the forest and the importance of *mālama 'āina.*

The fellow who once dropped out of Farrington High School was back on campus, a kind of troubadour-professor, urging island youngsters to listen to the *'i'iwi* bird and listen to their elders. But as is usual with Eddie, three or four things were going on at once. Back in Honolulu, his next film was already in the works.

This time the subject was *kī hōʻalu,* that unique style of tuning and chording called slack-key. To his ear it was a quintessential Hawaiian sound, thus another way to get at something definitive about his people. Like the chant and the *hula* and the poignant call of the steel guitar, the slack-key sound is another way to express the fullness of the Hawaiian heart.

Eddie would bring to the project a lifetime of personal experience, from early childhood memories to his formative years with Gabby and beyond. Several famous guitarists would be featured, all musicians he knew and had worked with, among them Ledward Kaʻapana, George Kahumoku, Auntie Alice Nāmakelua (filmed in her eighties), National Heritage Award winner Raymond Kāne, and two virtuoso pickers still playing with The Sons, Dennis Kamakahi and George Kuo. But the emphasis would not be on celebrity performance for its own sake. The film would look at how this music works, how musicians regard it, and what it reveals about the cultural life. Prior films on Hawaiian music tended to point the camera at a well-known band, or sometimes several bands at a concert or festival, and let the songs and instruments speak for themselves. Eddie wanted to take it to the next level, get in closer to the sources and the mystique.

opposite
Slack-key master Raymond Kāne, circa 1990.

He chose, for example, to film performers not in clubs or in concert settings, but in the backyards where this style of playing had been nurtured for a hundred years, and in the kitchens and living rooms where tunings and finger stylings are still passed along from one generation to the next. Once again his searches took him "out there," to the Big Island's upcountry Kohala district, to Molokaʻi, to remote Niʻihau, about as far as one can get from Honolulu and the music industry's commercial center. While voice-over narration describes the intimate, soothing sound itself, called *nahenahe,* characterized by a steady and resonant acoustic halo, the screen is filled with a guitarist's picking hand, the roving thumb, above the quivering of vibrant, open strings.

Throughout this film, vivid footage of open terrain, rural

Manu Kaha'iali'i and family at home on Maui in the late 1980s while filming The Hawaiian Way. *Willie (known to his many fans as "Willie K"), Manu, John, Ipo, and Nalani.*

valleys, and gleaming shorelines links the slack-key sound to a profound reverence for the *'āina,* the earth of these islands and their many inspirational features. Eddie interviewed Maui community leader and veteran guitarist, Manu Kaha'iali'i, who summed it up this way: "*Kī hō'alu* stems from the echo of winds and the rattle of leaves and sweet sound of our mountains . . . and when you play it you're not only playing for yourself, you're playing for all those who played before you, your grandparents and those who have taught you. They are right there with you, and they are saying, 'Hey, listen to that music! I *know* that music!'"[4]

They finished editing early in 1993. Eddie and Myrna called it *The Hawaiian Way,* which refers to the slack-key style, as well as to a certain way of being in the world. You might say it refers to the film, too, which had brought into clearer focus the nature of his approach to the medium. For Eddie and Myrna, *The Hawaiian Way* helped to clarify the path in front of them, a path that would be marked by an ongoing sequence of documentaries they now named "The Hawaiian Legacy Series."

Each one had been introduced by Eddie, as the personal quest of a man of Hawaiian ancestry in search of some essential truth about his own people. In each film there was an emphasis on music as a key, much of it performed by The Sons. There was the persuasive flow of Ka'upena's off-camera voice, the outdoor and rural settings that keep the natural world ever present, the intimate glimpses of family places and Hawaiian faces.

People who'd been following Eddie's work felt the time had come for some wider form of recognition, perhaps linked to the year 1993, which happened to be another of those emblematic moments in the reawakening of island consciousness. It was the one-hundredth anniversary of the overthrow of Queen Lili'u-okalani, which had ended the rule of Hawai'i by Hawaiians. In January there was a march and a rally in front of 'Iolani Palace, reigniting the long debate about the sovereign rights of native peoples. Throughout the year there would be forums and public meetings. Magazines and newspapers ran features covering the century of political and social change. President Bill Clinton chose 1993 as the year to sign a bill returning control of the small island of Kaho'olawe to the state, whereupon the legislature designated it a protected cultural and historic site. Clinton's bill ended a twenty-year struggle between Hawaiian activists and the U.S. Navy, which had been using the uninhabited island as a bombing and gunnery range since the early days of World War II.

The United Nations chose 1993 to be the International Year of Indigenous Peoples, and this in turn stirred a desire in Hawai'i's congressional delegation to bring something from the islands to the nation's capital, an event in keeping with this symbolic year.

One thing quickly led to another. Festival director Jeannette Paulson made some calls to the East Coast. The Visitors Bureau offered to help with travel. That May, Eddie and Myrna and the boys in the band were on their way to Washington, D.C., where *The Hawaiian Way* would have its premiere at the Kennedy Center. Retrospective screenings of *Li'a* and *Listen to the Forest* would follow, during a day devoted to Eddie's work, co-sponsored by the American Film Institute.

Hawaiian Day at Kennedy Center, May 8, 1993. Left to right: George Kuo, Dennis Kamakahi, Eddie, Braddah Smitty Smith, Gary Haleamau.

First stop was an afternoon reception on the fourth floor of the Hart Senate Office Building, hosted by Reps. Patsy Mink and Neil Abercrombie, together with Sens. Daniel Inouye and Daniel Akaka, the first native Hawaiian ever elected to national office. Heaped with *lei,* each member of Congress spoke. There was Hawaiian music on the soundtrack. Friends and supporters who'd flown in from Honolulu mingled with staffers and guests, sipping and nibbling at a buffet spread much like you'd see at a festive reception in the islands—jumbo prawns, spring rolls, sushi, sashimi, slices of pineapple and papaya, and teriyaki chicken wings—with springtime light streaming in across the treetops of the city.

The next day, called "Hawaiian Day at Kennedy Center," the AFI theater was jammed. The local community of expatriate islanders was represented by Mahina Bailey, composer and *kumu hula,* who'd lived in Washington for many years. In chanter's robes he delivered an opening Oli Aloha, his voice seeming to travel across time and across the far water to still the room and charge the air. Next came the long ritual call of a conch shell, summoning Clayton Hee. As chairman of Honolulu's Office of Hawaiian Affairs, which also co-sponsored this event, he welcomed the crowd.

Then The Sons took the stage, in their *lei* and red-checked *palaka* shirts. Eddie always figures the best way to introduce a film is to play some music. "It gets folks in the right mood," he says. "You come there, play with *aloha,* when the lights go down they're ready to see what's on the screen, and ready to hear."

The musicians he brought along had all performed in *The Hawaiian Way*—Dennis, Braddah Smitty, George Kuo, and Big Island guitarist Gary Hale'ama'u, famous both for his slack-key stylings and his heart-breaking falsetto. It became a kind of slack-key concert, with expert picking and Hawaiian lyrics to cast their spell. For the finale they brought out Sheldeen Hale'ama'u, Gary's young wife, and one of Hawai'i's most elegant dancers. She, too, appears in the film. At a recent Merrie Monarch Festival in Hilo she'd been named Miss Aloha Hula, a soloist's highest honor. She is one of those dancers whose effortlessly supple moves seem to be creating themselves. Her flowing hands and fluid hips held the audience transfixed, while five of the islands' best musicians filled the theater with the spirit of the music about to be celebrated on the screen. When the lights went down—as Eddie had predicted—the room was ready.

Afterward there was talk of taking the films and the band on a national tour. Maybe Europe, too. Jeanne Firstenberg, AFI's director, had given the "Hawaiian Legacy Series" an international dimension, calling it "an outstanding example of the many distinctive voices of innovative filmmakers from the Pacific, Asia, and America that the Institute is committed to support. These documentaries share the legacies of past generations with future generations from many countries and many cultures. Through the universal language of the moving image, they foster hope for even greater understanding between nations throughout the world."[5]

For Eddie it was a true high point, to have his work featured at the Kennedy Center in the middle of the Year of Indigenous Peoples, the first filmmaker of Hawaiian ancestry to be acknowledged at such a level. And yet, for all the heady atmosphere of the capital, he was already itching to get back to the islands. Never one to revel in large pronouncements, he was half-wishing he'd stayed home, where the next project was well under way: a film about a group of Hawai'i's finest composers. Getting close to the sources of slack-key had opened his ears to a new kind of hearing, to his own next level of musical awareness. The next film's opening scene had finally come to him.

On the morning of the day of screenings, he and Myrna were booked to do a radio interview, but something else was on Eddie's mind. They'd just stepped out of an elevator and into the buzzing lobby of the Sheraton, when he remembered a sound he'd heard a hundred times yet had never understood or even thought much about.

"Myrna, I just realized something. Write this down."

"Okay."

"It starts with the rocks."

"What starts?"

"Hawaiian music."

She looked at him, pen poised above her spiral notebook.

"You remember that cove on the Big Island?" he said. "Out by Smitty's place, north Kohala, where the whole beach is covered with round black rocks?"

"You mean Kupainaha?"

"That's it. There's a sound when the tide is high and the swell comes through the rocks so they clink, the surf rushing, and the whole beach clinking—not a hard clink, the soft kind you get when it's old porous lava that's rolled a long time in the surf . . . Are you writing this down?"

"As fast as I can."

"Well, that's it! That's where the whole thing starts. That sound right there. It's the first Hawaiian song!"

Eddie and Myrna at Waikahalulu in 2003.

BIG ISLAND MYSTERIES *You know, I've spent almost all my life here in Honolulu, born here, grew up here. Myrna and me, we been in the same building now, I guess, twenty-five years. But I keep going over to the other islands every chance I can. And it's not just to get out of the city for a while. Things happen over there that are different from what happens in Honolulu. Especially on the Big Island. Over there everything is different. It's wild country. They got the craters and the lava. They got their own music. They got their own stories. When I'm on the Big Island I hear stories like I never hear anywhere else.*

I know this one Hawaiian man, my friend Harry, he is in his eighties now. He knew Sam Li'a. He knew Luther Makekau. A few years back Harry was feeling a lot of pain in his head, his shoulders, down his arms. He went to see a Chinese doctor in Hilo who took some tests and came back with the results. It was cancer, he said, a brain tumor. Maybe they could try surgery, but it was already pretty far gone.

Harry didn't like the idea of surgery. He never went to a hospital in his life and figured he was too old to start. So he went back home to his place in Kohala, up on the north end of the island, where he lived by himself. His wife had passed away. According to what Harry told me, the next night a voice come to him in his sleep. He calls it his "Hawaiian voice." The voice tells him to get up and go outside. So Harry does that. He goes out into his yard and says, "What now? Where should I go?" And the voice says, "Go this way," guiding him across the yard and down the road and across a bridge above the stream, then out into the forest.

"Follow this path," the voice tells him, and Harry follows the path in the dark until the voice says, "Go over to that tree and stop." So Harry does that, and the voice says, "Now pick some leaves from that tree. Take some bark. This is what you need."

Harry takes the leaves and bark back to his house. The voice tells him how to prepare it and how to take it. For thirty days Harry goes back to that same tree and does the same thing. After a month all his pain is gone away. He goes back to Hilo to see the Chinese doctor, who checks him out and takes some tests and x-rays, and comes back to Harry and says it's amazing.

"There's nothing there," the doctor says. "All signs of the tumor went away." He'd never seen anything like it!

Some people might say Harry's "Hawaiian voice" was just Harry waking up in the middle of the night remembering things he already knew about what's out there in the forest. But either way, the medicine still worked. The day he told me this story, you would never believe he was eighty-six years old. His skin was so smooth, he looked like he was forty-five.

Princess Miriam Likelike (1851–1887), younger sister of Queen Lili'uokalani.

12

Who Was Guiding Me?

In the early days, when he first went into libraries and museums, Eddie was often looking for a single verse, for one lost melody. Year by year his researches had broadened, leading him into other realms of island life. *Listen to the Forest* had its roots in the songs, in their nature imagery, the celebration of places. He had embarked upon the slack-key project believing the sound itself reveals the essence of the Hawaiian soul. In each case, the making of the film had become, for Eddie, a personal journey and lesson.

Now he had in mind a documentary that would move beyond slack-key and examine the multiple sources of Hawai'i's long musical tradition, something not previously tried on film. It would honor the Hawaiian gift for transmuting foreign influences into a music that continues to be their own. And as this new project unfolded, other layers of Eddie's own past would be reclaimed. His past had been there all along, a region of distant voices, barely audible, but growing louder, getting closer.

Once again it was a season in his life marked by the passing of a member of the band. At age sixty-three Joe Marshall died. Like the passing of Feet Rogers, it brought Eddie to a temporary standstill. Among the original members he and Joe had been the closest in age. They'd been friends and fellow performers for over thirty years. At first Eddie thought the time had finally come to let the performing go.

"I went to the wake," he says, "where Joe's brother-in-law was the minister. I went up to the pulpit and shared my last conversation with Joe, about a morning when I stopped by to see him where he worked as a security guard. He was outside

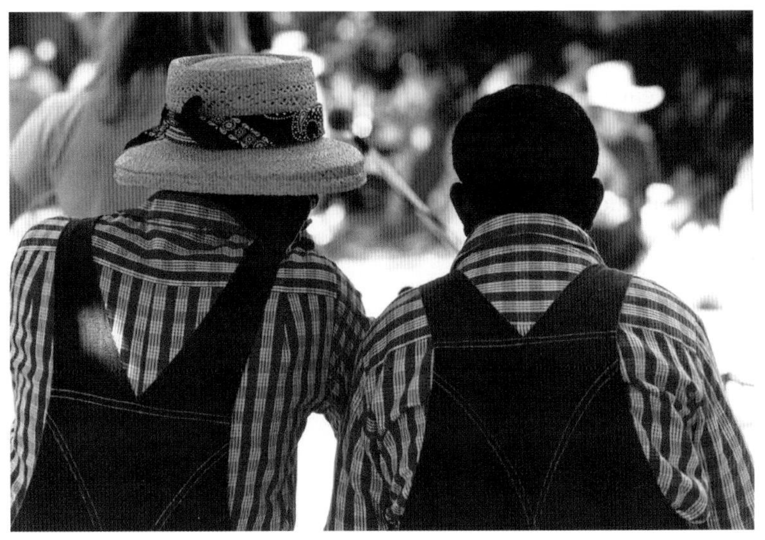

Feet Rogers and Joe Marshall, between sets, circa 1975.

his shack in his uniform, feeding the birds, and he says to me with that bossy tone of his, like he's giving me an order, 'Pops, I want no tears. I just want joy.' I said, 'What are you talking about?' Joe says, 'You know what I'm talking about. No tears. No pain. Just joy and happiness.' I told him, 'I don't know what you're talking about, so just cut it out.' But I did know. So did Joe. He could feel it in his body. It was just a few days later he slumped over, right there in the security guard shack in the middle of his shift. He had emphysema, you know. He always smoked too much. Anyhow, at the wake, I told them what I knew was Joe's last wish, that we celebrate his time with joy and *aloha.* After that I told myself this was the end. I don't have to work no more trying to set up gigs and worry about the business. I was thinking how Gabby had passed away back in 1980, just dropped dead on the golf course one morning when he was fifty-nine. Then Feet went. Then Joe. So I'm the last one, and now I can just tell the story."

Around this time Dennis Kamakahi and George Kuo were both approached by Dancing Cat, a new label out of Santa Cruz,

California. George Winston, the keyboard star and founder of Windham Hill Records, had been listening to Hawaiian music since the early 1970s, first awakened to its pleasures by a copy of The Sons' "Five Faces" album. He'd picked it up by chance while browsing one day at Tower Records on Sunset Boulevard.[1] Before long he'd discovered slack-key, developed a passion for its sound, and now he was starting to record the best island performers, asking them to play the tunes they most wanted to play. He had equipment that would enhance the intimacy and technical skill, and he was ready to give this music a big push, nationally and around the world. Called "The Slack Key Guitar Masters Series," it had opened with CDs by Sonny Chillingworth and Raymond Kāne and would soon include Cyril Pahinui (Gabby's oldest son), Ledward Ka'apana, Leonard Kwan, Keola Beamer, and George and Moses Kahumoku. It would become the biggest exposure for Hawaiian music since the heyday of the 1930s. For Dennis and George it was the kind of break every musician dreams about.

"By that time," Eddie says, "Dennis and me been together almost twenty years. George been playing with us going on ten. But The Sons, we're not doing any recording, and this was too good to pass up. I told them both it was time to move on. I said, 'Go. Do it. Make the most of it.' They went up to the mainland and recorded for Dancing Cat. Then they went all over the place with their CDs, doing concerts, the Hollywood Bowl, over to Japan."

For The Sons of Hawaii, it was the end of an era. But as things turned out, it was not the end of the band. While Eddie grieved for Joe Marshall, he couldn't really stop playing. He didn't want to stop. He was still a performer, a singer, a composer, an arranger. The band he'd led for all these years had shaped a big part of his life. The sound itself was a source of continuity. While the personnel had changed, the sound had continued from year to year, the mix of strings, fine musicianship, traditional lyrics, Hawaiian voices tightly blended.

He was still in touch with Braddah Smitty Smith. And Smitty had a good friend, Charlie Mahi, who lived in Hilo, a bassist and vocalist who sat in from time to time when The Sons had

Eddie with Braddah Smitty on the Big Island in 1998 to film The Sons of Hawaii.

a Big Island gig. On O'ahu there was another bassist who'd apprenticed with Joe, sometimes filling in on days when ill health kept Joe at home. A big, handsome fellow, with classic Hawaiian features, Ocean Kaowili was, for Eddie, something of a young Joe Marshall. He had picked up Joe's bass style. He, too, had attended Kamehameha School, had sung in the glee club there, and had his own affection for the early melodies.

Ocean's voice was deep, a rich baritone, soon to be balanced by the higher range of a new singer Eddie had started listening to. Pekelo Cosma had grown up in Hāna, on Maui's windward side, still lived there, and in 1994 had recorded his first solo album, *Pekelo's Hāna Jam.* On some of the cuts his voice was so similar to Gabby Pahinui's it carried Eddie back in time. He had to meet this fellow, and when he did, he discovered that Pekelo, like Dennis Kamakahi, had been listening to the music of The Sons from childhood. He had a connection to the band that went all the way back to the Ho'olaule'a Eddie and his friends had staged at Hāna in the spring of 1970. Ten years old that day, Pekelo had found himself captivated by the vitality of the band, and especially by Gabby, his wit, his style, his poignant voice slipping in and out of a tender falsetto.

"You know, it was funny," Pekelo recalls, "right while The Sons were playing, all the kids were going down to the beach watching this lady who was swimming in the water, swimming nude. There was this manta ray out there with its wings flapping. The kids were yelling at this lady to get out, get out! So for the kids, all this excitement was going on down at the water. But The Sons were playing, too. And Gabby was singing. I had to choose whether to go with the other guys or stay and listen to the music. I chose to stay, and that was such an important day for me. He really inspired me from that day on."[2]

In the intervening years Pekelo had perfected his own vocal style and also mastered slack-key guitar. When he and Eddie

The Sons play on (left to right): Ocean Kaowili, Smitty Smith, Eddie, Pekelo Cosma.

finally played a gig together, they found it was an effortless match. Before long the next incarnation of the band had found its shape, with Eddie on *'ukulele,* Ocean Kaowili on bass—or sometimes Charlie Mahi—Braddah Smitty on rhythm guitar, and Pekelo playing slack-key. Dennis and George would still sit in from time to time, if they happened to be in town. It would no longer be a full-time band. Pekelo played on Maui when he could. On the Big Island Smitty and Charlie had a trio of their own. Ocean sat in with other groups. They weren't taking long-term gigs, or cutting records, or touring. But if a concert came along, if it was time to cut the soundtrack for a film, or to travel with the film to a festival or to a special screening, Eddie had a group of like-minded performers he could call on, musicians who could deliver a sound he loved to hear.

Joe's passing had settled something. From now on, Eddie's main job would be to "tell the story," traveling among the islands to seek out elders, teachers, native speakers, gathering footage for his "Hawaiian Legacy Series." Music making would still have a part in this, since for Eddie music had always been his primary link to the culture. The work in progress, for example, grew out of his affection for certain songs he'd come to know in a visceral way, with the kind of understanding that is felt in the throat and in the play of fingers across a fretboard. He felt a kinship with the composers of these songs, whose poetry and melodies spoke to him almost person to person. They wrote in Hawaiian and, like Sam Li'a, they thought in Hawaiian.

It occurred to Eddie that through their songs one could chart a century of extraordinary adaptation. Such a film could start with the clink of surf-rolled stones in a remote cove well known to Big Island dancers who came in search of their *'ili'ili.* These stones are small and flat enough to be held, two in each hand, and used like castanets, to accompany *hula* and chant. As a basic piece of both nature and culture, the handheld stones introduce a percussive and vocal tradition that goes back two thousand years and more.

Early in the nineteenth century ancient rhythms began to merge with new instruments and other voices arriving by ship from farflung ports around the globe—violins from Germany, guitars from Spain and Mexico, gospel harmonies traveling around Cape Horn with the missionaries from New England. While many features of island life were gradually overwhelmed by foreign influence, something else happened in the realm of music. Thanks to an innate eclectic genius, this fusion gave rise to new forms of expression. The melodies were Western, the words and poetry would continue to be Hawaiian.

A key figure in this unfolding process was Alfred Unauna 'Alohikea, one of Eddie's favorite composers. Still known by many as "The Poet Laureate of Kaua'i," he was a taro farmer, a fisherman, a self-taught musician, and a charismatic showman with a taste for politics. From the mid-1920s until his death in 1936, he represented Kaua'i in the Territorial House of Representatives. But he is most remembered for songs that pay tribute to the spectacular terrain around Hanalei, on Kaua'i's north shore, songs filled with mist and cloud-layered peaks and rain-drenched moments that bring two lovers together.

'Alohikea composed dozens that hold a classic place in today's repertoire, songs written in the older poetic style, rich with word-play and double meaning. Among the best known is "Hanohano Hanalei," an excellent example of how 'Alohikea combined traditional sources with the music coming toward him from the mainland in the early twentieth century, the imported rhythms of ragtime and jazz.

The song has its origins in a welcoming chant composed in the 1880s for Queen Kapi'olani, the wife of King Kalākaua, when she returned to her family's island on a mission to promote the welfare of Hawaiian children. It's also an island-praising chant, in four stanzas, each keyed to a district of Kaua'i. The first stanza, celebrating the region around Hanalei, begins with these lines:

Hanohano Hanalei i ka ua nui
I pakika kahi limu o Manu'akepa

Majestic Hanalei in the pouring rain,
slippery with the moss of Manu'akepa . . .

Alfred 'Alohikea (1884–1936), the "Poet Laureate of Kaua'i," with the Wai'oli Church Choir, Hanalei, Kaua'i, circa 1921. Alfred is the tall fellow in the middle of the back row.

Thirty-five years later Alfred 'Alohikea used these same lines to open an upbeat, toe-tapping song of place that is also a song of love. In the next two lines, weather and courtship begin to intertwine:

I laila ho'i au i 'ike iho ai,
I ka hana hu'i konikoni i ka 'ili.

It was there I felt the chill
that penetrates the skin . . .

To help tell 'Alohikea's story Eddie called on Andy Cummings, the veteran composer and popular bandleader. Then in his eighties, still spry and alert, and ready to break into song at a moment's notice, Cummings had grown up on Kaua'i and had sung with the composer in his early years.

"I was seventeen," he said, "and he decided to take me under his wing and tutor me, teach me how to say the Hawaiian correctly. He was the finest single performer in Hawai'i that I have ever seen. And he was also a stickler for enunciation—and pronunciation!—to be distinct when you're saying the words. He always said the words were the most important part."[3]

When Cummings moved to Honolulu, he brought 'Alohikea's songs with him, including them in the repertoires of bands and combos he would lead from the 1930s onward. It was under Cummings's tutelage that Gabby Pahinui had learned 'Alohikea's songs, while playing with his Hawaiian Serenaders during the 1940s and 1950s. Gabby, in turn, brought them to the early jam sessions in Waimānalo, so that these musical poems from the north shore of Kaua'i were among the Hawaiian songs that first touched Eddie.

Here was another type of lineage—from performer to performer—another way that music survived from one era to the next, to feed the renaissance that would soon begin to flower. 'Alohikea's songs would be among the standards performed by The Sons of Hawaii from 1959 onward: "Hanalei Bay" (recorded on their first album), "Ka Ua Loku" (The Pouring Rain), "Pua Lilia" (The Lily Flower), "Nāmolokama" (honoring the great, flat-topped mountain that rises beyond the town).

"I always loved 'Alohikea's music," Eddie says. "Something about it just wakes you up! It's a kind of writing you don't hear much anymore. He was a man who joined the old with the new. Whenever I sing a song composed in that way, I know I help to keep the poetry alive. It's still in there, you know. There's music in the language, and it gives the song more life."

An earlier composer with a central role in this film is Queen Lili'uokalani, for whom Eddie holds a special reverence. She had come of age in the previous generation, just as the first waves of Western music reached her islands: Christian hymns, Spanish dances, light opera, folk songs, brass bands, pianos, bass drums, and bugles. While 'Alohikea was the self-taught son of a taro farmer, she was of the chiefly class, schooled in chant and oral poetry. At the same time she was among the first Hawaiians to receive an English education, beginning at the Chiefs' Children's School in Honolulu. Enrolled in 1842 at the age of four, she soon learned scales, chords, and harmony. A precocious sight-reader, she learned piano early and probably did her first composing there.

Lili'uokalani was part of a family of talented performers, all of whom composed songs still heard today: her sister Miriam Likelike and her brothers, William Leleiōhoku and David Kalākaua. But she was the most gifted of this group, sometimes called Nā Lani 'Ehā (The Four Chiefs). She was the most prolific and would eventually become the first Hawaiian composer to write down her songs, with both lyrics and accurate musical notation, thus the first to cross from oral poetry to the written page. She was the first Hawaiian composer to have a song published anywhere in the world: in 1869 the Oliver Ditson Company in Boston brought out "Nani Nā Pua" (Beautiful Are the Flowers). In 1878 she composed her famous song of farewell, "Aloha 'Oe," becoming the first island composer to be widely heard outside Hawai'i.

For Eddie, she was the first composer whose work caught his attention, when singer Haunani Kahalewai showed him the sheet music for "Ku'u Pua I Paoakalani" back in the late 1950s. A few years later, it was his compulsion to track down a melody that led him to the Bishop Museum, where he discovered that he had heard the queen's song "Tūtū." That fateful expedition had launched his lifelong pursuit of the messages lodged within the lyrics of these old Hawaiian songs.

And now that search was about to take another unexpected turn. The gathering of materials for this new film had sent him back to the museum, back to the archive of song sheets and notebooks and wax cylinders. He was looking for graphics, perhaps a manuscript page, to accompany some voice-over narration about the royal four, Nā Lani 'Ehā. Working his way through a box of elderly pages encased in glassine folders, he came across a document that sent chills through his body. It was the handwritten copy of a chant composed in Lahaina in 1868. The author was the queen's sister, Princess Likelike. Its title was "He Inoa No Kamae" (A Name Chant for Kamae). And it was dedicated to her grandmother, a woman named Kamae-o-ka-lani. Composed in four-line stanzas, the chant begins like this:

He inoa nō kēia
No ka wahine la'i o ka uka
I walea I ke kui pua
Pua lei Kāmakahala

This is indeed a name chant
for the serene lady of the uplands
who is adept at stringing flower lei,
flowers for the Kāmakahala lei

Eddie was astounded. The grandmother of Likelike and Lili'u-okalani had been named Kamae! It could mean that somewhere around the generation of his great-great-grandparents, there might have been a connection he'd never known about. In his family all the records from that far back were gone; genealogies had been forgotten. One thing was certain, though: Kamae is not a common name. He dug a little deeper and found that Kamae-o-ka-lani had been from the Big Island, perhaps with ties to Waipi'o and the region where Eddie's father and grandfather and great-grandfather had lived. Her husband, 'Aikanaka, was a chief from O'ahu, but descended from 'Umi-a-Līloa, Waipi'o's legendary leader, whose chiefly compound once stood along the beach where Eddie and Myrna had picnicked with Sam on the day they met.

This discovery started him thinking again about the song he'd heard in the marketplace in Kailua in 1961, how he went and woke up 'Iolani Luahine, then curator at the Royal Mausoleum in Nu'uanu, to ask if she recognized this song. She had told him to go see Tūtū, and he had thought she meant, "Go see Kawena." But as he was driving out of the manicured grounds and past the graves of Hawai'i's last royal family, something told him to change his course and head for the Bishop Museum, a place he'd never visited, at a time of day when its doors weren't open to the public. Yet the librarian happened to be there early and let him in, and that was how he had come upon the queen's packet of manuscripts tied with twine. The first song he turned to was the one he'd come looking for, composed by Lili'uokalani, an affectionate portrait of her *tūtū,* her grandmother, who—Eddie now surmised—may well have been the woman Likelike wrote her chant for, a woman named Kamae.

"It still makes me wonder," Eddie says now, "about that early morning forty years ago. They're all buried there, you know, Lili'uokalani, Likelike, the two brothers. And when I drove past those graves, somebody or something told me where to go. How do you explain stuff like that? Who was guiding me toward her song? Maybe it was some older voice, maybe an ancestor telling me where to go to find the name and the words, and from there all the rest of the songs down through the years, setting me on the course I have followed ever since."

DRAGONFLIES *A while back I noticed that everywhere I go, dragonflies follow me. I can be walking along by myself on a road over on the Big Island, and a dragonfly will show up right by my head. Sometimes they show up in front of my windshield while I'm at a stoplight, and just hang there on the other side of the glass like they came to check up on me. Myrna will say, "There's your* pinao, *Eddie, there's your dragonfly for today."*

Once I was back in Mānoa Valley at a place I like to go and sit and think, and all of a sudden half a dozen dragonflies were all around me. I couldn't believe it, everywhere I turned.

I guess what really got my attention was the time we were on Maui to play a concert. We stayed overnight at a motel. The next morning we're packing to get out of there and catch the plane back to Honolulu, and I see this dragonfly right outside my window. Its wings are quivering. It hangs in the air, shiny blue and green. I go over to look at it, and it doesn't move. The window is open. There are hibiscus flowers outside. I pull a chair up close and sit down and watch the dragonfly until my bass player Joe Marshall knocks on the door.

"Eddie," he says, "we gotta leave in five minutes."

Part of Joe was like the scoutmaster. He was the one who worried about getting everybody to a certain place at a certain time. I said, "Okay." But I didn't move, because that dragonfly was only about twelve inches away from me, and it wasn't moving. I sat there looking it right in the eyes, and pretty soon Joe is banging on the door again.

"Eddie! C'mon! We got all our stuff in the cars. We don't leave now, we gonna miss the plane!"

"Go on, then. I'll catch up with you."

"Whaddya mean, catch up?"

"I mean, I'm busy."

"What's going on in there?"

"I said I'm busy."

So they went on to the airport, and I sat there watching the dragonfly suspended in midair and watching me back. Another half-hour went by, maybe more, before it finally lifted up and flew away.

Then I had to call a cab. By the time I got to the airport, I missed the plane and had to wait for a later flight, but it was worth it because I finally understood something. Whenever I see the pinao, *I feel like there's no problem during that day. Everything is going to work out. And you know,* it does! *If you're on your way to a job somewhere, you hope everybody will show up, but you never know for sure. If I see my* pinao, *I know everything will go the way it's supposed to go.*

I asked some people about this, and they say the pinao *is my* 'aumakua, *an ancestral spirit guarding me. I don't know about that for sure. You see, on my mother's side it's the* mano, *the shark. All I know is, I see my* pinao *and things happen. Everything just opens up the right way. Things I hope for and wish for, they appear. I don't know how to explain it. But I have seen it so many times, all I can say is, "It's my friend," and I let it go at that.*

Ho'omau

They called the new film, *Words, Earth and Aloha: The Sources of Hawaiian Music.* This time the edited video footage was blown up to 35 mm, which gave the color more life and seemed to open out the sound. After the film's Honolulu premiere in 1995, the festival judges chose it for a Silver Maile Award. Sponsored by *American Film* magazine, and named for the fragrant vine found in upland rain forests, this award had been established two years earlier to encourage the new growth of film production in the islands. At a ceremony in the Monarch Room of the Royal Hawaiian Hotel, Eddie as director and Myrna as producer were heaped with *lei* and named "Hawai'i's Film Makers of the Year."

It was another time to celebrate. Yet for Eddie, the more meaningful moment had been the less public one, the discovery of Likelike's chant, composed in 1868, and what it seemed to verify, as if some wheel had come full circle, an unseen pattern suddenly made clear. Call it a message. Call it a synchronicity. It was another validation that he was on the right path, the kind of sign that kept him going from project to project. And he had five ahead of him now, five more documentaries in various stages of development, emerging from the hundreds of hours of video footage piling up in the apartment. Somehow they all lived together in his roaming imagination. Each idea seemed so urgent, he wished he knew how to produce five films at once. But he would have to take them singly, and they would come the way the albums came back in the 1970s after Eddie set up his own label.

First in line was the story he had promised to tell. *Luther*

 Kahekili Makekau: A One Kine Hawaiian Man premiered in 1997. Next they brought out *Hawaiian Voices* (1998). As Eddie's tribute to the spoken language and its essential role in the continuity of culture, this was another outgrowth of his long involvement with songs and lyrics and the work begun in 1960 with Kawena Pukui and Pīlahi Pākī. Following soon would be another musical documentary, the forty-year history of his influential band. And meanwhile, at the time of this writing, he was taking his cameras to Maui, to develop a film about Lahaina.

In the way that Sam Li'a was an emblematic Hawaiian man, and the slack-key sound an emblematic feature of Hawaiian music, Lahaina is, for Eddie, an emblematic region, containing in capsule form the whole history of these islands. By turns a capital of the kingdom, a major whaling port, a plantation and sugarmill town, and the home for contract workers from China, Japan, and the Philippines, it has become a tourist mecca, now trying to redefine itself, reimagine its relationship to a nearly lost heritage. At the center of this effort, near the center of the town, and central to Eddie's film-in-progress, there lies one of Hawai'i's most significant archeological sites. Once sacred and soon to be restored, the pond and island called Moku'ula was an ancient burial ground and habitat of chiefs, but since the 1920s had been completely covered by a softball field.

This complex legacy merges with Eddie's earliest memories of Lahaina as the region where his father met his mother, where both his father and grandfather went to school, where a raised oblong of lava stones marks his grandmother's grave. From that hallowed spot he can look toward the same view that filled his boyhood summers, six-thousand-foot Pu'u Kukui, west Maui's highest peak standing against the sky. In the long valley rising toward that peak the same rainbows arc through gauzy mist.

Once again Eddie's choice of material has combined a cultural search with a personal journey. In that sense his work and his life have been one and the same, a series of returnings, reclaimings, reawakenings to the people and places that have shaped his path. In the early years, looking past the imported mainland sounds that first appealed to him, he found a deeper grounding in Hawai'i's song-making tradition, and with that he helped to forge a musical renaissance. As he then moved from one medium to the next, he brought with him a Hawaiian way of seeing that offered guidance to new generations of island filmmakers.

Whatever the subject, he has stayed true to his original goal of preserving the voices, the gestures, the faces, songs, and memories of a generation of elders who are rapidly passing away. Though the traditional values of these people are as endangered as any of the species in the rainforest, those who voice them—the *kūpuna,* the singers, the dancers, the teachers, the storytellers—are never portrayed as victims. We see their compassion, their creativity, their dignity, their will for cultural survival, each film an affirmation of what it is to be Hawaiian.

Now move across the water from Maui to O'ahu, and move forward in time to another day when another part of Eddie's life will come full circle. It is March 23, 2000, four o'clock in the afternoon. In the atrium of Honolulu Hale, city hall, rows of chairs are filling up, underneath the high rotunda. The Commission on Culture and the Arts for the City and County of Honolulu is launching a series of annual awards to individuals and organizations who have contributed to the cultural life of the islands. As one of the first two recipients, Eddie is sitting in front of the podium, worrying about what he is going to say.

He almost didn't show up for this. "I'm too busy," he told Myrna. "I have too many things on my mind to drive all the way downtown and park my car and walk over there and have to say hello to all those people, and have to get up in front of the mike. It breaks my concentration. What am I supposed to say? Why can't I just stay home?"

Then he learned that some of his relatives were going to be there to wish him well, along with some of the musicians he had played with over the years, and that the other recipient would be Barbara Smith. She founded the Ethnomusicology Department at the University of Hawai'i and built it into a world-class program, all the while promoting musical awareness among Hawai'i's numerous ethnic communities. Fifty years ago, soon after she joined the faculty, and when Eddie was just starting out, she was the young teacher who traded *'ukulele* lessons for tutoring in music theory and chord structure.

Mayor Jeremy Harris welcomes the crowd, telling them these awards have been established to "recognize our living treasures, and to thank them for enriching lives throughout Hawai'i, for improving the quality of life for all our people."

Listening from the front row, Eddie feels the pressure building. Again he wonders if coming down here was the right thing to do. He worries until it's his turn to move to the podium. As he stands up, the city hall is filled with the sound of Moe Keale's voice. It's a musical salute to The Sons of Hawaii—the opening track from their "Five Faces" album, which has been visible again on record racks on all the islands, heard on the radio, and featured in stores going on two years now, ever since the CD rerelease. The first song is "No Ke Ano Ahiahi," a nostalgic ballad of ocean travel. It is preceded by a lusty sailor's call, chanted by Moe with great vigor:

> *E nā luina! Huki mai i ka heleuma!*
> *E ho'omākaukau e holo aku!*
>
> *Hey, sailors! Weigh anchor!*
> *Get ready to go!*

"I heard Moe's voice coming through the sound system," Eddie said later, "and it took me all the way back to the day we recorded that song, when all the boys were still together, Moe, me, Gabby, Feet, Joe. It took me even farther back, to the first time I heard that call, and the fellow who told me about it. His name was Kapo'o. Reverend Kapo'o. He was the one who offered to take me around to Nāhiku, on Maui's windward side, to meet that canoe maker who wanted to tell me all his stories, the old man who waited for me to come, then passed away before I could get there. Well, what popped into my mind was the day Reverend Kapo'o told me about the sailor's call, so by the time I got up to the mike, by golly, I knew what I was going to say."

At the podium he smiles with wistful pleasure, listening to the song begin—a chorus of power picking on the eight-string *'ukulele* Eddie played back then, Joe Marshall's driving bass line, Feet Rogers's steel adding little glints and silvery chips of sound, against the solid rhythm of Moe's uke and Gabby Pahinui's big twelve-string guitar.

He wears black shoes highly polished, pressed blue jeans, a freshly laundered denim shirt. Under the muted light from overhead his silver hair takes on a sheen. For a man who will soon turn seventy-three, his brown face is remarkably smooth and free of blemishes.

For someone of Eddie's age, this ceremony might be seen as the fitting culmination of a long and emblematic career. Eddie started out in a one-story frame house in a working-class compound less than a mile from this vaulting atrium where the City and County of Honolulu now honor his lifetime of achievement. No question, it's another high point, and in a way the most gratifying. How often do you get this kind of recognition from your own hometown?

But this is not a finale. Far from it. Last summer his band performed again in Washington, D.C., featured in the annual July 4th Folklife Festival on the Capitol Mall. In the fall they will play at the Convention Center in Honolulu, when Eddie's seventh film premieres at the Hawaii International Film Festival, a memoir spanning four decades of Hawaiian music, called *The Sons of Hawaii: A Sound, a Band, a Legend.* They will take it to the outer islands; then Eddie and Myrna will send video cassettes and study guides into the school system, where documentaries from the "Hawaiian Legacy Series" have so far been seen by over two hundred thousand youngsters. In all, more than a million viewers have seen at least one of Eddie's films, thanks to multiple screenings in schools and on television. With four more films in the works, his plate is still full, his mind still roaming, looking ahead, looking back, always looking both ways at once.

As the music fades, he begins to speak, with the softness of voice that causes a hush to fall over the room. He talks first about the children of Hawai'i, and the need to preserve a cultural memory they can build on. He honors all his teachers, calling them by their first names—Kawena, Pīlahi, Sam—his words full of reverence and characteristic humility. Whatever he has accomplished, he says, he owes to them, their guidance, their example. He pauses, smiles at the crowd with a self-effacing charm.

"And you know something else? I'm glad to hear that song again and that old chant. Now I remember the first time I heard it. This was maybe thirty-five years ago, when my friend Reverend Kapo'o was recuperating from a stroke. He played the guitar, and we used to trade songs and stories. I knew the music always lifted his spirits, so I went to see him, and this time while we were talking, I asked him what he did before he entered the ministry. He said he used to be a stevedore down at Honolulu Harbor. I asked him what he remembered from those days. Right away he reached over and grabbed his two *'ulī'ulī,* you know, the small gourds with the pebbles inside and the feathers, and he called out, 'E nā luina!' the way he used to hear it when he was a young man working along with all the other Hawaiian stevedores, and a ship was getting ready to pull away from the pier and set off on another voyage. He came alive then, shaking the gourds and shouting. It looked like he was going to get up and dance."

Again Eddie pauses, searching for a way to bring this to a close. His mind is full of the chant. He sees Reverend Kapo'o waving his feathered rattles as if about to rise from the chair. Over the Reverend's voice he hears the exuberance of Moe Keale, as it filled this hall just moments ago, a voice from the album they cut back in 1970, chanting a sailor's call much older than that, an ancient call from a mid-Pacific world of voyagers, announcing the start of yet another journey:

Hey, sailors!
Weigh anchor!
Get ready to go!

RESPECT—AN EPILOGUE

Around the time we started working on the Lahaina project, I heard about some folks from the Bishop Museum coming over to dig a hole in the old ball park that was built on top of Moku'ula. I called up my friend Jerry Kunitomo who helps us set up things whenever I work on Maui. Then I called the video crew to make sure they could shoot that day.

Going out to a place like that, you know, where they used to have shrines and heiau, *you have to be careful. In the old days it was a little island surrounded by shoreline ponds. Kings used to live there. Chiefs used to be buried there. Back at the hotel I made a* ho'okupu, *an offering to bring along, some taro and sweet potato wrapped in a ti leaf. Before the dig starts, I take that over to the site and set it on the ground and ask permission for us to film.*

When the museum people get there, I call my crew over. These are the guys I always used on Maui, one for sound, one with the handheld video camera, a haole *guy and a really good technician, the kind of guy I don't have to explain things to. He always seems to know the kind of shot I want, even before I tell him. So they come over and set up and get ready to film, but something is wrong, and his camera jams.*

He thinks maybe it's the battery. So he replaces all the batteries, and he starts again. And I can't believe it! The camera still isn't working. It jams again. I tell those guys to go back over by the van and wait.

I don't want to do anything to offend any of the bones or spirits around there. I think, maybe the first time I asked permission, I was in too much of a hurry. So I compose myself and stand there awhile alone and try to connect with that sacred place and speak directly to it.

Finally I say, "We want permission to film here. We want to make sure we're doing the right thing. We don't want to violate this place in any way. We come with respect. But we have to know it's okay for us to be here."

After a while I call my guys back. And this time, when he turns his camera on, it works! And we get the footage we're hoping for, an early peek at some of the old stonework that is still there, just a few feet under the ball field.

Later on it started me thinking about something else that happened to me years earlier, way before I knew about what was under there, before anybody knew or remembered. This was back in the 1970s. We were spending a few days in Lahaina, me and Myrna and some guys we used to run around with and all their families, and one afternoon we get into a softball game, just for the hell of it. I come up to bat and get a hit, and I'm halfway to first base when I fall and roll. By the time I'm back on my feet, the fielder has thrown the ball to first, and I'm out.

But that isn't what bothered me. Until today I still remember this because there was no reason for me to fall down. The base path was smooth. No rocks or low spots. I wasn't drinking any beer. I didn't stumble or miss my footing or anything. One moment I'm running, the next moment I'm down on the ground and rolling, like somebody tripped me. Myrna was watching that day, and she says I did a whole somersault, with red dirt flying through the air.

Then I remembered other stories I've heard from some of the old-timers around Lahaina, about other things that happened on that field through the years, people getting hurt—you know, sports injuries of one kind and another—but strange injuries, people who were in good shape, getting hurt for no reason.

For me, it's just one more reminder of what you have to do when you try to tell the story of these islands. Never forget the ones who came before you.

Acknowledgments

The Hawaiian Legacy Foundation Ho'okupu Project gratefully acknowledges the organizations and individuals who have made this book possible through their generous contributions. *Mahalo nui loa.*

STRONG FOUNDATION

ATHERTON FOUNDATION

COOKE FOUNDATION

HALEKULANI HOTEL

HAWAI'I COMMUNITY FOUNDATION

MOVIE MUSEUM

HARRIET "HAKU" BALDWIN

DWIGHT "KUAIKA" DAMON

ESME "ELEU" DAMON

JULIA "KULIA" DAMON

KIMO CAMPBELL

GORDON RUSSELL

BARBARA B. SMITH

MARTI AND DWAYNE "NAKILA" STEELE

Many more people have contributed to the making of this book than can be named here. But we want to offer a special word of thanks to William E. Aull, Samuel A. Cooke, Carol Fox, Cori Houston, Jeanne Houston, Carl Lindquist, Jeannette Paulson, Henry F. Rice, Madeleine Shaw, Hardy Spoehr, and Kelvin H. Taketa.

We are also very grateful to Fred Kalani Meinecke for the many hours he spent reviewing the manuscript and for his careful attention to a systematic approach for diacritical markings. (Note that personal names may not include diacritical markings according to individual preference, e.g., Mary Kawena Pukui.)

Finally, to Barbara Pope, Elizabeth Lee, Maureen Liu-Brower, and Janice Otaguro at Barbara Pope Book Design, *mahalo nui loa* for the insight, wisdom, and superb professional guidance.

Chronology

1927
4 August: Edward Leilani Kamae born in Honolulu

1942
A brother gives him his first *'ukulele*

1945–1947
Serves in U.S. Army, posted to New Caledonia

1948
Meets Shoi Ikemi, to form The Ukulele Rascals

1949
U.S. tour with Ray Kinney's Hawaiian Revue

1959
First album, *Heart of the Ukulele;* three-month jam session in Waimānalo, with Gabby Pahinui, Joe Marshall, and David "Feet" Rogers, forming The Sons of Hawaii

1960
First gig, at the Sandbox, Honolulu; meets mentors Mary Kawena Pukui and Pīlahi Pākī

1961
The Sons' first album, from Hula Records

1965
December: Meets Myrna Harmer in Lahaina

1970
August: Ho'olaulea, at Hāna, Maui; meets Sam Li'a

1971
December: "Five Faces" album released by Panini Records

1973
Dennis Kamakahi joins the band

1975
Hawaii Sons record label established, with the first album introducing "Morning Dew"

1979
Named a "Living Treasure of Hawai'i" by Honolulu's Honpa Hongwanji Mission

1982
David "Feet" Rogers passes away, at age forty-seven, and the band stops recording

1987
Meets Luther Kahekili Makekau

1988
October: First film, *Li'a: The Legacy of a Hawaiian Man,* opens at Kukuihaele Social Hall, Big Island

1992
Receives "Lifetime Achievement Award" from Hawai'i Academy of Recording Artists

1993
May: Hawaiian Day at Kennedy Center, Washington, D.C., featuring films in the "Hawaiian Legacy Series"; Hawaii Delegation of the U. S. Congress presents a Joint Resolution honoring Eddie and Myrna Kamae for service and accomplishments in leadership, music, and film

1995
November: Receives "Silver Maile Award" from the Hawaii International Film Festival for *Words, Earth and Aloha*

1996
January: Receives Charles Reed Bishop Award from Bishop Museum board of directors, for his "leading role in the renewal of pride, understanding and interest in Hawaii's musical heritage"

2000
March: Receives award from Commission on Culture and the Arts for the City and County of Honolulu, recognizing him as a living treasure and as a leader of the Hawaiian renaissance

2001
September: Inducted into the Ukulele Hall of Fame, Montclair, New Jersey

2002
November: Hawaii International Film Festival gives "Film in Hawai'i Award" to Eddie and Myrna Kamae for the ongoing contribution of their "Hawaiian Legacy Series"

Discography

1959
Heart of the Ukulele. Instrumental solos. Produced by Mel Murata. Bob Lang, recording engineer. Mahalo Records. M3002.

1961
Gabby Pahinui with The Sons of Hawaii. Gabby Pahinui, guitar and vocals; Johnny Maunawili (Eddie Kamae), *'ukulele;* David "Feet" Rogers, steel guitar; Joseph Kalei Marshall, bass and vocals. Produced by Don McDiarmid, Jr. Sound engineer, Bob Lang. Hula Records. H503.

1963
Music of Old Hawaii, Featuring The Sons of Hawaii. Gabby Pahinui, guitar and vocals; Eddie Kamae, *'ukulele* and vocals; David "Feet" Rogers, steel guitar; Joe Marshall, bass and vocals. Producer Don McDiarmid, Jr. Sound, Bob Lang. Hula Records. H506.

1965
This Is Eddie Kamae and The Sons of Hawaii. Eddie Kamae, *'ukulele* and vocals; David "Feet" Rogers, steel guitar; Joe Marshall, bass and vocals; Leland "Atta" Isaacs, slack-key guitar; Robert Larrison, vocals. Produced by Don McDiarmid, Jr. Sound, Bob Lang. Hula Records. H513.

1971
The Sons of Hawaii: The Folk Music of Hawaii. Gabby Pahinui, guitar and vocals; Eddie Kamae, *'ukulele* and vocals; Moe Keale, *'ukulele* and vocals; David "Feet" Rogers, steel guitar; Joe Marshall, bass and vocals. Produced by Steve Siegfried, Witt Shingle, and Lawrence Brown. Sound, Bob Lang. Panini Productions, in association with Island Heritage, Ltd. KN1001. Compact disc rerelease, 1998.

1974
The Music of Hawaii: A Sounds of the World Recording from the National Geographic Society. Featuring 'Iolani Luahine, Hoakalei Kamau'u, Keola and Kapono Beamer, The Sons of Hawaii—Eddie Kamae, Dennis Kamakahi, David Rogers, Joe Marshall. Producer, John M. Lavery. Sound, Marc J. Aubort. Production consultant, Eddie Kamae. National Geographic Society, Washington, D.C.

1975
Eddie Kamae Presents The Sons of Hawaii. Eddie Kamae, *'ukulele* and vocals; Moe Keale, *'ukulele* and vocals; Dennis Kamakahi, guitar and vocals; David Rogers, steel guitar; Joe Marshall, bass and vocals. Guest vocalists, Kulo and Harold Kaniho. Sound, Bob Lang and Herb Ono. Produced by Eddie Kamae. Hawaii Sons, Inc. HS1001.

On the following albums, engineered by Bob Lang and produced by Eddie Kamae on his Hawaii Sons label, the performers are Eddie, Dennis Kamakahi, David Rogers, and Joe Marshall.

1976
The Sons of Hawaii. HS2002.

1977
The Sons of Hawaii. With guest artists Diana Aki, vocals; Sonny Chillingworth, slack-key guitar; Joe Bourque, fiddle. HS3003.

1978
Christmas Time with Eddie Kamae and The Sons of Hawaii. With guest artists Diana Aki, vocals; and Honolulu Boy Choir. HS4004.
Compact disc rerelease, 1996. HSCD1014.

1979
The Sons of Hawaii: Ho'omau. Guest artist, Diana Aki, vocals. HS5005.

1980
The Sons of Hawaii: Grassroots Music. HS6006.

1981
The Best of The Sons of Hawaii. HS7007.

Filmography

1969
Bring Wood, Build a House. 30 min. docu-drama, independently produced by Carl Lindquist. Director, Steve Moore. Musical director, Eddie Kamae.

1977
Taro Tales. 30 min. documentary, produced and directed by Jeannette Paulson for State Dept. of Education. Music by The Sons of Hawaii, arranged by Eddie Kamae.

1978
Christmas Time with Eddie Kamae and The Sons of Hawaii. 30 min. documentary directed by Dennis Mahaffay, co-produced by Dennis Mahaffay and Eddie Kamae, for KHON-TV, Honolulu.

The Hawaiian Legacy Series
Director, Eddie Kamae.
Producer, Myrna Kamae.
Writer, James D. Houston.
Principal photography, Rodney Ohtani.
Narrator, Ka'upena Wong.
Hawaiian language consultants, Fred Kalani Meinecke and Lilia Wahinemaika'i Hale.
(Unless otherwise noted, each Legacy film listed below premiered at the Hawaii International Film Festival, Honolulu.)

1988
Li'a: The Legacy of a Hawaiian Man. 60 min. Editor, Ralph Biesmeyer. Camera, Gene Kois, W. E. Couvillon II, Boone Morrison.

1991
Listen to the Forest. 60 min. Rodney Ohtani, associate producer and editor, with Ralph Biesmeyer and Brian Burgess.

1993
The Hawaiian Way: The Art and Family Tradition of Slack Key Music. 70 min. Rodney Ohtani, co-producer and editor, with Dirk Fukushima. Premiere in the American Film Institute Theatre, Kennedy Center, Washington, D.C.

On Maui in 1995, filming Hawaiian Voices. *Left to right: Rev. David Ka'alakea (1920–1998), Eddie, Rodney Ohtani, Bob Cramer.*

1995
Words, Earth and Aloha: The Sources of Hawaiian Music. 60 min. Rodney Ohtani, co-producer and editor, with Dirk Fukushima.

1997
Luther Kahekili Makekau: A One Kine Hawaiian Man. 60 min. Editor Ralph Biesmeyer, with Paul Venus.

1999
Hawaiian Voices: Bridging Past to Present. 60 min. Co-producer, Rodney Ohtani. Editors, Stanford Chang, Robert Oshita.

2000
Sons of Hawaii: A Sound, a Band, a Legend. 80 min. Co-producer, Rodney Ohtani. Editors, Stanford Chang, Robert Oshita.

Notes

CHAPTER 2 *Awakening*

1. In 1792 the British captain, George Vancouver, picked up a few head of cattle while anchored at Monterey, California, then the capital of Mexico's northern province. He carried them to the Big Island as a goodwill offering from the king of England to King Kamehameha I. After he continued on his voyage, the Hawaiians weren't sure how to respond to this generosity, since they'd never seen such creatures. For many years the animals ran wild and multiplied. Eventually numbering in the thousands, they were known to trample gardens and taro ponds, sometimes toppling the grass houses. The cattle were finally brought under control when Hawai'i's king began importing vaqueros from Monterey and elsewhere.

2. "Masters of Hawaiian Music: David Rogers," in *The Musicians* (Norfolk Island, Australia: Island Heritage Music Ltd., 1971).

CHAPTER 3 *Guides*

1. Mary Kawena Pukui and Samuel H. Elbert, *Hawaiian Dictionary* (Honolulu: University of Hawai'i Press, 1957; revised and enlarged edition, 1986).

2. Interview with Don McDiarmid, Jr., Honolulu, August 4, 1996.

CHAPTER 5 *Out There*

1. E. S. Craighill and Mary Kawena Pukui, *The Polynesian Family System of Ka'ū, Hawai'i* (Wellington, New Zealand: Polynesian Society, 1958; Rutland, Vermont, and Tokyo: Charles Tuttle Co., 1972); Mary Kawena Pukui, E. W. Haertig, and Catherine A. Lee, *Nānā I Ke Kumu* (Look to the Source), 2 vols. (Honolulu: Queen Lili'uokalani Children's Center, 1972); *'Ōlelo No'eau: Hawaiian Proverbs and Poetical Sayings,* collected, translated, and annotated by Mary Kawena Pukui (Honolulu: Bishop Museum Press, 1983).

2. A protégé of Mary Kawena Pukui, James Ka'upena Wong had trained in the tradition of her lineage. In 1964 he chanted at the Newport Folk Festival, one of the first to bring this ancient art form to national attention.

3. *The Hawaiians,* directed and photographed by Bob Goodman, with text by Gavan Daws and Ed Sheehan (Norfolk Island, Australia: Island Heritage Limited, 1970).

CHAPTER 6 *Where the Songwriter Lives*

1. Keakaolani and J. M. Bright, *Ka Buke O Na Leo Mele Hawaii O Na Home Hawaii* (Honolulu: Pacific Commercial Advertiser, 1888).

CHAPTER 7 *"Five Faces"*

1. This and later excerpts from an interview with Moe Keale, Honolulu, April 1999.

2. Interview with Bob Goodman, Honolulu, 7 October 1997.

3. Interview with Herb Kawainui Kāne, Honolulu, 4 October 1997.

4. Herb Kawainui Kāne, "Waipi'o," in *Old Hawaiian Folk Music* (Norfolk Island, Australia: Island Heritage, Ltd., 1971).

5. George Kanahele, ed., *Hawaiian Music and Musicians: An Illustrated History* (Honolulu: University of Hawai'i Press, 1979), p. 364.

6. Toni Auld Yardley, "Sons of Hawai'i: 'The Folk Music of Hawai'i'," *Hawaiian News,* Honolulu, November 1998.

7. Samuel Elbert and Noelani Mahoe, *Na Mele O Hawai'i Nei: 101 Hawaiian Songs* (Honolulu: University of Hawai'i Press, 1970).

CHAPTER 8 *The Soul Comes Home*

1. This and later excerpts from interviews with Dennis Kamakahi, Honolulu, 21 and 22 April 1994.

2. Interview with Jackie Kaho'okele Burke, Honolulu, 6 November 2000.

CHAPTER 9 *Do It Now*

1. From "Kōke'e," words and music by Rev. Dennis D. K. Kamakahi, copyright 1979 and 1983 by Naukilo Publishing Co., Honolulu.

2. From "Composing the Islands," by Sharla Manley, *Honolulu* Magazine, November 1998.

3. Interview with Tony Good, Honolulu, 6 April 1999.

4. Elizabeth Buck, *Paradise Remade: The Politics of Culture and History in Hawai'i* (Philadelphia: Temple University Press, 1993). On p. 176 she writes, "In 1975 only five Hawaiian albums were released; in 1977, fifty-three were released. The peak year for record production was

1978; 110 albums were released. . . . Although record production slowed in the 1980s, it remained fairly steady with from thirty-five to fifty albums produced each year."

5. Dennis Kamakahi, "E Hihi Wai," copyright 1980, Naukilo Publishing Co., Honolulu.

CHAPTER 10 *A Way of Seeing*

1. Interview with Ruth Makaila Kaholoa'a, Waipi'o, 2–4 May 1987.

CHAPTER 11 *It All Connects*

1. John Charlot, "Films of the Pacific," in *Viewers Guide: The Eighth Annual Hawaii International Film Festival* (Honolulu, 1988).

2. This and later excerpts from an interview with Henry 'Auwae, Keaukaha, 10 March 1991.

3. This and later excerpts from an interview with Pualani Kanahele, Hilo, 14 April 1991.

4. Interview with Manu Kaha'iali'i, Maui, May 1992.

5. "Hawaiian Day at Kennedy Center," program guide (Honolulu: Hawaii Sons, Inc., 1993).

CHAPTER 12 *Who Was Guiding Me?*

1. Constance Hale, "George Winston: The Saviour of Slack Key," *Honolulu* Magazine, November 2001. She describes George Winston's "first Hawaiian music epiphany, after he had started playing guitar in the mid-70s, messing around with what he calls American-traditional-folk-with-some-prewar-country-blues-thrown-in. 'I was floundering,' he recalls. 'I was looking for something. I knew it wasn't American. I'd go to the international record bin at Tower Records on Sunset Boulevard. I used to pass from Haiti to Israel in the alphabet, and skip Hawaiian music, which I thought was just too commercial. But someone had put this red box in the Hawaiian bin—the groundbreaking 1971 recording *Sons of Hawaii,* accompanied by booklets on Hawaiian music and musicians'" (p. 52).

2. Interview with Pekelo Cosma, Honolulu, 2 July 1996.

3. Interview with Andy Cummings, Honolulu, 10 March 1993.

The Sons celebrate the seventy-seventh anniversary of the Honolulu Academy of Arts, April 2004, when Eddie Kamae and his teachers (Kawena Pukui, Pīlahi Pākī, and Sam Liʻa) were honored.

Left to right: Pekelo Cosma, Eddie, Smitty Smith, Ocean Kaowili.

Glossary

'āina the earth, the Hawaiian land, or lands
ali'i nui high chiefs, chiefesses; or high chief, chiefess
aloha a word of complex meaning, including welcome, love, and appreciation
aloha 'āina literally, "affection for the land," love for the earth's ancestral power
'aumakua guardian spirit
'awa plant used to make a traditional drink, also called kava
hānai foster child
haole Anglo-American, Caucasian, foreigner
hapa-haole a person of mixed race, part-white, part-Hawaiian
heiau temple
ho'okupu ceremonial gift or offering
ho'olaule'a celebration
ho'omau to continue, carry on
hula traditional Hawaiian dance form, today done in two styles: *auwana* (modern) and *kahiko* (ancient)
hula mele a song to be performed in dance
'ie'ie an endemic, woody climbing plant *(Freycinetia arborea)*
'i'iwi native Hawaiian species of bird, the scarlet honeycreeper *(Vestiaria coccinea)*
'ili'ili small, flat stones held by *hula* dancers and used like castanets
'ilima native Hawaiian shrub (various species of *Sida*) with many uses; its flower, used in *lei,* is the official flower of O'ahu
kahuna kālai wa'a master canoe builder
kahuna lapa'au master of Hawaiian medicine
kahuna pule master of the praying chant
kālua baked
kapa *tapa,* bark cloth
kī hō'alu slack-key style
kukui candlenut tree *(Aleurites moluccana)*
kumu hula teacher of the dance, leader of a *hula* troupe
kupuna (plural *kūpuna*) grandparent, ancestor, relative or friend of grandparent's generation
lama hardwood trees, endemic types of ebony

lānai porch or veranda

laulā broad, wide; hence, to give freely or share

laulau packages of food (meat, fish, taro) wrapped in *ti* or banana leaves and baked

lehua flower of the *'ōhi'a* tree *(Metrosideros macropus),* also the tree itself; official flower of the island of Hawai'i

lei garland, wreath, necklace, traditionally made of flowers, leaves, nuts/berries, shells, etc.

lū'au traditional Hawaiian style of feast

mahalo thank-you

mālama to nurture, care for, preserve, protect

mālama 'āina literally, "care for the earth"

mana inner power, spiritual power

mana'o intention, feeling

mano shark

mele song

mele inoa name song, honoring a particular person or deity

mele pana song celebrating a particular place

mo'o lizard

mu'umu'u long, loose dress worn by women

nahenahe soft, sweet, melodious

'ōkolehao a Hawaiian form of home-brewed alcoholic drink

'ō'ō native Hawaiian species of bird, a type of honey eater (*Moho* spp.)

'o'opu goby

'ōpae shrimp

'ōpiko native species of trees belonging to genus *Psychotria;* also *kōpiko*

pahu round temple drum

palaka a checkered pattern of cloth used for work shirts

pali cliff

palupalu soft, supple

paniolo Hawaiian cowboy

pilikia trouble

pinao dragonfly

poi food made of cooked taro corms, pounded and thinned with water

pū conch shell *(Charonia tritonis)* used as a musical instrument

tūtū grandparent, mentor, guide, elder

'ukulele literally, "leaping flea"; stringed instrument originally brought to Hawai'i by the Portuguese

'ulī'ulī gourd rattle

Selected References

Buck, Elizabeth. *Paradise Remade: The Politics of Culture and History in Hawai'i.* Philadelphia: Temple University Press, 1993.

Charlot, John. "Films of the Pacific." In *Viewer's Guide: The Eighth Annual Hawaii International Film Festival.* Honolulu, 1988.

———. *The Hawaiian Poetry of Religion and Politics.* Monograph No. 5. Honolulu: Institute for Polynesian Studies, Brigham Young University, Hawai'i Campus, 1985.

Elbert, Samuel H., and Noelani Mahoe, eds. *Na Mele O Hawai'i Nei: 101 Hawaiian Songs.* Honolulu: University of Hawai'i Press, 1970.

Houston, James D. "Grass Roots Renaissance." *Los Angeles Times,* Sunday Travel Section, 7 March 1999.

———. "Kaua'i: An Island in Song." *Hana Hou,* the Magazine of Hawaiian Airlines, Winter 1999.

———. "The Songwriter of Waipi'o Valley." *Honolulu* Magazine, October 1987.

———. "Wayfinders of the Future." In *Discovery: A Hawaiian Odyssey.* Honolulu: Bishop Museum Press, 1993.

Johnny Noble's Collection of Ancient and Modern Hulas. New York: Miller Music Company, 1935.

Kanahele, George, ed. *Hawaiian Music and Musicians: An Illustrated History.* Honolulu: University of Hawai'i Press, 1979.

Keakaolani and J. M. Bright. *Ka Buke O Na Leo Mele Hawaii O Na Home Hawaii.* Honolulu: Pacific Commercial Advertiser, 1888.

Klieger, P. Christian. *Moku'ula: Maui's Sacred Island.* Honolulu: Bishop Museum Press, 1995.

Lindquist, Carl. *The Musicians.* Norfolk Island, Australia: Island Heritage Limited, 1971. (Booklet to accompany *The Sons of Hawaii* [Honolulu: Panini Records, 1971].)

Pahinui, Gabby. Interview with Dave Guard, 1961. Recorded on *Pure Gabby: I Just Play the Way I Feel.* Honolulu: Panini Records, 1978.

Pukui, Mary Kawena, trans. *Nā Mele Welo, Songs of Our Heritage: Selections from the Roberts Mele Collection.* Arranged and edited by Pat Namaka Bacon and Nathan Napoka. Honolulu: Bishop Museum Press, 1995.

Ronck, Ronn. *Celebration: A Portrait of Hawaii through the Songs of The Brothers Cazimero.* Honolulu: Mutual Publishing, 1984.

Ruymar, Lorene, ed. *The Hawaiian Steel Guitar and Its Great Hawaiian Musicians.* Anaheim Hills, Calif.: Centerstream Publishing, 1996.

Tadaro, Tony. *The Golden Years of Hawaiian Entertainment: 1874–1974.* Honolulu: Tony Tadaro Publishing, 1974.

Tatar, Elizabeth. *Strains of Change: The Impact of Tourism on Hawaiian Music.* Bishop Museum Special Publication No. 78. Honolulu: Bishop Museum Press, 1987.

Thornton, Brian. "Eddie Kamae: The Sons and Music of Hawaii." *Hawai'i Observer,* 5 September 1977.

Wittig-Harby, Bill. "Gabby Pahinui: Twelve Years Gone." *Honolulu* Magazine, November 1992.

Index

Note: Page numbers in italics refer to illustrations.

Illustrations are from the collection of Eddie and Myrna Kamae unless otherwise noted. Illustrations are used with permission. Photographers and artists listed hold the copyright for their work.

FRONTMATTER. Eddie Kamae, page ii, photograph by Philip Spalding III, 1999. Eddie Kamae, page vii, photograph by Boone Morrison. Mary Kawena Pukui, page viii, photograph by George Bacon. Mock Chew house steps, page x, photograph by Franco Salmoiraghi, 1974.

CHAPTER ONE. Eddie Kamae, page xx, photograph by Boone Morrison. Eddie Kamae's brother and parents in front of Kaumakapili Church, page 6, Alfred Kamae collection.

CHAPTER TWO. Gabby Pahinui, pages 26, 28-29, 30, photographs by Ken Sakamoto, circa 1975.

CHAPTER THREE. Mary Kawena Pukui at Waimānalo, page 44, 1939, © Bishop Museum. Pīlahi Pākī, page 47, photograph by Francis Haar, 1972. Mary Kawena Pukui at Bishop Museum, page 50, 1957, © Bishop Museum. 'Iolani Luahine with Tom Hiona, page 54, photograph by Francis Haar, 1961. 'Iolani Luahine at Nāpō'opo'o, page 55, photograph by Francis Haar, circa 1975. Queen Lili'uokalani, page 58, circa 1902, Hawai'i State Archives. "Tutu" handwritten manuscript, page 59, © Bishop Museum.

CHAPTER FOUR. *Music of Old Hawaii* album cover, page 60, circa 1960s, courtesy of Hula Records. The Sons of Hawaii recording at KPOI studio, pages 66-67, circa 1960s, courtesy of Hula Records. Eddie Kamae's grandmother's house in Lahaina, page 74, courtesy of Alice Greenwood.

CHAPTER FIVE. *'Āpi'i* taro—Waipi'o, page 80, photograph by Franco Salmoiraghi, 1974. *First Light, Huelo, Maui,* page 82, photograph by Boone Morrison.

CHAPTER SIX. Sam Li'a Kalainaina, page 100, photograph by Boone Morrison. Sam Li'a and his wife, Sarah, page 111, hand-colored photograph, circa 1920, photograph of original artwork by Shuzo Uemoto, 2004.

CHAPTER SEVEN. *The Folk Music of Hawaii,* page 114, album cover illustrations by Herb Kāne, 1971, courtesy of Panini Records. David "Feet" Rogers, page 118, photograph by Robert B. Goodman, 1971. Moe Keale, page 121, illustration by Herb Kāne, 1971. *Hi'ilawe,* page 123, painting by Herb Kāne, 1977, collection of the State Foundation on Culture and

the Arts. Feet Rogers, page 126, illustration by Herb Kāne, 1971, courtesy of Panini Records.

CHAPTER EIGHT. Eddie Kamae and Sam Li'a, pages 128, 130, photographs by Boone Morrison, 1972. The Sons of Hawaii in 1973, page 135, photograph by Boone Morrison. The Sons of Hawaii at Seven Sacred Pools, page 140, photograph by Bob Jamieson, 1976, courtesy of Hawaii Sons, Inc.

CHAPTER NINE. Dennis Kamakahi, Eddie Kamae, and a Big Island youngster, page 148, photograph by Boone Morrison, 1986. *Cloud Visiting the Valley*, page 152, photograph by Franco Salmoiraghi, 1977. The Sons of Hawaii in Hāna, Maui, page 155, photograph by Bob Jamieson, 1976, courtesy of Hawaii Sons, Inc.

CHAPTER TEN. Eddie Kamae, page 162, photograph by Boone Morrison. John K. Purdy and John Holi Mae, page 164, photograph by Boone Morrison. Luther Kahekili Makekau, page 174, photograph by Tomas Belsky and Lloyd Jeffrey Mallan. Making *'ōkolehao,* page 181, photograph by Boone Morrison. Roy Toko, Eddie Kamae, and Eddie Thomas, page 182, photograph by Boone Morrison.

CHAPTER ELEVEN. Pualani Kanaka'ole Kanahele and Nalani Kanaka'ole Zane, page 186, photograph by Franco Salmoiraghi, 1998. Ray Kāne, page 201, photograph by Lynn Martin, circa 1997, collection of the State Foundation on Culture and the Arts. Eddie and Myrna Kamae, page 207, photograph by Philip Spalding III, 2003. Princess Miriam Likelike, page 210, photograph by A. A. Montano, circa 1881, Hawai'i State Archives. Alfred 'Alohikea and Wai'oli Church Choir, page 218, circa 1921, © Bishop Museum.

NOTES. The Sons of Hawaii at Honolulu Academy of Arts, page 244, photograph by Shuzo Uemoto, 2004.

AUTHOR BIO. James D. Houston, page 259, photograph by Greg Pio.

James D. Houston

The author of fifteen works of fiction and nonfiction, James D. Houston has been recognized in Hawai'i and nationwide for his broad understanding of the history and cultures of the western United States and the Asia/Pacific region. With his wife, Jeanne Wakatsuki Houston, he co-authored the classic *Farewell to Manzanar.* Based upon the experiences of her family during and after the World War II internment, this book is now a standard work in schools and colleges across the country. His recent novel *Snow Mountain Passage* was named by the *Los Angeles Times* and the *Washington Post* as one of the year's best books. He has also served as writer for the seven cultural documentaries in Eddie Kamae's "Hawaiian Legacy Series." His works have earned numerous honors, among them a Wallace Stegner Fellowship at Stanford University, an American Book Award, and the Humanitas Prize. For some years, while getting started as a writer, he made his living as a musician, playing string bass and acoustic guitar. A frequent visitor to Hawai'i, he lives in Santa Cruz, California. (For more, visit his website at www.jamesdhouston.com.)